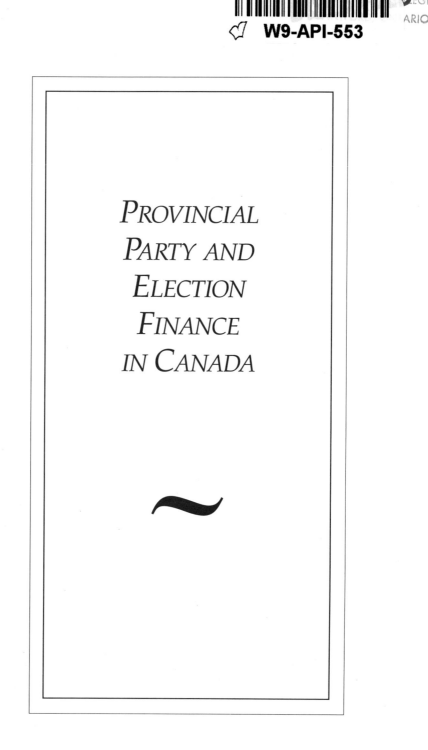

PROVINCIAL PARTY AND ELECTION FINANCE IN CANADA

This is Volume 3 in a series of studies
commissioned as part of the research program
of the Royal Commission on Electoral Reform
and Party Financing

PROVINCIAL PARTY AND ELECTION FINANCE IN CANADA

~

F. Leslie Seidle
Editor

Volume 3 of the Research Studies

ROYAL COMMISSION ON ELECTORAL REFORM
AND PARTY FINANCING
AND CANADA COMMUNICATION GROUP –
PUBLISHING, SUPPLY AND SERVICES CANADA

DUNDURN PRESS
TORONTO AND OXFORD

© Minister of Supply and Services Canada, 1991
Printed and bound in Canada
ISBN 1-55002-099-4
ISSN 1188-2743
Catalogue No. Z1-1989/2-41-3E

Published by Dundurn Press Limited in cooperation with the Royal Commission on Electoral Reform and Party Financing and Canada Communication Group – Publishing, Supply and Services Canada.

Canadian Cataloguing in Publication Data

Main entry under title:
Provincial party and election finance in Canada.

(Research studies ; 3)
Issued also in French under title: Le Financement des partis et des élections de niveau provincial au Canada.
ISBN 1-55002-099-4

1. Campaign funds – Canada – Provinces. 2. Elections – Canada. 3. Political parties – Canada. I. Seidle, F. Leslie. II. Canada. Royal Commission on Electoral Reform and Party Financing. III. Series: Research studies (Canada. Royal Commission on Electoral Reform and Party Financing) ; 3.

$24.95

JL198.P76 1991   324.271   C91-090515-0

Dundurn Press Limited
2181 Queen Street East
Suite 301
Toronto, Canada
M4E 1E5

Dundurn Distribution
73 Lime Walk
Headington
Oxford, England
OX3 7AD

CONTENTS

TABLES

5. PARTY FINANCING IN ALBERTA: LOW-IMPACT LEGISLATION

FOREWORD

THE ROYAL COMMISSION on Electoral Reform and Party Financing was established in November 1989. Our mandate was to inquire into and report on the appropriate principles and process that should govern the election of members of the House of Commons and the financing of political parties and candidates' campaigns. To conduct such a comprehensive examination of Canada's electoral system, we held extensive public consultations and developed a research program designed to ensure that our recommendations would be guided by an independent foundation of empirical inquiry and analysis.

The Commission's in-depth review of the electoral system was the first of its kind in Canada's history of electoral democracy. It was dictated largely by the major constitutional, social and technological changes of the past several decades, which have transformed Canadian society, and their concomitant influence on Canadians' expectations of the political process itself. In particular, the adoption in 1982 of the *Canadian Charter of Rights and Freedoms* has heightened Canadians' awareness of their democratic and political rights and of the way they are served by the electoral system.

The importance of electoral reform cannot be overemphasized. As the Commission's work proceeded, Canadians became increasingly preoccupied with constitutional issues that have the potential to change the nature of Confederation. No matter what their beliefs or political allegiances in this continuing debate, Canadians agree that constitutional change must be achieved in the context of fair and democratic processes. We cannot complacently assume that our current electoral process will always meet this standard or that it leaves no room for improvement. Parliament and the national government must be seen as legitimate; electoral reform can both enhance the stature of national political institutions and reinforce their ability to define the future of our country in ways that command Canadians' respect and confidence and promote the national interest.

In carrying out our mandate, we remained mindful of the importance of protecting our democratic heritage, while at the same time balancing it against the emerging values that are injecting a new dynamic into the electoral system. If our system is to reflect the realities of Canadian political life, then reform requires more than mere tinkering with electoral laws and practices.

Our broad mandate challenged us to explore a full range of options. We commissioned more than 100 research studies, to be published in a 23-volume collection. In the belief that our electoral laws must measure up to the very best contemporary practice, we examined election-related laws and processes in all of our provinces and territories and studied comparable legislation and processes in established democracies around the world. This unprecedented array of empirical study and expert opinion made a vital contribution to our deliberations. We made every effort to ensure that the research was both intellectually rigorous and of practical value. All studies were subjected to peer review, and many of the authors discussed their preliminary findings with members of the political and academic communities at national symposiums on major aspects of the electoral system.

The Commission placed the research program under the able and inspired direction of Dr. Peter Aucoin, Professor of Political Science and Public Administration at Dalhousie University. We are confident that the efforts of Dr. Aucoin, together with those of the research coordinators and scholars whose work appears in this and other volumes, will continue to be of value to historians, political scientists, parliamentarians and policy makers, as well as to thoughtful Canadians and the international community.

Along with the other Commissioners, I extend my sincere gratitude to the entire Commission staff for their dedication and commitment. I also wish to thank the many people who participated in our symposiums for their valuable contributions, as well as the members of the research and practitioners' advisory groups whose counsel significantly aided our undertaking.

Pierre Lortie
Chairman

INTRODUCTION

THE ROYAL COMMISSION'S research program constituted a comprehensive and detailed examination of the Canadian electoral process. The scope of the research, undertaken to assist Commissioners in their deliberations, was dictated by the broad mandate given to the Commission.

The objective of the research program was to provide Commissioners with a full account of the factors that have shaped our electoral democracy. This dictated, first and foremost, a focus on federal electoral law, but our inquiries also extended to the Canadian constitution, including the institutions of parliamentary government, the practices of political parties, the mass media and nonpartisan political organizations, as well as the decision-making role of the courts with respect to the constitutional rights of citizens. Throughout, our research sought to introduce a historical perspective in order to place the contemporary experience within the Canadian political tradition.

We recognized that neither our consideration of the factors shaping Canadian electoral democracy nor our assessment of reform proposals would be as complete as necessary if we failed to examine the experiences of Canadian provinces and territories and of other democracies. Our research program thus emphasized comparative dimensions in relation to the major subjects of inquiry.

Our research program involved, in addition to the work of the Commission's research coordinators, analysts and support staff, over 200 specialists from 28 universities in Canada, from the private sector and, in a number of cases, from abroad. Specialists in political science constituted the majority of our researchers, but specialists in law, economics, management, computer sciences, ethics, sociology and communications, among other disciplines, were also involved.

In addition to the preparation of research studies for the Commission, our research program included a series of research seminars, symposiums and workshops. These meetings brought together the Commissioners, researchers, representatives from the political parties, media personnel and others with practical experience in political parties, electoral politics and public affairs. These meetings provided not only a forum for discussion of the various subjects of the Commission's mandate, but also an opportunity for our research to be assessed by those with an intimate knowledge of the world of political practice.

These public reviews of our research were complemented by internal and external assessments of each research report by persons qualified in the area; such assessments were completed prior to our decision to publish any study in the series of research volumes.

The Research Branch of the Commission was divided into several areas, with the individual research projects in each area assigned to the research coordinators as follows:

F. Leslie Seidle	Political Party and Election Finance
Herman Bakvis	Political Parties
Kathy Megyery	Women, Ethno-Cultural Groups and Youth
David Small	Redistribution; Electoral Boundaries; Voter Registration
Janet Hiebert	Party Ethics
Michael Cassidy	Democratic Rights; Election Administration
Robert A. Milen	Aboriginal Electoral Participation and Representation
Frederick J. Fletcher	Mass Media and Broadcasting in Elections
David Mac Donald (Assistant Research Coordinator)	Direct Democracy

These coordinators identified appropriate specialists to undertake research, managed the projects and prepared them for publication. They also organized the seminars, symposiums and workshops in their research areas and were responsible for preparing presentations and briefings to help the Commission in its deliberations and decision making. Finally, they participated in drafting the Final Report of the Commission.

On behalf of the Commission, I welcome the opportunity to thank the following for their generous assistance in producing these research studies – a project that required the talents of many individuals.

In performing their duties, the research coordinators made a notable contribution to the work of the Commission. Despite the pressures of tight deadlines, they worked with unfailing good humour and the utmost congeniality. I thank all of them for their consistent support and cooperation.

In particular, I wish to express my gratitude to Leslie Seidle, senior research coordinator, who supervised our research analysts and support staff in Ottawa. His diligence, commitment and professionalism not only set high standards, but also proved contagious. I am grateful to Kathy Megyery, who performed a similar function in Montreal with equal aplomb and skill. Her enthusiasm and dedication inspired us all.

On behalf of the research coordinators and myself, I wish to thank our research analysts: Daniel Arsenault, Eric Bertram, Cécile Boucher, Peter Constantinou, Yves Denoncourt, David Docherty, Luc Dumont, Jane Dunlop, Scott Evans, Véronique Garneau, Keith Heintzman, Paul Holmes, Hugh Mellon, Cheryl D. Mitchell, Donald Padget, Alain Pelletier, Dominique Tremblay and Lisa Young. The Research Branch was strengthened by their ability to carry out research in a wide variety of areas, their intellectual curiosity and their team spirit.

The work of the research coordinators and analysts was greatly facilitated by the professional skills and invaluable cooperation of Research Branch staff members: Paulette LeBlanc, who, as administrative assistant, managed the flow of research projects; Hélène Leroux, secretary to the research coordinators, who produced briefing material for the Commissioners and who, with Lori Nazar, assumed responsibility for monitoring the progress of research projects in the latter stages of our work; Kathleen McBride and her assistant Natalie Brose, who created and maintained the database of briefs and hearings transcripts; and Richard Herold and his assistant Susan Dancause, who were responsible for our research library. Jacinthe Séguin and Cathy Tucker also deserve thanks – in addition to their duties as receptionists, they assisted in a variety of ways to help us meet deadlines.

We were extremely fortunate to obtain the research services of first-class specialists from the academic and private sectors. Their contributions are found in this and the other 22 published research volumes. We thank them for the quality of their work and for their willingness to contribute and to meet our tight deadlines.

Our research program also benefited from the counsel of Jean-Marc Hamel, Special Adviser to the Chairman of the Commission and former

Chief Electoral Officer of Canada, whose knowledge and experience proved invaluable.

In addition, numerous specialists assessed our research studies. Their assessments not only improved the quality of our published studies, but also provided us with much-needed advice on many issues. In particular, we wish to single out professors Donald Blake, Janine Brodie, Alan Cairns, Kenneth Carty, John Courtney, Peter Desbarats, Jane Jenson, Richard Johnston, Vincent Lemieux, Terry Morley and Joseph Wearing, as well as Ms. Beth Symes.

Producing such a large number of studies in less than a year requires a mastery of the skills and logistics of publishing. We were fortunate to be able to count on the Commission's Director of Communications, Richard Rochefort, and Assistant Director, Hélène Papineau. They were ably supported by the Communications staff: Patricia Burden, Louise Dagenais, Caroline Field, Claudine Labelle, France Langlois, Lorraine Maheux, Ruth McVeigh, Chantal Morissette, Sylvie Patry, Jacques Poitras and Claudette Rouleau-O'Toole.

To bring the project to fruition, the Commission also called on specialized contractors. We are deeply grateful for the services of Ann McCoomb (references and fact checking); Marthe Lemery, Pierre Chagnon and the staff of Communications Com'ça (French quality control); Norman Bloom, Pamela Riseborough and associates of B&B Editorial Consulting (English adaptation and quality control); and Mado Reid (French production). Al Albania and his staff at Acart Graphics designed the studies and produced some 2 400 tables and figures.

The Commission's research reports constitute Canada's largest publishing project of 1991. Successful completion of the project required close cooperation between the public and private sectors. In the public sector, we especially acknowledge the excellent service of the Privy Council unit of the Translation Bureau, Department of the Secretary of State of Canada, under the direction of Michel Parent, and our contacts Ruth Steele and Terry Denovan of the Canada Communication Group, Department of Supply and Services.

The Commission's co-publisher for the research studies was Dundurn Press of Toronto, whose exceptional service is gratefully acknowledged. Wilson & Lafleur of Montreal, working with the Centre de Documentation Juridique du Québec, did equally admirable work in preparing the French version of the studies.

Teams of editors, copy editors and proofreaders worked diligently under stringent deadlines with the Commission and the publishers to prepare some 20 000 pages of manuscript for design, typesetting and printing. The work of these individuals, whose names are listed elsewhere in this volume, was greatly appreciated.

Our acknowledgements extend to the contributions of the Commission's Executive Director, Guy Goulard, and the administration and executive support teams: Maurice Lacasse, Denis Lafrance and Steve Tremblay (finance); Thérèse Lacasse and Mary Guy-Shea (personnel); Cécile Desforges (assistant to the Executive Director); Marie Dionne (administration); Anna Bevilacqua (records); and support staff members Michelle Bélanger, Roch Langlois, Michel Lauzon, Jean Mathieu, David McKay and Pierrette McMurtie, as well as Denise Miquelon and Christiane Séguin of the Montreal office.

A special debt of gratitude is owed to Marlène Girard, assistant to the Chairman. Her ability to supervise the logistics of the Commission's work amid the tight schedules of the Chairman and Commissioners contributed greatly to the completion of our task.

I also wish to express my deep gratitude to my own secretary, Liette Simard. Her superb administrative skills and great patience brought much-appreciated order to my penchant for the chaotic workstyle of academe. She also assumed responsibility for the administrative coordination of revisions to the final drafts of volumes 1 and 2 of the Commission's Final Report. I owe much to her efforts and assistance.

Finally, on behalf of the research coordinators and myself, I wish to thank the Chairman, Pierre Lortie, the members of the Commission, Pierre Fortier, Robert Gabor, William Knight and Lucie Pépin, and former members Elwood Cowley and Senator Donald Oliver. We are honoured to have worked with such an eminent and thoughtful group of Canadians, and we have benefited immensely from their knowledge and experience. In particular, we wish to acknowledge the creativity, intellectual rigour and energy our Chairman brought to our task. His unparalleled capacity to challenge, to bring out the best in us, was indeed inspiring.

Peter Aucoin
Director of Research

PREFACE

TWENTY-FIVE YEARS AGO, following a review of the costs of election campaigns, the pattern of party finance and related issues, the Committee on Election Expenses (Barbeau Committee) issued its report. The Committee's conclusions provided the basis for the 1974 *Election Expenses Act*, which led to what was then considered Canada's most comprehensive regulatory framework for party and election finance. The main elements of the 1974 reforms were: limits on the election expenses of registered political parties and candidates; disclosure of parties' and candidates' revenue and spending; and public funding through post-election reimbursements to parties and candidates, as well as an income tax credit for contributions to either.

While amendments in 1977 and 1983 did not alter the main lines of the federal regulatory framework, developments during the past 15 years or so have led to calls for an assessment of its operation and effects. Some have asked whether the objectives on which the 1974 legislation was based are still being met – or, indeed, remain valid. A number of factors account for this, among them changes in party and campaign management techniques, the implications of the adoption of the *Canadian Charter of Rights and Freedoms* in 1982, the role of interest groups in elections and developments in the regulation of political finance at the provincial level.

The Royal Commission on Electoral Reform and Party Financing was mandated to consider, among other issues, "the appropriate principles and process that should govern ... the financing of political parties and of candidates' campaigns, including ... the means by which political parties should be funded, the provision of funds to political parties from any source, the limits on such funding and the uses to which such funds ought, or ought not, to be put." To assist it in carrying out these aspects of its mandate, an extensive series of research studies on party and election finance was undertaken by members of the academic profession, consultants and research analysts employed by the Commission. The principal studies are published in this volume and the four others in this research area.

The research projects in the party and election finance area were intended to assist the Commission in taking decisions on a number of issues at the heart of its mandate. In this regard, the studies in these five volumes are relevant to three of the six objectives of electoral reform referred to in Volume 1, chapter 1 of the Final Report: promoting fairness in the electoral process; strengthening the parties as primary political organizations; and enhancing public confidence in the integrity of the electoral process. These studies canvass issues relevant to these objectives, draw on comparative experience (both within Canada and elsewhere) and discuss possible reforms. In so doing, they address fundamental questions such as how to circumscribe the influence of money in politics; how to encourage greater participation in the financing of parties and candidates and in the electoral process, including the nomination stage; how to ensure a high degree of transparency in relation to political finance; and whether and in what ways public funding should be part of the system.

In considering possible reforms, the Commission reviewed developments in this area in other democracies (see Volume 4 of the Research Studies) and at the provincial level in Canada. This volume includes five research studies on political finance and its regulation in Quebec, Ontario, Alberta, New Brunswick and British Columbia. These provinces were chosen to illustrate the variety of approaches provincial governments have adopted to regulate the role of money in politics. Taken as a whole, the studies demonstrate that, in this area as in other areas of public policy, the Canadian federal system sometimes serves as a 'laboratory': provincial initiatives may influence policy makers at the federal level and vice versa; in addition, developments in a province may have an impact on public policy adopted by another province.

Louis Massicotte's study documents the steps taken by Quebec, which can be justly labelled the pioneer in the regulation of political finance in Canada. The Quiet Revolution was marked by a rejection of many of the mores long associated with Quebec politics. The 1963 amendments to the *Election Act* fit within this pattern: parties' and candidates' election spending was limited, and reimbursement of a share of the expenses of candidates who had received 20 percent of the vote was instituted. Disclosure requirements (broadened in 1977) were intended to remove the suspicion about political finance based on *caisses occultes* ('slush funds'). Quebec was a pioneer in two other ways: in 1975 it instituted annual allowances from public funds for political parties; in 1977 it restricted to qualified electors the right to make political contributions (and also adopted limits on the size of donations). Dr. Massicotte's analysis of annual financial reports since 1977 provides a number of interesting insights into the pattern of political finance in Quebec.

Quebec was not, however, the first province to pass legislation limiting the size of political contributions. In this case, Ontario was the pioneer. As David Johnson explains, Ontario's approach contrasted with the federal legislation, centred on spending limits for parties and candidates, adopted in 1974. The Ontario legislation was based on the report of the Camp Commission, which was less concerned with the cost of campaigns and the effect on access to elected office than with the possibility of undue influence being exercised by generous donors. This was reflected in the contribution limits adopted in 1975 and in the extensive disclosure system put in place; the registration and reporting requirements for constituency associations were also a first step for Canada. At the same time, Ontario's *Election Finances Act* restricted advertising spending by parties, candidates and constituency associations. As Dr. Johnson explains, the adoption of comprehensive spending limits was part of the accord struck between the Liberal and New Democratic parties following the election of a minority government under David Peterson in 1985; this reform was achieved in 1986.

The research studies on Alberta and New Brunswick illustrate how some provinces have been influenced by other provinces' initiatives. Indeed, Doreen Barrie suggests that the "contagion effect," rather than any particular event (such as the Fidinam scandal in Ontario), accounts for the rise in interest in reform in Alberta. She explains that Ontario's 1976 Act was "most persuasive," although the Alberta *Election Finances and Contributions Disclosure Act* (adopted in 1977) included neither limits on advertising expenses nor reimbursements. The key principles of the Alberta Act – contribution limits and broad disclosure (including by constituency associations) – remain unchanged.

As Hugh Mellon recounts, fund-raising scandals lay behind the reforms reflected in New Brunswick's 1978 *Political Process Financing Act*. In this case, the architects of the legislation were most influenced by Quebec's approach. New Brunswick adopted limits on the size of contributions but, unlike Quebec, did not restrict to qualified electors the right to make political contributions. Otherwise the principles behind New Brunswick's legislation parallel those of Quebec: spending limits for candidates and parties, reimbursements for candidates, annual allowances for political parties and disclosure (including by constituency associations).

Regulation of party and election finance in Canada: federal and provincial levels

	Spending limits (candidates and parties)[a]	Contribution limits (size)	Election reimbursements		Parties: annual allowances	Income tax credits	Constituency association registration/ reporting[b]
			Candidates	Parties			
Canada	X	X	X	X		X	
British Columbia						X	
Alberta		X				X	X
Saskatchewan	X		X	X			
Manitoba	X		X	X		X	
Ontario	X	X	X	X		X	X
Quebec	X	X[c]	X		X	X	X
Nova Scotia	X		X			X	
New Brunswick	X	X	X		X	X	X
Prince Edward Island	X		X		X	X	
Newfoundland[d]							

Source: Author's review of relevant legislation.

[a] All jurisdictions indicated limit the election expenses of both candidates and parties.

[b] In British Columbia, constituency associations wanting to issue tax receipts are required to register with the Commissioner of Income Tax at the Income Taxation Branch in Victoria; no reporting of constituency association finances is required.

[c] Quebec also limits the source of political contributions: only qualified electors may make such donations.

[d] In December 1991, legislation with the following provisions was introduced in Newfoundland: spending limits for candidates and parties, limits on the size of political contributions, reimbursements for candidates, disclosure and an income tax credit.

The study by Terry Morley examines political finance in British Columbia, the province where, apart from Newfoundland, the least regulation applies. (See, however, note "d" below the accompanying table.) Candidates and "recognized political parties" must report their election expenses to the chief electoral officer, but no disclosure of contributions is required (either post-election or otherwise). In direct contrast to the four other provinces reviewed in this volume, British Columbia has neither spending limits nor contribution limits. Furthermore, there is no public funding of the political process except a tax credit for political contributions, which applies in all other provinces but Newfoundland and Saskatchewan.

These five studies help explain why, in seeking to regulate the role of money in the political and election processes, each province has taken a particular path. Political culture, scandal, independent commissions, leading political activists and even the search for political advantage have, to a greater or lesser degree, all played a role in the development of reforms in these and other provinces. The result is a diversity of regulatory systems – as illustrated in the accompanying table, which indicates the main principles behind the relevant legislation at the provincial level in Canada.

The Commission owes a considerable debt of gratitude to the researchers who agreed to undertake the studies in this area. Through their dedication and professionalism, their responsiveness to the Commission's priorities and their cooperation in meeting deadlines, all those whose work appears in these volumes have contributed greatly to the research program. A number of the researchers presented their findings at Commission seminars and/or meetings. We valued their participation on these occasions, as well as their willingness to respond to a range of questions and requests for information, particularly during the period when the Commission's Final Report was being prepared. I would also like to express my personal gratitude to Peter Aucoin, whose suggestions and counsel helped in so many ways as these research studies were planned, discussed and carried forward for publication.

The Commission's publication program reflects the central role research played in the work of the Royal Commission on Electoral Reform and Party Financing. It is hoped these studies will illuminate debate on the Commission's recommendations and, in so doing, help chart the way to a modern and responsive regulatory framework for party and election finance that will bolster electoral democracy in Canada.

F. Leslie Seidle
Senior Research Coordinator

PROVINCIAL
PARTY AND
ELECTION
FINANCE
IN CANADA

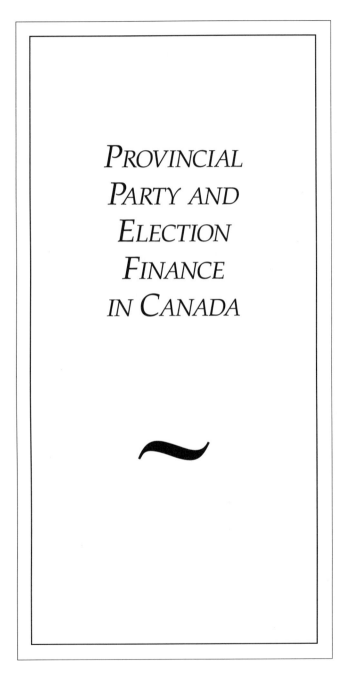

1

PARTY FINANCING IN QUEBEC
An Analysis of the Financial Reports of Parties 1977–89

Louis Massicotte

WHETHER PEOPLE PERCEIVE the ultimate goal of political parties as gaining and holding office or as promoting ideas and principles, political parties remain, first and foremost, organizations. Like any organization, political parties vitally need financial resources to carry out their activities properly. This need becomes even more pressing during an election period. Not all parties, however, are equally successful at mobilizing and using their financial resources. In addition, parties use different fund-raising methods. Because these differences often offer insight into the interests the parties represent,[1] a study of party financing sheds some light on the controversial issue of relations between state and society.

Authors writing on the subject disagree on the scope of the light that is shed. While some perceive corporate contributions as a vital link between economic and political decision makers, others attribute what they believe to be the dependency of politicians on economic interests to more fundamental factors (Miliband 1969, 151, 171ff.; and Meynaud 1969, 81).

THE BACKGROUND TO THE QUEBEC LEGISLATION

In Quebec, as in other liberal societies, debate on the financing of political parties and election campaigns has been going on for a long time. As early as 1875, an attempt was made to regulate candidates' spending during provincial elections. However, it was not until the Quiet Revolution that the province began adopting comprehensive legislation to regulate such activities. The current system in relation to the financing of political parties was built in three stages.

In 1963, new provisions on election spending were added to the Quebec *Election Act*. The idea of an official agent responsible for all of a candidate's spending was borrowed from Great Britain, as was the idea of limiting and disclosing money spent in constituencies during election periods. However, the Quebec Act introduced two major innovations. First, it instituted a partial reimbursement of expenses to candidates receiving 20 percent of the vote; second, it recognized the existence of political parties and imposed on them the same requirements as candidates during an election period: appointing an official agent, and limiting and declaring expenses. Party spending was not, however, to be reimbursed. This legislation was copied in other parts of the country, partly because some people involved in drafting it later worked for the Barbeau Committee on Election Expenses.

In 1975, the Bourassa government added an annual allowance for political parties, which was initially set at $400 000 but was changed two years later to $0.25 per registered voter. (Today, this amounts to about $1.2 million.) The allowance has always been distributed according to the number of votes obtained by each party in the preceding election. At the time Quebec added this allowance, no other jurisdiction in Canada had such a system, although two provinces, New Brunswick and Prince Edward Island, have since adopted it.

Finally, in 1977, *An Act to govern the financing of political parties and to amend the Election Act* was adopted with the objective of limiting contributions. As in 1963, Quebec both borrowed ideas and originated them. The mechanism for authorizing parties, riding associations and candidates originated in Ontario, while Ottawa already required that the identity of major contributors be disclosed and allowed tax credits for donations. However, the essential feature of the legislation, a ban on donations from legal entities such as corporations, did not exist anywhere in Canada.

The law was later amended, but there was no change in the fundamentals. In 1982 the principal technical flaws of the Act, which had been adopted rather hastily, were corrected. In addition, the position of director general of political party financing was abolished and the responsibilities added to those of the chief electoral officer. In 1984, a further change allowed eligible candidates to receive advances on refunds of election expenses. Later in this study we will look at more recent amendments to the Act. Although the parliamentary opposition was initially critical of the public servant who was responsible for applying the Act, and doubts are often expressed about whether the Act is being respected, the two larger parties continue officially to support the legislation.

The 1977 Act was imposed by a party that already financed itself exclusively and successfully through the support of voters. On the other hand, the three main federal parties received (then as now) a significant share of their funds from companies or unions. Since big business in Quebec was dominated by anglophones at the time, a nationalist party would probably have had fewer scruples about closing the corporate taps that supplied its rivals, a situation that is quite unlike today's federal scene. These differences in context probably explain (at least in part) why there is not strong support within federal parties for the idea of "grassroots financing."

THEORETICAL AND PRACTICAL INTEREST OF THE QUEBEC SYSTEM

K.Z. Paltiel (1981, 142–43) observed 10 years ago that parties had generally been unable to collect adequate funds through personal contributions; the help of corporate, union or government bureaucracy was necessary. In this respect, the province of Quebec is an interesting case in that no legal entity of any type can make political contributions; this privilege is restricted to voters, with government providing additional incentives.[2]

Although unique in Canada, such a legal framework is not unusual. In the United States, direct contributions by legal entities are also prohibited at the federal level, while corporate contributions are forbidden in 19 states and union contributions in nine states (Council of State Governments 1988, 193–202). The sharp criticism surrounding the activity of political action committees (PACs) (see Stern 1988; Wright 1982; U.S. News & World Report 1984, 1988; Time 1984) tends to obscure facts familiar to the experts: PACs contribute little to presidential campaigns; they remain a minority source of funds for congressional elections. Most important, PACs collect only personal contributions not exceeding $5 000, which they pool for maximum effect. It is revealing that the sharpest complaint in the United States is not about the prohibition of contributions by legal entities, but rather about the possibility that such contributions could, through PACs, influence the financial strength of campaigns (see Sabato 1984, 1985; Grenzke 1988, 1989; Jacobson 1980, 1985; Lacorne 1984; Lassale 1986, 124–31; Epstein 1986, 284–300).

Proponents of the Quebec and American systems were, respectively, the Parti québécois (PQ) and the Progressive Movement, under whose influence corporate contributions were prohibited in the United

States as early as 1907 (Ontario, Commission 1988, 112–13). Despite their obvious policy differences, the two movements shared a significant reason for their keen interest in the rules of the political process. As middle-class parties, they could not rely on solid corporate or union support.[3] This did not mean that the parties received no support or money from the two groups; rather, it meant simply that the parties could not claim to *represent* either in the same way that Conservative and Labour party members in Britain represent, respectively, business and unions. Economic leaders, often anglophones, saw the idea of Quebec's independence as heresy, and from 1971, at least, it became obvious that the PQ would keep its distance from union leaders. As a result, grassroots financing was the only alternative, and the party experimented with it successfully before imposing it on all other parties shortly after coming to power (on the origins of grassroots financing in the PQ, see Léger 1986, 54–61).

Regardless of what we think of the arguments for or against this system,[4] it does raise questions of a practical nature. Are the parties able to gather the resources required without resorting to unlawful methods? Does the system augment the parties' financial dependency on the state? Does it make parties "more independent" of financial powers? Does it mean that internal party finances become more centralized? An analysis of the financial reports produced in accordance with the law over the past 12 years helps answer these questions and evaluate the financial health of parties. This analysis will focus on party revenues rather than expenditures. The ground rules for expenditures have already been analysed since the coming into force of new provisions on electoral expenses in 1963; there were no changes as a result of the 1977 Act (although the provisions have been enforced more stringently since then).[5]

The parties' financial reports for the period 1 April 1978 to 31 December 1989 consist of thousands of pages. Extracting information from them requires careful attention. The summary tables presented in this study are based on information contained in these reports.[6]

THE OVERWHELMING DOMINATION OF THE TWO LARGER PARTIES

On the surface, Quebec has a multitude of parties. Since 1978, no fewer than 38 different parties have been authorized[7] to receive contributions and incur expenses. However, 24 parties have also had their authorizations revoked during the same period. From libertarians to communists, from the proponents of independence to the supporters of freedom of choice, not to mention the Green Party and others, there is hardly an ideological movement that has not been constituted as a political party in Quebec since the Act came into force (see table 1.1).[8]

Table 1.1
Number of authorized entities (excluding independent candidates) as of 31 March
each year, 1978–91

| Year | Political parties | Party organizations | | | Total |
		Electoral districts	Regions	Quebec	
1978	6	0	0	0	6
1979	7	255[a]	36	0	298
1980	9	257[a]	36	0	302
1981	12	292[b]	13	0	317
1982	12	291[b]	13	0	316
1983	15	294[a]	14	1	324
1984	17	298[a]	14	1	330
1985	17	309	14	1	341
1986	12	376	14	2	404
1987	14	392	14	1	421
1988	17	394	14	1	426
1989	17	395	14	1	427
1990	16	339	13	0	368
1991	14	313	15	0	342

Source: Quebec, Director General of Political Party Financing (1978–82) and Chief Electoral Officer
(1982–91), Rapports annuels.
[a] At that time called "district associations."
[b] Includes 12 "local organizations," all others being "district associations."

On closer examination, however, this multiplicity is more illusion
than reality. Consider the example of local- and regional-level entities
authorized since 1978 (see table 1.2). Only the Quebec Liberal party (QLP)
and the Parti québécois (PQ) have managed to establish and maintain
authorized associations in all constituencies over those years. The NDP-
Quebec (NDPQ) has authorized associations in 58 constituencies. Before
its demise in 1989, the Union nationale (UN) had between 33 and 58 authorized associations.[9] The Parti indépendantiste managed to organize itself
in approximately 30 electoral districts before it disappeared. Five other
parties have obtained authorization for a few local associations, while
the remainder have had none. At the regional level, only the QLP and the
PQ had authorized associations throughout the entire province.[10]

While authorizations help to evaluate the strength and geographic
distribution of the parties, these numbers are only vague indicators.

Table 1.2
Number of authorized riding associations, by party, as of 31 March each year, 1978–91

Year	QLP	PQ	UN	Créd.	PNP	UQ	PI	PCPQ	NDPQ	EP	Total
1978	—	—	—	—	—	—	—	—	—	—	0
1979	110	110	34	—	1	—	—	—	—	—	255
1980	110	110	33	3	1	—	—	—	—	—	257
1981	122	122[a]	44	3	1	—	—	—	—	—	292
1982	122	122[a]	45	2	—	—	—	—	—	—	291
1983	122	122	48	2	—	—	—	—	—	—	294
1984	122	122	52	2	—	—	—	—	—	—	298
1985	122	122	57	2	—	6	—	—	—	—	309
1986	122	122	58	—	—	—	4	7	63	—	376
1987	122	122	49	—	—	—	29	7	63	—	392
1988	122	122	49	—	—	—	31	7	63	—	394
1989	126[b]	126[b]	49	—	—	—	31	—	63	—	395
1990	125	125	—	—	—	—	27	—	58	4	339
1991	125	125	—	—	—	—	—	—	58	5	313

Source: Quebec, Director General of Political Party Financing (1978–82) and Chief Electoral Officer (1982–91), *Rapports annuels.*

Notes: Parties not listed in the chart had no authorized riding associations on the dates indicated.

QLP = Quebec Liberal party; PQ = Parti québécois; UN = Union nationale; Créd. = Ralliement créditiste (les Démocrates); PNP = Parti national populaire; UQ = Parti Unité Québec; PI = Parti indépendantiste; PCPQ = Progressive Conservative party of Quebec; NDPQ = NDP-Quebec; EP = Equality party.

[a]Includes 12 "local organizations," all others being "district associations."

[b]The number of riding associations for these two parties was higher than the number of electoral districts that existed at the time, following the expected redistribution.

Many local associations, and even provincial parties, are little more than inactive "legal shells." Eleven parties lost their authorizations in November 1985 for failing to run 10 candidates, as required under the *Election Act*, even though no deposit is required from candidates.[11]

As a source of information, the financial reports of authorized parties and party authorities are much more revealing. Over the past 12 years the reports have sketched the portrait of a political scene that is clearly two-party. The five indicators we used for analysis all point to the same conclusion (see table 1.3). Since 1978, the two major political parties combined have collected over 97 percent of the revenue, contributions and membership fees reported by all authorized entities,

Table 1.3

Combined revenues and expenditures of the Quebec Liberal party and the Parti québécois, 1978–89

(percentage of total)

Year	Total revenue	Money contributions	Number of contributors (receipts issued)	Membership fees	Expenditures
1978	95.7	97.1	96.7	95.7	93.3
1979	97.2	98.3	98.7	96.2	94.9
1980	98.2	98.4	99.4	98.4	96.7
1981	94.2	93.2	96.9	99.2	95.6
1982	97.6	97.6	96.7	96.5	95.8
1983	97.9	97.6	99.0	98.6	96.9
1984	99.0	99.1	99.4	99.2	98.0
1985	97.1	96.7	96.3	99.3	96.4
1986	98.3	98.2	96.6	99.4	96.7
1987	97.7	98.2	91.5	95.0	96.6
1988	98.4	98.8	98.3	93.7	97.8
1989	96.2	95.2	95.6	95.6	97.4
Total	97.3	97.4	97.1	97.2	96.3

and their contributors represent 97.1 percent of the total number. Predictably, their expenditures represent 96.3 percent of the total amount. Although the two parties clearly dominate the political scene between elections, this domination is less pronounced during election years.

Among minor parties (see table 1.4), the UN ranks highest, with aggregate revenue for 1978 to 1989 of $975 631, or less than 3 percent of revenue reported during the same period by the weaker of the two larger political parties. The NDPQ collected $476 647 over five fiscal years: its best annual performance (in 1987) amounted to less than one-tenth that of the PQ, which was then experiencing a slump. The hegemony of the two major parties during the period under study was never seriously challenged, even though opinion polls conducted in the fall of 1987 offered a glimmer of hope – which later vanished – to the NDPQ. A good dozen or so groups registered since 1978 could rightly be described as "micro-parties" of little importance.

Table 1.4
Principal small parties, 1978–89
(dollars)

Name	Total revenues	Highest revenue reported in a single year
Union nationale	975 631	219 691 (1981)
New Democratic party of Quebec	476 647	158 401 (1987)
Equality party	254 807	254 807 (1989)
Progressive Conservative party of Quebec	217 932	195 885 (1985)
Quebec Communist party	182 879	32 687 (1981)
Parti indépendantiste	125 659	54 655 (1985)
Parti des travailleurs du Québec	112 957	16 735 (1989)
Mouvement socialiste	105 050	24 364 (1989)
Freedom of Choice party	50 459	29 618 (1981)
Ralliement créditiste / Les Démocrates/ Parti démocrate créditiste	41 213	19 588 (1979)
Workmen's Communist party (Quebec section)	37 086	34 836 (1981)
Parti humaniste du Québec	20 676	7 861 (1985)
Parti national populaire	14 136	7 741 (1978)

These indications simply confirm the evidence from election statistics. The two larger parties have won all the seats contested since the 1976 general election, except for four won by the Equality party in 1989. Their combined share of votes reached 92.4 percent during the 1978–80 by-elections, 95.3 percent in 1981, 89.7 percent during the 1982–85 by-elections, 94.7 percent in 1985, 91.1 percent during the by-elections of the 33rd Legislature and 90.1 percent in 1989. Because of their dominance, the remainder of this study focuses almost exclusively on the Quebec Liberal party and the Parti québécois.

Is the 1977 Act a major cause of the duopoly established under its authority (Angell 1988, 3)? Large organizations are undoubtedly better equipped than smaller ones to fulfil the complex obligations imposed by such legislation. However, it would not be justified to criticize the Act for favouring larger parties. Existing organizations, other than those led by the Premier and the Leader of the Opposition, were not obliged to meet overly stringent authorization requirements; they simply had to present 10 candidates in the subsequent general election. Parties whose members were elected to the National Assembly gained access to a proportion of the government allowance[12] and could delegate members to the committee responsible for advising the director general who applied the Act. The UN, the Créditistes and the Parti national populaire were squeezed because of the strong polarization generated by the referendum (this was apparent as early as 1978), their aging personnel and, in one case, the inability of the party to broaden its base outside one South Shore riding of Quebec. At the same time, the impact of the single-member plurality system should not be overlooked.

ADEQUATE INCOME?

The introduction of a new party financing system ruffled a few feathers. Some of the new Act's provisions threatened to dry up the parties' sources of income, or at least some of them. Contributions by legal entities, traditionally a major source of income for the QLP and the UN, were now prohibited. There was a ceiling of $3 000 on annual contributions from a single elector, and disclosure of the names of electors who gave contributions over $100 was mandatory.[13] In a society where legal entities had been a significant source of party income and where the fear of partisan reprisals was still deeply felt, there was reason to fear, if not a general dearth of funds, much difficulty for parties unfamiliar with grassroots financing. By increasing the annual government allowance to parties from $400 000 to more than $1 million, and by introducing fiscal incentives for political contributions, the legislators were clearly trying to alleviate fears and smooth the transition.

From a historical perspective, the new mechanism had the good fortune to be introduced during a lively period in Quebec politics. The importance of the referendum on separation made it easier to foster widespread public mobilization. Contrary to expectations, the QLP adjusted well to the new system during the crucial years following its introduction. During the first three fiscal years after adoption of the Act, the QLP reported revenues amounting to 89 percent of those of the PQ, an experienced practitioner of the system. Though the Liberals had troubles in 1981 that went beyond simple financing, they have since surpassed their rival.

In 12 years, the various authorized entities reported revenues totalling almost $111 million (see table 1.5). This amount would have been even higher if sources of income other than those explicitly mentioned in the Act had been reported prior to 1982.[14]

Were these revenues adequate? We can gain a better idea by examining the pattern of party revenues under a less restrictive legal framework. The revenues of Quebec provincial parties amounted to

27 percent of those of Canadian federal parties during the same 12-year period, a percentage somewhat greater than Quebec's demographic weight within the federation (for data concerning the federal level, see Paltiel 1988; Stanbury 1986, 1989; Seidle 1985). Such a comparison, however crude, at least suggests that the ban on corporate financing by no means led to the financial downfall of Quebec's parties.

This impression is borne out by the total expenditures by authorized entities from 1978 to 1989: at $118.9 million, they barely exceeded the revenues collected. However, this comparison obscures the following fact: while the QLP rarely spent more than it received, the PQ during its first term of office spent almost twice as much as it received and as the QLP spent. In the absence of a sizable contingency fund, this practice of overspending revenues is probably not unrelated to the party's subsequent financial woes.

The distribution of revenues of the two major parties is almost identical (see tables 1.6 and 1.7). Money contributions represent

Table 1.5
Reported revenues of all authorized entities, 1978–89
(dollars)

Year	Contri-butions	Membership fees	Admission / registration fees	Anon. donors	Election expense refunds	Other revenues	Total
1978	3 760 957	557 007	276 666	68 738	*	*	4 663 368
1979	5 070 458	848 958	251 780	75 005	*	*	6 246 201
1980	6 085 200	1 186 350	186 365	75 959	*	*	7 533 874
1981	4 402 038	1 705 864	205 258	59 128	*	*	6 372 288
1982	3 052 390	1 112 174	384 002	20 655	*	1 750 619	6 319 840
1983	3 529 929	1 054 784	543 349	18 248	*	1 653 875	6 800 185
1984	5 216 555	1 270 306	628 110	19 417	*	1 722 732	8 857 120
1985	10 703 941	1 894 233	553 565	39 958	2 669 338	1 688 573	17 549 608
1986	7 521 116	896 274	323 234	13 791	773 451	1 468 052	10 995 918
1987	7 522 201	881 084	324 774	5 713	70 870	1 609 361	10 414 003
1988	8 568 505	1 018 697	739 879	7 363	51 808	1 813 987	12 200 239
1989	6 568 782	1 339 130	276 856	23 993	2 631 301	2 169 122	13 009 184
Total	72 002 072	13 764 861	4 693 838	427 968	6 196 768	13 876 321	110 961 828
%	64.9	12.4	4.2	0.4	5.6	12.5	100.0

*This item, not then covered by the Act, was not included in the financial report.

approximately two-thirds of total revenues (66 percent for the QLP and 63 percent for the PQ). Membership fees come a distant second, at 12 percent of the total (10 percent for the QLP and 16 percent for the PQ). Other revenues, including the annual government grant, account for 16 percent of revenues collected since 1982 (the year the disclosure thereof became mandatory). Admission fees to political activities, demonstrations and conventions represent 4.2 percent of the total (5.2 percent for the QLP and 2.4 percent for the PQ). Election expense reimbursements made up approximately 5 percent of revenues (more in election years).

Major fluctuations were observed in revenues among the large parties. The QLP went from a low of $1.1 million in 1981 (an unusual phenomenon for an election year) to a high of $10.1 million in 1985. The PQ peaked, financially speaking, with a remarkable surge in 1985, when its revenues reached $6.9 million. Two years later, its revenues tumbled to $1.8 million, a figure it barely surpassed the

Table 1.6
Reported revenues: Quebec Liberal party, 1978–89
(dollars)

Year	Contri- butions	Membership fees	Admission / registration fees	Anon. donors	Election expense refunds	Other revenues	Total
1978	1 757 740	226 220	165 270	45 848	*	*	2 195 078
1979	2 587 460	411 580	111 510	40 142	*	*	3 150 692
1980	2 387 067	546 057	119 549	53 282	*	*	3 105 955
1981	717 619	283 238	64 440	11 574	*	*	1 076 871
1982	997 880	351 547	310 168	10 441	*	961 841	2 631 877
1983	1 807 369	609 796	461 818	11 371	*	856 485	3 746 839
1984	3 459 241	874 679	535 472	14 397	*	979 973	5 863 762
1985	6 407 233	999 300	422 133	19 899	1 340 794	940 660	10 130 019
1986	6 550 267	619 090	242 793	5 878	435 114	948 805	8 801 947
1987	6 543 846	528 780	208 145	2 263	39 077	1 041 980	8 364 091
1988	7 242 687	568 080	608 457	740	36 562	1 297 149	9 773 675
1989	2 997 152	700 545	151 530	565	1 320 582	1 546 369	6 716 743
Total	43 455 561	6 718 912	3 401 285	216 400	3 197 129	8 573 262	65 537 549
%	66.3	10.3	5.2	0.3	4.8	13.1	100.0

*This item, not then covered by the Act, was not included in the financial report.

following year, despite Jacques Parizeau's efforts to revive the party's fortunes. These swings are much bigger than those observed at the federal level. They do not always correspond to opinion poll or election results. The financial collapse of the QLP in 1981, for example, did not reflect their respectable showing in the general election held that year. A comparison of the party's ratings in the polls and its financial performance suggests that the latter indicator exaggerates both the lows and highs of the parties.

The scope of the financial fluctuations created concern among certain observers, who believed that the swings supported the case for reinstating corporate contributions (Angell 1982, 88; 1987, 377; and 1988, 16). Such a move probably would have solved the QLP's financial problems in 1981, but it is difficult to see how it could have helped the PQ later. In addition, in the context of the years 1985–88, the reinstatement of corporate contributions would probably have

Table 1.7
Reported revenues: Parti québécois, 1978–89
(dollars)

Year	Contri-butions	Membership fees	Admission / registration fees	Anon. donors	Election expense refunds	Other revenues	Total
1978	1 892 670	306 729	60 571	6 448	*	*	2 266 418
1979	2 394 548	405 000	96 047	22 406	*	*	2 918 001
1980	3 601 585	621 279	56 571	16 500	*	*	4 295 935
1981	3 384 152	1 408 210	122 157	13 152	*	*	4 927 671
1982	1 981 048	721 720	58 266	5 106	*	770 591	3 536 731
1983	1 638 919	429 743	60 733	3 775	*	777 104	2 910 274
1984	1 709 577	385 843	73 196	2 306	*	731 396	2 902 318
1985	3 940 487	881 340	86 460	11 727	1 276 630	709 386	6 906 030
1986	836 089	271 493	69 047	5 101	321 200	507 417	2 010 347
1987	839 756	308 115	85 433	1 954	22 951	547 227	1 805 436
1988	1 222 226	386 142	122 129	5 597	12 870	491 726	2 240 690
1989	3 257 811	580 209	120 519	20 807	1 288 614	535 384	5 803 344
Total	26 698 868	6 705 823	1 011 129	114 879	2 922 265	5 070 231	42 523 196
%	62.8	15.8	2.4	0.3	6.9	11.9	100.1**

*This item, not then covered by the Act, was not included in the financial report.
**Percentages do not add to 100.0 because of rounding.

aggravated the already worrisome imbalance between the two larger parties, not to mention raising ethical objections about destroying the cornerstone of the 1977 Act. It is interesting to note that, during the 1987–89 revision of the *Election Act*, the Liberal government did not even consider such an option (Quebec, Electoral Reform Secretariat 1988, 85–150; Quebec, Parliamentary Commission 1988).

ANALYSIS OF FINANCIAL CONTRIBUTIONS

In keeping with the spirit of the Act, money contributions have become the standard source of party income. None of the other financing sources provided in the Act is regulated so closely or secures similar advantages. Given their relative importance (see table 1.8), it is not unreasonable to consider money contributions as the major indicator of a party's financial health (see table 1.9).

The major development since 1978, therefore, is the marked decline in the number of contributors (see table 1.10). On average, 211 000 receipts were issued each year between 1978 and 1981,[15] compared with 96 487 annually between 1985 and 1988. *The financial base of the*

Table 1.8
Contributions as a percentage of total revenues of authorized entities, 1978–89

Year	All authorized entities	Quebec Liberal party	Parti québécois
1978	80.6	80.1	83.5
1979	81.2	82.1	82.1
1980	80.8	76.9	83.8
1981	69.1	66.6	68.7
1982	48.3	37.9	56.0
1983	51.9	48.2	56.3
1984	58.9	59.0	58.9
1985	61.0	63.2	57.1
1986	68.4	74.4	41.6
1987	72.2	78.2	46.6
1988	70.3	74.3	54.6
1989	50.5	44.6	56.1
Total	66.1	65.5	62.1

Table 1.9
Overall contributions collected, 1978–89
(dollars)

Year	All authorized entities	Quebec Liberal party	Parti québécois	Other parties	Independent candidates
1978	3 760 957	1 757 740	1 892 670	110 547	—
1979	5 070 458	2 587 460	2 394 548	88 450	—
1980	6 085 200	2 387 067	3 601 585	96 502	46
1981	4 402 038	717 619	3 384 152	269 571	30 696
1982	3 052 390	997 880	1 981 048	73 462	—
1983	3 529 929	1 807 369	1 638 919	72 885	10 756
1984	5 216 555	3 459 241	1 709 577	40 834	6 903
1985	10 703 941	6 407 233	3 940 487	322 851	33 370
1986	7 521 116	6 550 267	836 089	127 520	7 240
1987	7 522 201	6 543 846	839 756	138 599	—
1988	8 568 505	7 242 687	1 222 226	103 510	82
1989	6 568 782	2 997 152	3 257 811	257 913	55 906
Total	72 002 072	43 455 561	26 698 868	1 702 644	144 999

political parties therefore shrank by half during the period examined. However, since 1985, the overall amount of contributions was much higher than during the early years of the Act because after 1983 the average size of contributions increased (see table 1.11). Before 1983, electors contributed an average of $20. In 1983 this figure climbed to $35, then to $52 in 1984, $83 in 1985, $105 in 1986, $78 in 1987 and $96 in 1988. Inflation alone cannot explain such a sharp increase, which began in a period of economic stagnation.

During the same period, the relative importance of "small contributions" ($100 and less) constantly diminished (see table 1.12). Small contributions represented 78 percent of the total amount in 1978, but only 23 percent in 1988. Receipts for small contributions were 98 percent of the total receipts issued in 1978, but only 77 percent 10 years later.

These developments did not affect the two parties equally. Based on either of the indicators mentioned above, the PQ has remained closer to its earlier practices. With the exception of 1985, the average size of contributions to the PQ varied between $20 and $49 during the 12-year

Table 1.10
Number of receipts issued for contributions, 1978–89

Year	All authorized entities	Quebec Liberal party	Parti québécois	Other parties	Independent candidates
1978	163 910	64 535	93 941	5 434	0
1979	235 139	124 439	107 569	3 131	0
1980	259 072	103 337	154 170	1 564	1
1981	185 803	11 049	168 910	5 652	192
1982	111 235	29 815	77 748	3 672	0
1983	100 181	50 009	49 143	882	147
1984	99 680	54 120	44 963	565	32
1985	128 391	61 791	61 895	4 469	236
1986	71 354	45 286	23 620	2 441	7
1987	96 864	66 524	22 118	8 222	0
1988	89 339	53 349	34 355	1 634	1
1989	82 027	11 821	66 582	3 367	257
Total	1 622 995	676 075	905 014	41 033	873

Table 1.11
Average contribution, 1978–89
(dollars)

Year	All authorized entities	Quebec Liberal party	Parti québécois	Other parties	Independent candidates
1978	22.95	27.24	20.15	20.34	N/A
1979	21.56	20.79	22.26	28.25	N/A
1980	23.48	23.09	23.39	61.70	46.25
1981	23.85	64.95	20.19	47.69	159.88
1982	27.44	33.47	24.62	20.01	N/A
1983	35.24	36.14	33.35	82.64	73.17
1984	52.33	63.92	38.02	72.27	215.73
1985	83.37	103.69	63.66	72.24	141.40
1986	105.41	144.64	35.40	52.24	1 034.35
1987	77.65	98.37	37.97	16.86	N/A
1988	95.90	135.76	35.57	64.82	82.00
1989	80.08	253.54	48.93	76.60	217.53

N/A = not applicable; there were no contributions to independent candidates in those years.

period. Contributions of $100 or less were still the most numerous, with little change since 1978. The QLP, on the other hand, experienced significant changes. In 1979, the average contribution to the QLP was slightly less than that to the PQ ($20.79 compared with $22.26). From this level, it leapt past the hundred dollar mark in four out of five years since 1985, to a level in the same neighbourhood as contributions *by individuals* to the traditional federal parties. As a result, the relative importance of small contributions to the QLP fell from 82 percent in 1978 to 15 percent 10 years later.

While the PQ has strayed less from its earlier practices, the QLP has not returned to its own. With several thousand contributors having made an average annual contribution of $132 since its return to power in 1985, it remains much closer to grassroots financing than its counterparts in Ottawa or in the other provinces. In terms of the number of contributors, it outranked the PQ in all but two years since 1983 (see table 1.10).

For the PQ, the most disturbing indicator is not the average size of contributions, but rather the steep decline in the number of donors. The number of PQ contributors reached 154 170 in 1980 and 168 910 (a level since unparalleled) in 1981. That figure tumbled to 77 748 in

Table 1.12
Contributions of $100 or less as a percentage of total contributions, 1978–89

Year	All authorized entities		Quebec Liberal party		Parti québécois	
	Receipts issued	Amounts paid	Receipts issued	Amounts paid	Receipts issued	Amounts paid
1978	98	78	98	82	97	75
1979	98	75	98	78	97	73
1980	97	73	98	74	97	73
1981	97	72	94	69	97	75
1982	97	72	96	73	96	72
1983	94	64	95	69	94	60
1984	90	48	89	45	93	55
1985	86	29	82	23	90	40
1986	82	29	75	19	95	58
1987	79	29	72	17	94	60
1988	77	23	66	15	95	66
1989	88	33	60	8	94	55

1982, 44 963 in 1984, 23 620 in 1986 and 34 451 in 1988. However, the party could still stage a comeback, as it did in 1985 and 1989 with a well-managed fund-raising campaign (Léger 1986, 290–93). The QLP also experienced a decline in its number of donors since 1979, its best year (124 439), but after scraping bottom in 1981 with 11 049 contributors, it subsequently stabilized around the 50 000 mark long before it came to power.

FUND-RAISING METHODS

The fund-raising methods used by the PQ and QLP illustrate the diversity of practices authorized under Quebec's Act. By and large, the PQ has stuck to the method it introduced in the early 1970s under the leadership of Marcel Léger, based on small contributions raised from among the membership. The QLP prefers social activities (dinners, brunches, cocktail parties, golf tournaments, etc.), for which it charges a wide range of admission fees (in 1988, the charge varied from $2 to $2 500). This practice, introduced on a large scale after the Act was amended in this regard in 1984,[16] proved so successful that it became the party's chief source of contributions (see table 1.13). From 139 in 1985, the number of such social activities climbed to 264 in 1988, or an average of five each week. Contributions collected through social events grew from $1.9 million in 1985 (30.4 percent of total party contributions) to $5.9 million in 1988 (82.6 percent).

The PQ and some observers have criticized this fund-raising

Table 1.13
Contributions with or without receipts collected during social events: Quebec Liberal party, 1983–89

Year	Number of social events	Amount of contributions given at those events	As a % of total contributions to the party
1983	112	0	N/A
1984	79	0	N/A
1985	139	1 944 794	30.4
1986	211	4 370 600	66.7
1987	221	4 810 857	73.5
1988	264	5 985 044	82.6
1989	32	178 383	6.0

N/A = not applicable.

method as contrary to the spirit of the Act. Some have referred to fund-raising dinners where, for the "modest" sum of $1 000, voters can rub elbows with cabinet ministers. Such events are not unusual. In 1988, 50 or so of the Liberals' 264 social activities set admission fees of $1 000 or more, and these accounted for approximately 35 percent of contributions from social events. The average estimated number of participants at these high-cost activities was about 30. This being said, we should point out that the legality of this type of activity is beyond question, as long as participants are not fronting for bigger financial backers.

Does the success of grassroots financing depend on the number of party members? This is what Angell (1988) strongly argues; he considers that the number of members is the most important feature of a mass party, the essential tool enabling it to collect funds. Indeed, it is not unlikely that a party requires a certain membership "cushion" to conduct a successful fund-raising campaign. However, in light of the Quebec experience, it is questionable whether a direct relation exists between membership growth and financing success. From 1985 to 1987, the QLP lost almost half its membership, dropping from 190 068 to 105 756, while total contributions climbed during the same period from $6.4 million to $6.5 million. In May 1988, the PQ under Jacques Parizeau managed to catch up with the Liberals in membership, with 102 223 members in good standing; however, the same year, it collected only $1.2 million in contributions.[17]

The success of a fund-raising campaign depends on a host of factors: political and economic conditions, whether the party is in power or in opposition, the degree of grassroots mobilization and conviction, the personalities of the leader and campaign organizers, the party's popularity among the electorate, and the wealth of its members and supporters. Among this complex group of factors, the total number of party workers is not a decisive factor. At least, this seems to be the lesson that emerges from the QLP's success in fund-raising since 1983. Compared with the PQ's door-to-door technique, which requires a large number of active, motivated supporters, the QLP's social activities need fewer workers yet have produced concrete results.

PUBLIC FUNDING OF PARTIES: SUBSTITUTE OR COMPLEMENT?

As yet, the sharp drop in the number of contributors has not, as some observers had feared, created a revenue void, a void that should have to be filled with an increase in the annual government subsidy. The subsidy has remained unchanged at $0.25 per voter since 1977. The virtual elimination of the annual enumeration of voters since then has not permitted any adjustment of this subsidy, except following an election. From 1982 to 1988, this subsidy and election expense reimbursements represented 7.2 percent to 19.8 percent of the QLP's revenues (see tables 1.14 and 1.15). The Parti québécois has relied more heavily on these sources, which represented 15.8 percent to 38.9 percent of its revenues during the same period. When times are hard, outside sources of financing dry up, inflating the relative weight of the more stable allowance.

Tax Credits

Public funding also takes the form of tax credits for individuals who contribute to the parties. The Quebec scheme has always been less generous than the formula at the federal level and in most of the provinces, even after legislative amendments in 1983 increased the Quebec credit to 50 percent of the first $280 contributed.[18] The cost of these tax credits has exceeded the annual subsidy ($16.4 million compared with $11.5 million over an 11-year period) and would have exceeded it even more if every eligible taxpayer claimed the credit, which was not actually the case.

Data available from the Quebec Department of Revenue show that a majority of donors did *not* claim the tax credit to which they

Table 1.14
Direct government subsidies: Quebec Liberal party, 1982–89

Year	Election expense reimbursements ($)	Annual subsidy ($)	Reimbursements and subsidy as a % of total party revenues
1982	Not included	520 413	19.8
1983	Not included	525 611	14.0
1984	Not included	525 447	9.0
1985	1 340 794	557 665	18.7
1986	435 114	661 202	12.5
1987	39 077	665 642	8.4
1988	36 562	665 642	7.2
1989	1 320 582	646 166	29.3

Table 1.15
Direct government subsidies: Parti québécois, 1982–89

Year	Election expense reimbursements ($)	Annual subsidy ($)	Reimbursements and subsidy as a % of total party revenues
1982	Not included	559 080	15.8
1983	Not included	558 612	19.2
1984	Not included	561 712	19.4
1985	1 276 630	571 326	26.8
1986	321 200	461 593	38.9
1987	22 951	469 189	27.3
1988	12 870	461 189	21.1
1989	1 288 614	461 306	30.2

were entitled under the Act (see table 1.16). Since 1978, the number of individuals who obtained a tax credit for political contributions has varied between one-third and one-half of the number of receipts issued (50 percent in 1989).

Several factors might explain this phenomenon. While the numerator (individual contributors identified for tax credits) on which the above percentages are based is unquestionably correct, the denominator may be artificially inflated if a single individual has made many contributions, because the data only indicate the number of receipts, not whether more than one has been issued to any individual.

However, while it is possible that the denominator is inflated, it is unlikely, for two reasons. First, as mentioned earlier and in the Appendix, nothing in the financial reports indicates that the number of receipts (except for the QLP from 1985–88) is markedly higher than the number of contributors, at least for contributions over $100, the only contributions that can be verified. Second, since 1983 it has been possible to know not only the number of contributors and the amount of the tax credits paid to them, but also the total amount of contributions they reported paying. This latter amount represents only two-thirds to four-fifths of the value of money contributions received by authorized entities during the same period; hence the conclusion that not all tax credits are claimed.

It is quite possible that some electors lose receipts that are issued on the spot, or that people who do not pay income tax fail to take advan-

Table 1.16
Tax credits for political contributions, 1978–89

Year	Taxpayers having a tax credit			Total contributions reported in tax returns		
	Number	As a % of receipts issued	Tax credits (thousands of $)	Amount declared by parties (thousands of $)	As a % of contributions	Average amount per taxpayer
1978	50 401	31	1 125	n.a.	n.a.	n.a.
1979	77 631	33	1 508	n.a.	n.a.	n.a.
1980	90 358	35	1 727	n.a.	n.a.	n.a.
1981	69 034	37	1 267	n.a.	n.a.	n.a.
1982	50 708	46	926	n.a.	n.a.	n.a.
1983	32 671	33	1 045	2 501	71	76.55
1984	43 103	43	1 454	3 930	75	91.18
1985	54 449	42	2 237	7 738	72	142.11
1986	37 023	52	1 749	5 054	67	136.51
1987	29 813	31	1 525	5 078	67	170.33
1988	44 543	50	1 936	6 750	79	151.54
1989	41 028	50	1 546	5 195	79	126.62

Source: Compiled from data provided by the Quebec Department of Revenue, Direction des études, recherches et statistiques, July and August 1989; May 1991.

n.a.= not available.

tage of the tax reduction to which their contribution entitles them (more than one-quarter of Quebec taxpayers do not pay provincial income tax). If we cannot accept such explanations, difficult as they are to substantiate, there is yet another hypothesis: many taxpayers may not claim the credit to which they are entitled on their income tax return for fear of political reprisals. Such behaviour, however, appears most common among contributors of $100 or less, to whom the Act guarantees anonymity. The same fear is no longer a factor for persons contributing more than $100, because their names must in any case be disclosed in the party's financial report; hence, there is no point in hiding their contribution from the Department of Revenue.[19] This explanation is made more plausible by the fact that the average contribution reported on tax returns has been higher each year than the average contribution to authorized entities (see table 1.17). Some years, the former is twice as high as the latter.

Table 1.17
Comparison of contributions made and contributions
reported on tax returns, 1983–89
(dollars)

Year	Amount of average contribution	
	Given to authorized authorities (financial report)	Reported on tax return
1983	35.24	76.55
1984	52.33	91.18
1985	83.37	142.11
1986	105.41	136.51
1987	77.65	170.33
1988	95.90	151.54
1989	80.00	126.62

Source: Compiled from data provided by the Quebec Department
of Revenue, Direction des études, recherches et statistiques,
July and August 1989; May 1991.

If this analysis is correct, we are confronted with a significant paradox. In principle, the tax credit aims to encourage small contributions because it applies only to the portion of contributions under $280. Yet, for one reason or another, it seems that small contributors are most reluctant to claim the contribution. We may therefore question the effectiveness of such tax credits, even though they are lower than those elsewhere in the country. More than half the contributors do not care whether they receive the credit or not; they do not seem to be financially motivated.

FINANCIAL CENTRALIZATION WITHIN THE PARTIES

Both at the provincial level and in the constituencies, do the QLP and the PQ differ significantly in terms of financial centralization? Some interesting indications come from computing the portion collected or spent centrally for each revenue item and for total expenditures (see tables 1.18 and 1.19).

The QLP demonstrates a clear trend toward centralization, since almost all of its 1988 revenues (98 percent) were collected centrally. Within the PQ, only 32 percent of revenues were collected centrally during the same year. The basic reason for this difference is that all QLP contributions and membership fees are raised at the central level, while the PQ collects most of them in the constituencies. Nonetheless, a distinct trend toward centralization can be observed in both parties: even within the PQ, headquarters ("le national") collected only 17 percent of revenue in 1978, but 25 percent in 1983 and 32 percent in 1988. The scope of this phenomenon cannot be exaggerated, since each party has internal rules governing the redistribution of funds among the different levels.

As for expenditures, the differences between the two parties are much less obvious, with most expenditures being made at the central level in both cases: the PQ was traditionally less centralized than the QLP in expenditures, but the gap has been closing over the years.

Finally, it must be emphasized that expenditures vary according to electoral conditions: on average, expenditures are twice as high

Table 1.18
Financial centralization: Quebec Liberal party, 1978–89
(percentage collected or spent by headquarters)

Year	Contri-butions	Member-ship fees	Admis-sion fee	Regis-tration fee	Anon-ymous dona-tions	Reimburse-ment of election expenses	Other income	Total income	Total expendi-tures
1978	100	32	7	100	86	N/A	N/A	90	86
1979	100	10	0	100	93	N/A	N/A	85	75
1980	100	23	20	94	92	N/A	N/A	85	77
1981	99	21	0	0	83	N/A	N/A	72	52
1982	99	0		25[a]	36	N/A	86	72	71
1983	98	83		61	61	N/A	87	88	75
1984	100	88		52	86	N/A	88	92	79
1985	100	95		71	91	0	90	84	71
1986	100	100		50	3	0	94	93	78
1987	100	100		66	97	0	94	98	75
1988	100	100		93	0	0	91	98	81
1989	100	100		83	0	0	89	77	66

Note: As an example of how to read this table, in 1978, 90% of revenues reported by the Liberal party were collected centrally, 10% by local or regional party authorities.

[a]Since 1982, the admission and registration fees have been amalgamated for accounting purposes.

N/A = not applicable; this item, not then covered by the Act, was not included in the financial report.

Table 1.19
Financial centralization: Parti québécois, 1978–89
(percentage collected or spent by headquarters)

Year	Contri-butions	Member-ship fees	Admis-sion fee	Regis-tration fee	Anon-ymous dona-tions	Reimburse-ment of election expenses	Other income	Total income	Total expendi-tures
1978	4	100	0	0	9	N/A	N/A	17	47
1979	3	100	0	57	26	N/A	N/A	18	43
1980	1	100	0	0	11	N/A	N/A	15	49
1981	2	52	0	65	0	N/A	N/A	17	51
1982	2	2		28[a]	48	N/A	87	21	55
1983	4	1		32	0	N/A	80	25	54
1984	4	3		36	0	N/A	82	24	59
1985	20	48		24	0	N/A	86	27	64
1986	10	2		0	0	0	89	27	60
1987	7	9		58	0	0	95	36	74
1988	10	12		57	0	0	95	32	74
1989	22	4		24	0	0	89	22	37

Note: As an example of how to read this table, in 1978, 17% of revenues reported by the Parti québécois were collected centrally, 83% by local or regional party authorities.

[a]Since 1982, the admission and registration fees have been amalgamated for accounting purposes.

N/A = not applicable; this item, not then covered by the Act, was not included in the financial report.

during election and referendum years (see table 1.20). This observation corresponds to others made elsewhere in the country (see Nassmacher 1989, 225).

OVERALL FINANCIAL BALANCE

Since 1982, Quebec political parties have been required to produce an overall report of all their revenues and expenditures (see table 1.21)[20] (Quebec, Chief Electoral Officer 1985). The overall financial situation of the QLP, still in the black, has consistently been better than that of the PQ, which has reported deficits since 1985. In 1988, the gap between the two parties reached gigantic proportions when the QLP reported a surplus of $7.8 million and the PQ a deficit of $312 707. The financial troubles of the PQ are an alarming indicator: the party that introduced the system is having the most difficulty

Table 1.20
Expenditures by authorized entities, 1978–89
(dollars)

Year	All authorized entities	Quebec Liberal party	Parti québécois	Other parties	Independent candidates
1978	5 565 308	1 465 370	3 728 049	371 889	N/A
1979	8 809 645	2 811 013	5 550 033	448 599	N/A
1980	13 417 645	5 172 982	7 802 151	442 466	46
1981	17 024 500	6 143 899	10 134 543	693 727	52 331
1982	6 361 837	2 919 475	3 171 996	270 366	N/A
1983	6 894 704	3 763 625	2 916 652	191 067	23 360
1984	7 765 206	4 602 996	3 003 741	150 182	8 287
1985	11 869 439	7 197 380	4 249 929	348 894	73 236
1986	6 002 635	4 199 635	1 602 528	199 221	1 251
1987	7 321 085	5 079 554	1 995 240	246 291	N/A
1988	9 098 030	6 989 152	1 891 009	217 787	82
1989	18 789 033	12 202 222	6 091 621	401 888	93 302
Total	118 919 067	62 547 303	52 137 492	3 982 377	251 895

N/A = not applicable; no expenditures reported by independent candidates.

Table 1.21
Surplus (or deficit) at the fiscal year-end for Quebec Liberal party and Parti québécois, 1982–89
(dollars)

Year	Quebec Liberal party	Parti québécois
1982	1 066 113	98 361
1983	953 965	244 280
1984	1 104 871	65 470
1985	97 002	(457 144)
1986	2 865 006	44 184
1987	5 609 946	(293 887)
1988	7 777 949	(312 707)
1989	4 132 996	(450 895)

Note: Parentheses indicate a deficit.

financing itself under that system! If the political factors that have led to this problem persist, the party will have no alternative but to ask for full public funding of political parties.

1989 Financial Statements

Statements for 1989, made public the following year, reveal developments that temper criticisms that have been made of "grassroots financing" for some years.

First of all, the "stranglehold" of the two main parties was loosened when the Equality party (with an income of $254 807) achieved the best annual showing of a smaller party since the Act came into force, while still lagging well behind the weaker of the two larger parties. With its individual contributions averaging $71, this third party was not appreciably different from the others. The Equality party appears to receive very little financial support from francophones.

The main development for the QLP was the drop in the number of social events from 264 to 32. The money raised by such events, $178 383, was less than 6 percent of total contributions to the QLP. As well, the admission fee for each event was lower than in the past.

Criticism no doubt led to the decline of the social activities that were once so lucrative. The decline partially restored the balance between the incomes of the two larger parties, which was another major change in 1989. The total income of the QLP fell from $9.7 million the previous year to $6.7 million, while that of the PQ rose to $5.8 million from $2.2 million. For the first time since 1982, the PQ outclassed even the QLP in contributions received ($3.2 million as opposed to $2.9 million for the Liberals). The PQ also easily outdid the QLP in number of donors. These new developments confirm that the QLP does not depend exclusively on fund-raising dinners, although they have contributed to its prosperity when in power, and that the PQ is not doomed to poverty: its renewed financial upsurge coincided with a year-long rise in its popularity. Still, the $450 000 deficit remains a worry for party headquarters.

One trend that grew clearer in 1989, despite an election that year, was the decline in the number of contributors. The number of receipts (82 000) issued by all authorized bodies was the lowest since the law was enacted (except in 1986). The average annual number of subscribers (211 000 in 1978–81) fell to 85 000 for 1986–89. The PQ regained the lead, with 66 582 donors as opposed to 11 821 for the QLP, which would not have made a good financial showing except that the average contribution it received was $253, as opposed to $49 for the PQ.

Finally, in 1989, the sums provided by the government in the form of annual allowances and reimbursements for election expenses accounted for the highest proportion ever of each of the two parties' income (about 30 percent). The higher reimbursements for expenses in this election year explain this situation, which seems to be an exception.

In support of his categorical statement that the Quebec system "wasn't working," Harold Angell pointed out two facts in a letter to *La Presse* on 30 August 1990. First, he emphasized, the PQ was unable to attract the funding it needed; second, the QLP financed itself with social events. These assertions were no longer true in 1989.

CONCLUSION

This analysis is based on financial reports submitted annually by authorized entities. Only the reports submitted by parties to comply with the Act are audited. Nothing guarantees the absolute accuracy of reports prepared at the local level by volunteer workers who were obliged to take account of 14 directives, 11 recommendations, 9 inter- pretation bulletins and 5 reminders, not to mention the 13 princi- ples (Quebec, Chief Electoral Officer 1985) inscribed in a digest of jurisprudence! Nevertheless, the preceding analysis assumes that the people involved acted with honesty and competence, and checked each other. In the absence of clear evidence, we disregarded insin- uations that the Act was a mere "Potemkin village" concealing less honourable practices.

Sceptics will note, in light of the information analysed, that grassroots financing places the parties at greater risk than does corpo- rate or union financing. The income curve of the parties has taken sharp turns which, like a roller coaster, can dampen the enthusiasm of all but the most hardy. Others will reply that there is nothing wrong with a party being punished by its supporters for certain ideological or governmental choices. In other words, the grassroots financing method is not responsible for a party's financial disap- pointments; it merely allows basic political problems to reverberate directly at the financial level. There is no reason why the parties should be protected against all hazards or their own mistakes. This reasoning, of course, offers no comfort to those most directly affected.

The parties' shrinking financial base, demonstrated by the decline in the number of donors, is unquestionably the most disturbing development over the past 10 years. However, the number of donors seems to be stabilizing at a respectable level, one that far surpasses, on a per capita basis, the number of donors to the federal parties in Canada.[21]

The practical application of the Act has dispelled many of the concerns expressed in 1977 about its effects. The parties have not fallen under government control, and electors are still by far the main source of party revenues, although this study raises questions about the effectiveness of tax credits for those who make small donations.

Both parties that have held office since 1977 have occasionally had to defend themselves against accusations of corruption. However, these accusations were not always founded, and there were never as many as those made against previous provincial governments or against federal parties. It is difficult to distinguish the relative roles that various factors played in these developments: the personal integrity of René Lévesque, the introduction of contract-award mechanisms that theoretically ended favouritism, and the Act itself. But the psychological and practical impact of this legislation is undeniable. Indeed, the Bourassa government was very careful not to challenge its provisions after 1985.

People who perceive corporate financing as one of the major strings used by economic interests to ensure the perpetuation of capitalism and their domination of society will find little support for such theories in the Quebec experience. Few societies have gone as far in controlling party financing. Few have experienced simultaneously such infatuation with private enterprise and the values of capitalism. Few societies have seen unions so discredited and dealt with so harshly by a government party that had so "clean" a war chest.[22] This may be the chief myth that vanished with the "slush funds."

By prohibiting transfers between federal parties and Quebec parties, the Act accentuated a trend (already clear in 1964) of separation between the federal and provincial wings of the Liberal party. This slackening of ties that were formerly close (many authors have stressed the profound implications of this)[23] reached unprecedented levels during the 1988 federal election.

Given its originality, the model of Quebec's political party financing deserves more thorough examination. Two promising avenues for exploration are the profile of contributors and the relationship between financial success and electoral performance at the local level.

APPENDIX
THE NUMBER OF CONTRIBUTORS

How many individuals made political party contributions is one of the chief questions left unanswered by the financial reports. Unlike the *Canada Elections Act*, the Quebec Act does not require disclosing the number of *contributors*: it requires only disclosure of the *number of receipts issued* for contributions and the names of electors who gave larger contributions. A few sources (Angell 1987, 365; Quebec, Director General 1980, 39) considered the number of receipts and the number of contributors to be the same, as did we for this study.

However, differences are theoretically possible. The wording of section 83 of the 1977 Act did not clearly specify whether the identity of electors who made several donations of less than $100 but totalling more than $100 had to be disclosed. This ambiguity was not resolved until 1984, when parties were required to disclose the identity of a voter making one or more contributions totalling over $100. In 1977, nothing obliged the parties to consolidate the moneys paid to their provincial and local organizations: each voter could contribute $100 to a party and $100 to *each* of its local authorities in a given year without having his or her identity disclosed. This possibility was not eliminated until 1989, when the parties were required to consolidate such funds (Quebec *Election Act*, ss. 115–30).

It is impossible to determine accurately the extent to which these loopholes were used. Receipts for contributions of $100 and less are not open to public inspection. We examined the lists of electors who since 1978 had contributed more than $100 to the various authorized entities of the two larger parties, in order to locate names that were included more than once on the same list or that appeared on several lists during the same year. The findings are listed in tables 1.A1 and 1.A2. Clearly, the number of receipts for contributions over $100 slightly exceeds the number of contributors. The only major discrepancies (in the neighbourhood of 30 percent) relate to the Liberal party from 1985 to 1988. We should point out, however, that in 1985 and 1986 this party actually reported the number of contributors under the heading "number of receipts"!

These irregularities do not distort the fundamental conclusion of our research in this area, namely, that the financial base of the parties is half what it was 10 years ago. In fact, to the extent that the number of receipts reported by the QLP (in 1987 and 1988) artificially inflated the number of contributors, the decline in the number of contributors over the past 12 years is even greater than it appears.

Table 1.A1

Estimated difference in number of receipts issued and number of contributors of over $100 to the Quebec Liberal party, 1978–88

Year	Number of receipts issued	Estimated number of contributors[a]	Difference	Difference as a % of receipts issued
1978	1 175	1 162	13	1.1
1979	1 904	1 888	16	0.8
1980	1 974	1 959	15	0.8
1981	637	628	9	1.4
1982	906	879	27	3.0
1983	2 341	2 273	68	2.9
1984	5 915	5 883	32	0.5
1985	15 947[b]	10 970	4 977	31.2
1986	15 660[b]	11 312	4 348	27.8
1987	18 480	approx. 12 300	approx. 6 150	33.3
1988	18 204	approx. 13 000	approx. 5 200	28.6

[a]The number of contributors estimated after eliminating names entered two and three times, following a review of the list of contributors.
[b]The number of receipts reported by the party actually reflected the number of contributors. The number in this column is indeed the number of receipts.

Table 1.A2

Estimated difference in number of receipts issued and number of contributors of over $100 to the Parti québécois, 1978–88

Year	Number of receipts issued	Estimated number of contributors[a]	Difference	Difference as a % of receipts issued
1978	2 557	2 533	24	0.9
1979	3 389	3 380	9	0.3
1980	4 851	4 848	3	0.1
1981	4 281	4 270	11	0.3
1982	2 716	2 706	10	0.4
1983	2 701	2 697	4	0.1
1984	2 969	2 951	18	0.6
1985	5 942	5 742	200	3.4
1986	1 141	1 134	7	0.6
1987	1 267	1 244	23	1.8
1988	1 616	1 599	17	1.1

[a]The number of contributors was estimated after eliminating names entered two and three times, following a review of the list of contributors.

ABBREVIATIONS

c.   chapter
R.S.C.   Revised Statutes of Canada
S.Q.   Statutes of Quebec
s(s).   section(s)

NOTES

This study was completed in September 1991.

Louis Massicotte is a professor of political science at the Université de Montréal. The first draft of this study was prepared while he was a doctoral candidate at Carleton University and presented at a memorial conference in honour of Professor K.Z. Paltiel, February 1990.

In this study, quoted material that originated in French has been translated into English.

1. The following contain some useful theoretical pointers on party financing: Von Beyme (1985, 196–211); Duverger (1961, 83ff.); Epstein (1980, 242–50); Heidenheimer (1970, chap. 1); Key (1964, 486–519); Lemieux (1985, 186–92); Sartori (1976, 93ff.); Ware (1987, 98–104).

2. *An Act to govern the financing of political parties*, 1977. The provisions of this statute were integrated into the *Election Act* in 1984. The Act took effect in its entirety on 1 April 1978.

3. The situation of the Parti québécois in this regard is similar to that of the Union des électeurs, the Ralliement créditiste and the Bloc populaire. Concerning the first two, see Paltiel (1970, 70–74) and Stein (1966). Concerning the Bloc populaire, see Comeau (1982, 273–77). These three parties may be considered true pioneers of grassroots funding in Quebec, although for a long time their lack of success discouraged others from following their lead.

4. On this, see the debates during the bill's second reading in the *Débats de l'Assemblée nationale* (Quebec, Assemblée nationale 1977, 1845–54, 1926–55, 1994–2003, 2160–64, 2921–25, 2944–55, 2971–3007 and 3161–70, as well as the proceedings in committee (1977, B-3567–607 and B-4204–47). See especially interventions by Burns, Lavoie and Fontaine.

5. Concerning the *Election Act*, 1963, see Paltiel (1970, 124–32) and Angell (1966). The lax enforcement of this Act before 1977 is pointed out in Massicotte (1984, 48).

6. Like all statistics, those found in the financial reports may contain errors. For example, 21 reports by 11 parties were not submitted between 1978 and 1988, although all were very small organizations. Only the official

party reports were subject to a certified audit (Quebec *Election Act*, 1989, s. 110), not those of regional and constituency associations. Sometimes, the figures used one year change the next, due to the correction or late filing of a report (this author systematically checked this). As well, official representatives in ridings are not necessarily professional accountants. Nothing indicates that these flaws were extensive enough to affect the overall picture appreciably. On receipts, see the Appendix of this study.

7. The Act provides for authorizing three types of entities: parties; their organizations ("instances") at the electoral district, regional or Quebec levels; and independent candidates. The relevant provisions now appear in ss. 41–80 of the *Election Act*, 1989.

8. Criteria governing the authorization of new parties have frequently been revised. In 1977, parties were required to have a leader elected during a congress, to have 10 riding associations and to agree to run candidates in at least 10 electoral districts in subsequent general elections. In 1984, the requirements for an elected leader and 10 riding associations were eliminated, but parties had to submit (for an equal number of electoral districts) the names, addresses and signatures of 60 electors in each district, stating their membership or support of the party and their approval of the authorization request. The 1989 Act simply requires a total of 1 000 signatures, with no specific geographic distribution.

9. The chief electoral officer revoked the authorization of the Union nationale on 19 June 1989 for failure to pay its debts.

10. However, the authorization of the regional associations of the Liberal party were revoked on 31 December 1980 at the party leader's request (Quebec, Director General 1981, 14).

11. Deposits were abolished for provincial elections by the 1979 *Election Act*.

12. The *Election Act*, 1989 (s. 81) extended to all authorized parties the right to receive a proportional share of the government subsidy, a right formerly reserved for authorized parties *represented in the National Assembly*. The right to participate in the work of the *Election Act* advisory committee was similarly broadened (s. 515). The chief bias toward established parties can be found in the chapter on election expense reimbursements (Massicotte 1984, 56). The difference between new and established organizations was accentuated by the introduction in 1984 of a reimbursement advance for candidates of the established parties.

13. Sections 62, 64 and 83(*g*) of the 1977 Act, which now are ss. 87, 91 (amended) and 115–30 of the *Election Act*, 1989.

14. Before 1982, the parties were required to disclose only contributions, membership fees, admission fees to political events or conventions, and anonymous donations received during the fiscal year. Amendments passed in 1982 added an overall statement of revenues to this list, which

made it possible to take account of the annual government subsidy. Beginning in 1985, election expense reimbursements were reported in a separate column of the financial reports.

15. On the number of receipts and contributors, see the methodological note in the Appendix of this study.

16. Before 1984, moneys paid for admission to political events were not considered contributions unless they exceeded a certain amount, below which they were not entitled to a tax credit. An amendment made in 1984 enabled official representatives to consider any amount to be a contribution, as they deemed appropriate.

17. The membership figures are taken from Angell's presentation to the International Political Science Association, Washington (1988, 7 and 15).

18. As introduced in 1977, the tax credit amounted to 50 percent of the first $100 of a contribution and 25 percent of the second $100; therefore, it could not exceed $75. In contrast, the Canadian federal formula, also used in most provinces, allows 75 percent of the first $100 of contribution, 50 percent of the next $450 of a contribution and 33⅓ percent of subsequent portions of a contribution, to a maximum tax credit of $500.

19. A document prepared by the Electoral Reform Secretariat (March 1988) refers to this fear among electors, pointing out that receipts issued by the parties bear the party logo.

20. The chief electoral officer specifies that these figures reflect the situation of the political parties, *not including their organizations*.

21. Granted, the comparison is not a fair one to the extent that eliminating federal contributions by legal entities would probably result in a substantial increase in the number of individual donors.

22. We refer here to the laws by which the Parti québécois imposed salary cuts and new working conditions on unions in the public sector in 1982–83 because of the recession.

23. Paltiel (1966) shed light on the integrating effects of the former party financing model. For an overview of recent Canadian trends in this area, see Smiley (1987, 113–15) and (Dyck).

REFERENCES

Angell, H. 1966. "The Evolution and Application of Quebec Election Expense Legislation." In Canada, Committee on Election Expenses, *Report*. Ottawa: Queen's Printer.

———. 1982. "Le financement des partis politiques provinciaux du Québec." In *Personnel et partis politiques au Québec: Aspects historiques*, ed. V. Lemieux. Montreal: Boréal Express.

———. 1987. "Duverger, Epstein and the Problem of the Mass Party: The Case of the Parti Québécois." *Canadian Journal of Political Science* 20:363–78.

———. 1988. "Financing Quebec's Parties: Further Organizational and Financial Decline of the Parti Québécois: Buoyancy of the Quebec Liberal Party." Presentation to the International Political Science Association, Washington, DC.

———. 1990. Letter to the Editor, *La Presse,* 30 August, B2.

Canada. *Canada Elections Act,* R.S.C. 1985, c. E-2.

Comeau, P.-A. 1982. *Le Bloc populaire 1942–1948.* Montreal: Québec-Amérique.

Council of State Governments. 1988. *The Book of the States, 1988–89.* Lexington, KY.

Duverger, M. 1961. *Les partis politiques.* 4th ed. Paris: Armand Colin.

Dyck, R. 1989. "Relations between Federal and Provincial Parties." In *Canadian Parties in Transition: Discourse, Organization and Representation,* ed. A.G. Gagnon and B. Tanguay. Scarborough: Nelson Canada.

Epstein, L. 1980. *Political Parties in Western Democracies.* New Brunswick, NJ: Transaction Books.

———. 1986. *Political Parties in the American Mold.* Madison, WI: University of Wisconsin Press.

Grenzke, J. 1988. "PACs, Money and Politicians." *Election Politics* 5 (4): 24–27.

———. 1989. "PACs and the Congressional Supermarket: The Currency Is Complex." *American Journal of Political Science* 33:1–24.

Heidenheimer, A., ed. 1970. *Comparative Political Finance: The Financing of Party Organizations and Election Campaigns.* Lexington, MA: D.C. Heath.

Jacobson, G. 1980. *Money in Congressional Elections.* New Haven: Yale University Press.

———. 1985. "Parties and PACs in Congressional Elections." In *Congress Reconsidered,* 3d ed., ed. L. Dodd and B. Oppenheimer. Washington, DC: Congressional Quarterly.

Key, V.O. 1964. *Politics, Parties and Pressure Groups.* 5th ed. New York: Thomas Y. Crowell.

Lacorne, D. 1984. "Point de liberté de parole sans liberté de dépenser: Le financement des élections fédérales américaines et le déclin des partis." *Pouvoirs* 29:99–109.

Lassale, J.-P. 1986. "La campagne présidentielle de 1984 aux États-Unis." *Revue du droit public* 102:87–140.

Léger, Marcel. 1986. *Le Parti québécois: Ce n'était qu'un début...* Montreal: Québec-Amérique.

Lemieux, V. 1985. *Systèmes partisans et partis politiques.* Sillery: Presses de l'Université du Québec.

Massicotte, Louis. 1984. "Une reforme inachevée: Les règles du jeu électoral." *Recherches sociographiques* 25 (1): 43–81.

Meynaud, J. 1969. "Groupes de pression et politique gouvernementale au Québec." In *Réflexions sur la vie politique au Québec,* ed. J. Meynaud. Montreal: Cahiers Ste-Marie.

Miliband, R. 1969. *The State in Capitalist Society.* London: Quartet.

Nassmacher, K.H. 1989. "The Costs of Party Democracy in Canada – Preliminary Findings for a Federal System." *Corruption and Reform* 4:217–43.

Ontario. Commission on Election Finances. 1988. *A Comparative Survey of Election Finance Legislation 1988.* Toronto.

Paltiel, K.Z. 1966. "Federalism and Party Finance: A Preliminary Sounding." In Canada, Committee on Election Expenses, *Studies in Canadian Party Finance.* Ottawa: Queen's Printer.

———. 1970. *Political Party Financing in Canada.* Toronto: McGraw-Hill.

———. 1981. "Campaign Finance: Contrasting Practices and Reforms." In *Democracy at the Polls,* ed. D. Butler, H. Penniman and A. Ranney. Washington, DC: American Enterprise Institute for Public Policy Research.

———. 1988. "The 1984 Federal General Election and Developments in Canadian Party Finance." In *Canada at the Polls, 1984: A Study of the Federal General Elections,* ed. H. Penniman. Durham, NC: Duke University Press.

Quebec. *An Act to govern the financing of political parties and to amend the Election Act,* S.Q. 1977, c.11.

———. *Election Act,* S.Q. 1963, c. 13.

———. *Election Act,* S.Q. 1979, c. 56.

———. *Election Act,* S.Q. 1984, c. 51.

———. *Election Act,* S.Q. 1989, c. 1.

Quebec. Assemblée nationale. 1977. *Journal de débats.* Quebec.

Quebec. Chief Electoral Officer. 1985. *Guide des intervenants: Le financement des partis politiques et le contrôle des dépenses électorales.* Quebec.

Quebec. Director General of Political Party Financing. 1980. *Rapport annuel 1979–1980.* Quebec.

———. 1981. *Rapport annuel 1980–1981.* Quebec.

Quebec. Electoral Reform Secretariat. 1988. "Document de réflexion et de consultation sur la révision de la Loi électorale." Quebec.

Quebec. Parliamentary Commission on Revisions to the Election Act. 1988. "S'ouvrir à une démocratie de qualité." Submission by the Quebec Liberal Party. Quebec.

Sabato, L. 1984. *PAC Power: Inside the World of Political Action Committees.* New York: W.W. Norton.

———. 1985. "PACs, Parties and Presidents." *Society* 22 (May–June): 56–59.

Sartori, G. 1976. *Parties and Party Systems: A Framework for Analysis.* Vol. 1. Cambridge: Cambridge University Press.

Seidle, F.L. 1985. "The Election Expenses Act: The House of Commons and the Parties." In *The Canadian House of Commons, Essays in Honour of Norman Ward,* ed. J. Courtney. Calgary: University of Calgary Press.

Smiley, D. 1987. *The Federal Condition in Canada.* Toronto: McGraw-Hill Ryerson.

Stanbury, W.T. 1986. "The Mother's Milk of Politics: Political Contributions to Federal Parties in Canada, 1974–1984." *Canadian Journal of Political Science* 19:795–821.

———. 1989. "Financing Federal Political Parties in Canada." In *Canadian Parties in Transition: Discourse, Organization and Representation,* ed. A.G. Gagnon and B. Tanguay. Scarborough: Nelson Canada.

Stein, M. 1966. "The Structure and Function of the Finances of the Ralliement des Créditistes." In Canada, Committee on Election Expenses, *Studies in Canadian Party Finance.* Ottawa: Queen's Printer.

Stern, P. 1988. *The Best Congress Money Can Buy.* New York: Pantheon Books.

Time, 20 August 1984.

U.S. News & World Report, 28 May 1984, 7 November 1988.

Von Beyme, K. 1985. *Political Parties in Western Democracies.* Aldershot: Gower.

Ware, A. 1987. *Citizens, Parties and the State: A Reappraisal.* Cambridge: Polity Press.

Wright, J. Skelly, 1982. "Money and the Pollution of Politics: Is the First Amendment an Obstacle to Political Equality?" *Columbia Law Review* 82:609–45.

2

THE ONTARIO PARTY AND CAMPAIGN FINANCE SYSTEM
Initiative and Challenge

David Johnson

THE ELECTORAL SYSTEMS in Canada are at once extremely important and quite controversial. They are important for the simple reason that they are integral components of the procedural rules and normative understandings of democracy within this country. The electoral systems, in all their federal, provincial and municipal manifestations, are intended to establish free, fair and honest methods to periodically measure public opinion respecting the degree to which citizens seek to continue or change their political representatives. The systems are designed to provide ordinary Canadians with the power to control the fate of governments and thus the direction of public policy. As such, these systems are expected to put into practice the democratic theory of rule by, for and of the people.

The importance of the theoretical and practical dynamics within these systems, however, guarantees controversy. Debate exists over the degree to which electoral systems actually do turn democratic ideals into reality. Can the current electoral process fairly reflect popular opinion? Are current electoral distribution systems legitimate? What is the relationship between money, electoral politics and democracy?

All these matters are important to an understanding and analysis of the Canadian electoral system. The focus of this study is on the set of relationships surrounding the party and campaign finance system in Ontario. The Ontario system is worthy of close study for a number of reasons. First, it is comprehensive: the system in this province established legislative provisions that regulate the registration of candidates, constituency associations, parties and leadership candidates; the manner and amount of contributions that may be given to these political actors; the manner and amount of campaign expenditures that may be made by these actors; and the types of financial reports that must be filed with the Election Finances Commission. Moreover, the legislation establishes the structure, function and power of this Commission. The Ontario party and campaign finance system is thus one of the most elaborate systems in this country.

Second, because this system developed in stages, a review of its historical origins provides an informative study of the various approaches to such financial regulation and the reasons for their adoption, as well as an opportunity to review the strengths and weaknesses of the system over the past 16 years.

Finally, this system makes an intriguing case study: it became enmeshed in a crisis of legitimacy because of various scandals over recent years. Since the system has been subject to abuse, it is educational to review the problems that have arisen and the various responses and calls for reform these problems have elicited.

This study will examine a number of important historical developments. It will demonstrate that the development of the party and campaign finance system in Ontario was the product of deep anxiety over the ethics of the province's electoral process. The initial regulatory system designed to remedy this problem was substantial and involved but had its own difficulties. Certain problems led political authorities to amend the regulatory system significantly in the mid-1980s, while others have come to figure prominently in recent scandals. However, although the integrity of the system has been questioned, current popular understandings of the nature of this system are really misunderstandings. Although the system has its problems, its legislative foundation, in general, is sound and just. The administration of the system has proven to be quite effective as well as sensitive, and recent difficulties arising from scandals are exaggerated. In short, as with any human creation, the Ontario party and campaign finance system has both strengths and weaknesses. A review and analysis of the history of this system will lead to a better appreciation of the system as it is, the successes it has had and the tensions that confront it.

THE *ELECTION FINANCES REFORM ACT*: ORIGINS AND PROVISIONS

The party and campaign finance system in Ontario was a child of scandal. In June 1972, the government of Ontario, under the premiership of

William Davis, established the Ontario Commission on the Legislature
(Camp Commission) with formal terms of reference "to study the function of the Legislative Assembly with a view to making such recommendations as it deems advisable with respect thereto, with particular
reference to the role of the Private Members and how their participation in the process of Government may be enlarged" (Ontario, Legislative
Assembly 1972, 117).

The composition of the Commission was tripartite: the chair was
Dalton Camp, a prominent Conservative strategist. His fellow commissioners were Farquhar Oliver, a former leader of the Ontario Liberal
party, and Douglas Fisher, a former New Democrat member of
Parliament.

Initially, the terms of reference did not direct the Camp Commission
to study and report on the system of party and campaign financing.
This state of affairs was not to last long. While the Camp Commission
was getting under way the government became enmeshed in two scandals involving allegations of questionable fund-raising by the Progressive
Conservative party from very wealthy interests and of favouritism
being displayed to large corporate interests with close financial ties to
the governing party.[1] After months of persistent opposition party and
media criticism of the ethical standards of the government, the Premier
announced in December 1972 that he was adding the entire subject of
party financing to the Camp Commission's terms of reference and that,
in particular, he was instructing the Commission to make recommendations on contribution disclosure (Ontario, Commission on Election
Contributions and Expenses (CECE) 1982b, 105–106).

After a year and a half of close analysis, the Camp Commission
published its findings on party financing in its *Third Report*. In this
report, the commissioners said that they were concerned about the
closed nature of party financing and the preponderance of influence
exerted by "big money," whether corporate or union sourced, over the
three major parties. The commissioners' research led them to believe that
fully 90 percent of the Conservatives' and the Liberals' financial support came from limited corporate sources, while nearly 40 percent of NDP
financing came from a few major trade unions (Ontario, Commission
on the Legislature 1974, 6). This intimate relationship between parties
and large, powerful financial interests threatened the integrity of the
political system because it made parties susceptible to the politics of
favouritism and lowered public confidence in the role of parties and
the morality of the political process. In an effort to alleviate these problems, the Camp Commission advocated contribution limitations as follows: "We strongly recommend that the substantial dependence of our

political parties upon the substantial contributions of a few be terminated. We propose a system which relies on the support of many, at all levels of society, and in which, in the end result, no particular group or segment can be deemed to wield more influence, or bear more of the cost of political financing than another" (ibid., 31).

The Camp Commission believed that strict limitations on contributions would eliminate the ability of wealthy individuals and corporate donors to unduly influence the activities of parties, thereby enhancing public respect for the political process. As Camp said, "I thought that if you first of all drained the big money out of the system, you'd have no more of the 'Fidinam' syndrome. After this was achieved, we would build a structure that would accommodate this principle, built on full disclosure and accountability" (Ontario, CECE 1982b, 113).

The Camp Commission viewed the process of disclosure, therefore, as being inherently related to the contribution-making process. It argued that full disclosure of contributions over a nominal amount was essential both to enforce the contribution limitations set out in the proposed *Election Finances Reform Act* (*EFRA*) and to open the political fund-raising system to public scrutiny. This latter point was considered extremely important. If a failing of the old system was that it had been closed, thereby allowing "big money" to secretly influence parties and candidates, such a state of affairs would cease with disclosure. Through disclosure, the major financial supporters of all political actors would be known, allowing political competitors, the media and the public at large to evaluate the relationship between specific parties and candidates and their financial supporters (Ontario, CECE 1982b, 123–25). Camp emphasized the importance of the Act's disclosure provisions in his assertion that they underpinned all reform to the party and campaign finance system: "You couldn't make any fundamental changes in a system that needed change unless you had disclosure. The public interest is best protected by disclosure. Once you have this, however, it's going to be more difficult for the parties to finance themselves. Against this hazard you introduce some form of incentive to contribute and a subsidy. Once you do *that*, you're into public accountability" (ibid., 123–24).

The concluding remarks alluded to the Commission's fear that a strict system of public disclosure would act as a disincentive to contribution-making. To prevent such a result and to enhance broad-based political fund-raising from the general public, the Camp Commission recommended both a tax credit scheme and a process of limited public funding through candidate subsidies. Both these initiatives would be crucially important to the task of democratizing the electoral system. The tax credit would encourage large numbers of ordinary Ontarians who had hitherto refrained from making political contributions to do so, and it would provide parties, constituency associations and candidates with large sources of new funds, which would both support heightened political activities by these actors and diminish the influence of large financial interests over these actors (Ontario, Commission on the Legislature 1974, 40). The candidate subsidy provision would ensure that candidates and constituency associations capable of mounting a respectable political campaign would be guaranteed a level of funding sufficient to provide a good base for such campaigns. This would assist in revitalizing constituency-level political activity. As Camp and his colleagues said, "In our opinion this will provide a greater opportunity for parties to broaden their base by going out to organize new support. Consequently, the health of the constituencies will be improved and they too will have fresh incentives to solicit funds and maintain strong local organizations" (ibid, 11). It was hoped that candidate subsidies would enhance democratic participation and competition in party and electoral activities throughout the province.

The guiding principle flowing through the work of the Camp Commission was thus democratization. The reformed system would eliminate the reality and the perception of the influence of the wealthy few in politics, enhance the political activities of ordinary citizens and promote party activity directed to the interests of the general public.

While this principle was not and is not unique to Ontario, the political finance system proposed for the province was very distinct from its federal counterpart and became a model for other provinces.[2] The Ontario system of political financing would be geared primarily to the regulation of system inputs, namely contributions. In contrast, the federal system was rooted to outputs, namely expenditures. In 1974, Parliament, following the recommendations of the Barbeau Committee (Canada, Committee 1966) and the Chappell Committee (Canada, House of Commons 1971), had enacted the *Election Expenses Act* (now incorporated in the *Canada Elections Act*). The main thrusts of this legislation were the establishment of contribution disclosure provisions, the creation of a limited public funding scheme as well as a fund-raising process assisted by tax credits, and the imposition of strict limitations on election campaign expenditures. This legislation, however, did not countenance contribution limitations. Contributors were left free to donate any amount of money, goods or services to the party or candidate of their choice, subject only to the legislation's disclosure provisions (Canada *Election Expenses Act*, s. 4).

The federal and the Camp proposals thus stood in stark contrast to each other. While the Camp Commission and the Ontario legislature held that contribution limitations were necessary to eliminate the undue influence of wealthy interests in party and campaign activities and to enhance public trust in the fairness and integrity of the political process, federal study groups and Parliament rejected this approach.

Although the Camp Commission had the example of the 1974 federal legislation before it, the Commission itself, with Oliver dissenting, recommended against following the federal lead on spending limitations. Although Oliver supported the logic underpinning the federal initiative, both Camp and Fisher rejected expenditure limits for a number of reasons. On practical grounds, they echoed the fears expressed by the Barbeau Committee about how to evaluate the monetary value of volunteer labour, goods and services. More theoretically, these commissioners were also concerned about the effect expenditure limitations might have on the ability of parties and candidates to wage effective electoral campaigns. They were afraid spending limits would circumscribe the ability of political actors to take their message to the people, thereby making these actors dependent on the media and impugning their independence. Furthermore, Camp and Fisher expressed concerns that expenditure limitations in general and advertising limits in particular would constitute violations of the freedom of expression of parties and candidates. Such violations, in turn, would be untenable in a democratic society (Ontario, Commission on the Legislature 1974, 16–20).

Beyond these factors, both Camp and Fisher felt a regime of expenditure limitation was simply not necessary to reform the Ontario political financing system. They argued that the increasing rate of campaign spending observed by the Commission was only a reaction to general increases in the cost of living and specific increases in the cost of advertising. Moreover, this increase in campaign spending, they felt, was not sinister. While "excessive" campaign expenditures were undesirable because they were wasteful and unnecessary, such excesses could be eliminated by reducing both the general campaign period and the period during which campaign advertising was permissible (ibid., 41–42).

Finally, Camp and Fisher believed that if there was any move to impose expenditure limitations on parties, constituency associations and candidates, the state would eventually have to consider regulating and prohibiting special interest group campaign advertising. The reason for this was that if expenditures were limited, regulated political actors could either establish "independent" groups of their own to engage in supportive and unregulated campaign advertising or simply benefit from the actions of supportive, unaffiliated private groups who were interested in the actor's mission. In either case, election advertising would be taking place, demonstrably affecting election outcomes, and this advertising would be unregulated, since it would not be that of a registered party, constituency association or candidate. Yet, if the state were to subject such advertising to the expenditure provisions found in the Act, if not to an outright prohibition, then the same problem concerning the morality of the state's restricting freedom of expression would arise once again, this time with reference to a much larger body of individuals and groups. According to Camp and Fisher, the easiest and most morally correct way to avoid this entire set of problems was simply to refrain from imposing any expenditure limitations at all upon political actors (ibid., 21–22).

The recommendations of the Camp Commission greatly influenced the thinking of the government when it came to drafting relevant legislation. Indeed, the structure and substance of the *Election Finances Reform Act* closely followed the advice of Camp and his colleagues. This Act, which received Royal Assent on 2 May 1975, marked the beginning of the "reformed" era in Ontario political financing.

The provisions of the *Election Finances Reform Act* were many. The Act established a Commission on Election Contributions and Expenses (henceforth referred to as the Commission) with a chair appointed by the Lieutenant Governor in Council for a term of five years, two representatives from each of the parties having four or more members in the Assembly, a bencher from the Law Society of Upper Canada and the chief election officer. This Commission had broad powers under the Act to hire staff to administer the Act, to supervise the operation of the Act and to draft regulatory guidelines to interpret the meaning of the Act (Ontario *EFRA*, ss. 2–4).

The Act created a registration system applicable to all parties, constituency associations and candidates, who were required to register with the Commission to gain official recognition as bona fide political actors with entitlements and obligations under the Act (ibid., ss. 10, 11, 13, 14). The legislation furthermore provided for an extensive system of regulating contributions. The Act stipulated that individuals, corporations and trade unions were allowed to make contributions to registered parties, constituency associations and candidates. The amounts that could be donated, however, were restricted. Annual monetary contributions from a particular source were not to exceed $2 000 to each registered party and $500 to any one registered constituency association, with total annual contributions to such associations not to exceed $2 000.

During election campaign periods, these limits were to be doubled (ibid., s. 19).

Closely related to these contribution limitations was a tax credit system established through provisions in the Ontario *Income Tax Act* and the Ontario *Business Corporations Act*. Under these acts, the Legislative Assembly created a tax credit scheme identical to that found in the federal *Income Tax Act*, namely that there was to be a tax credit of 75 percent of contribution amounts up to $100. For contributions between $100 and $550, the credit was $75 plus half the amount. For contributions over $550, the credit was $300 plus one-third of the amount by which the contribution exceeded $550. Contributions over $1 150, however, ceased to provide a credit. The maximum tax credit was thus $500.

A number of other contribution regulations are worth noting. Campaign fund donations from a candidate's personal wealth constituted a contribution subject to the limitation provisions (Ontario *EFRA*, s. 19(3)). All contributions from any donor had to come from the actual property of the donor. Donors were thus not allowed to act as conduits for funds not their own (s. 20). Parties were not to accept contributions from any donor residing outside the province (s. 30). Federal parties could not make contributions to provincial parties, constituency associations and candidates except during a campaign period, when federal parties could contribute $100 for each registered candidate endorsed by their provincial counterpart (s. 21). The Act countenanced contributions of goods and services, but they were subject to regulation. Goods and services over the value of $100 constituted a contribution subject to the prescribed limitations. The value of these contributions would be the cost of these goods and services if purchased on the open market (s. 22). Advertising undertaken by any individual, corporation or trade union on behalf of any registered party or candidate, with the knowledge and consent of such party or candidate, also constituted a contribution subject to limitation if the value of the advertising exceeded $100 (s. 23).

Furthermore, party membership fees, trade union checkoffs and fund-raising dinners were also subject to special provisions. Under the Act, annual party and constituency association membership fees did not constitute donations provided such fees did not exceed $25 (Ontario *EFRA*, s. 31). Similarly, in the case of trade union payroll deductions, contributions of not more than 15 cents per month per bargaining unit employee did not constitute contributions from these individuals, but the total funds so raised and provided to a registered party, constituency association or candidate did constitute a contribution from the responsible trade union (s. 32). As for fund-raising dinners, if the charge was less than $50 per person, half that amount was an allowable expense, and the other half, if over $10, was a contribution. If the charge was over $50, the amount over $25 was a contribution (s. 24). The Act also stipulated that all contributions over $10 had to be by cheque to bank accounts registered with the Commission; receipts were to be issued for these contributions (s. 26). Finally, as a provision related to contributions, the legislation made allowance for the intraparty transfer of funds from a registered party's central office to registered constituency associations and vice versa. Such transfer funds were neither contributions nor expenditures and were therefore left unregulated except that such transfers had to be duly recorded for the Commission (s. 28).

While these provisions on contribution-making formed the heart of the Act, there were a number of other important legislative initiatives. Foremost was the process of disclosure. The legislation required that the registered party, constituency association or candidate record all contributions over $10 and that they report the name and address of donors for contributions over $100 to the Commission. Moreover, the Act required the chief financial officers of all registered parties, constituency associations and candidates to file with the Commission after every election, both the annual financial statements and the campaign finance statements showing the assets and liabilities as well as the income and expenses of the filing agent. Once filed with the Commission, these reports would become public records (s. 35(3)).

The Act also contained provisions for limited public funding of electoral activity by means of a reimbursement right. Those candidates able to garner 15 percent of the popular vote in their constituencies were entitled to a reimbursement from the public treasury of 16 cents per registered elector for the first 25 000 electors in the constituency, and 14 cents per elector for each elector in excess of the 25 000 (Ontario *EFRA*, s. 45(1)).

The Act further established limitations on election campaign commercial advertising. This was the one major initiative in the Act that the Camp Commission did not endorse. Contrary to the position taken by Camp and Fisher, the Conservative government called for limitations on the amount of commercial advertising allowed in any campaign. The government sought such limits because various members expressed concern that advertising was becoming excessively expensive and thus placed an unwarranted financial burden on all candidates. The advertising limitation restricted all registered political actors to advertising only during the 21 days preceding but not including the day before polling day. Additionally, there were restrictions on the amount political actors could expend on such advertising: registered parties could spend a maximum of 25 cents per elector in constituencies in which the parties fielded candidates; registered constituency associations and candidates could spend a maximum of 25 cents per elector per constituency (s. 39). While they ultimately accepted this proposal, the Liberals and the New Democrats advocated that the legislation should contain general limitations on all campaign expenditures so that no one party could gain electoral advantage by dramatically outspending its rivals. The Conservatives rejected this proposal for the same reasons that Camp and Fisher found this suggestion unacceptable, as well as on the grounds that general expenditure limitations discriminated against wealthy parties. The Conservatives could see no reason why a party should be limited in its campaign activities simply because it was proficient at fund-raising (Ontario, CECE 1982b, 158–60).

Finally, the Act called for the Commission to have various enforcement powers and outlined a schedule of penalties for those found guilty of violations. The Act gave the Commission the power to examine all financial returns filed by registered political actors and to conduct periodic examinations and investigations of the financial affairs and records of any registered party, constituency association or candidate. In order to enable it to undertake such investigations, the Commission was vested with the powers of a commission under the Ontario *Public Inquiries Act* (Ontario *EFRA*, s. 5). The Commission had the duty to report any apparent contravention of the Act to the Attorney General, and furthermore, no prosecution under the Act was to be initiated without the consent of the Commission (s. 54).

THE PARTY AND CAMPAIGN FINANCE SYSTEM: PRACTICE AND PROBLEMS

The *Election Finances Reform Act* of 1975 was heralded by all parties in the legislature as progressive legislation. The Act thereby stood as a pre-eminent piece of legislation governing a crucial part of the democratic process in Ontario. The Act existed with minor amendments until 1986, when it was substantially amended and renamed. The *Election Finances Act 1986* now governs the Ontario political finance system. This Act incorporated most of the provisions found in the 1975 Act while making certain additions, so that the amendments of 1986 denote a continuation with the past rather than a sharp break from it.

Over these 16 years, this system has known both success and difficulties. The system has met the challenges and eliminated the problems it was designed to address, and therefore, various political participants and knowledgeable observers regard it as being progressive, desirable and effective. The system, however, has not been without problems. There were criticisms from the very beginning over what some believed to be the limited provisions regarding campaign expenditure regulation. This criticism was instrumental in leading the Liberal minority government, with the support of the New Democrats, to amend the legislation in 1986. Other perceived weaknesses with the enabling legislation and the working of the system have been identified over the past 16 years: arguably, the greatest difficulty the system has faced revolves around the recent contribution scandal known as the "Starr affair."

The Elements of Success

By far the greatest successes of the Ontario political financing system relate to the contribution-making and disclosure provisions that formed the heart of the 1975 legislation. From the very inception of the system, there were marked transformations in the pattern of political financing, the nature of fund-raising and the general ambience surrounding the contribution-making process. The Camp Commission's criticism that the political financing system was, prior to 1975, a closed system changed dramatically as a result of the *Election Finances Reform Act*. Strict limitations on contributions forced parties and their constituency associations to broaden their bases of financial support. And this they did.

Table 2.1 illustrates that from the inception of the Act until 1988, all parties have generally seen their levels of funding increase dramatically. The NDP has consistently had strong fund-raising capability, while the fund-raising strengths of the Progressive Conservative and Liberal parties have been greatest when these parties have held office. This demonstrates, therefore, that the Act's contribution limitations have not hindered the ability of parties to raise substantial funding. While tensions between central party organizations and constituency associations have existed, and still do, the evidence suggests that parties over time have demonstrated strong abilities to raise enough funding to undertake effective party and campaign activities.

The influence of the Act, however, extends far beyond this finding. Tables 2.2 and 2.3 indicate that in the 10 years following 1975, the pattern of party financing changed significantly. While total contributions from major contributors (those donating more than $100) increased, the proportions attributed to the major donor types changed significantly. The proportion of such total funding received by the Progressive Conservative and Liberal parties from corporations declined from 76 percent and 69 percent respectively in 1975 to 59 percent and 61 percent respectively in 1985. The proportion of such total funding received by the NDP from trade unions also declined, from 30 percent in 1975 to 18 percent in 1985. Concurrent with this development was a general marked

Table 2.1
Total contributions to political parties (including constituency associations)
(constant July 1990 dollars)

	Progressive Conservative	Liberal	New Democrat
1976	3 270 906	340 711	1 602 727
1977	5 336 088	1 387 599	1 351 568
1978	3 321 550	549 158	1 149 566
1979	4 927 621	1 390 142	2 584 817
1980	5 672 737	1 568 462	2 809 966
1981	11 762 510	5 814 007	3 234 278
1982	6 164 260	2 122 971	3 940 468
1983	6 823 956	1 937 411	3 604 414
1984	7 817 412	1 841 038	3 592 027
1985	12 688 266	5 938 016	4 289 515
1986	2 523 946	1 807 921	2 334 472
1987	4 474 288	7 469 546	3 123 329
1988	1 177 746	2 858 049	2 389 446

Source: Ontario, Commission on Election Contributions and Expenses, and Commission on Election Finances, Annual Reports.

increase in the proportion of total party funding from individuals. In 1975, individual contributions over $100 accounted for 23 percent of Conservative funding, 31 percent of Liberal funding and 65 percent of New Democrat funding. By 1985, these figures had become 41 percent, 39 percent and 79 percent respectively. Equally marked was the absolute increase in the numbers of donors. In 1975, the Conservatives received a total of 3 749 donations of more than $100 from corporate contributors, with the Liberals receiving a total of 1 386. By 1985, these figures had increased to 6 144 and 3 507 respectively. In 1975, the NDP received donations of more than $100 from 225 trade unions and locals, and in 1985, this figure had increased to 537. The most dramatic increases, though, were in the number of individual contributors. In 1975, the Progressive Conservatives received a total of 2 200 contributions over $100 from individuals, the Liberals 1 398 and the NDP 898. By 1985, these figures had jumped to 7 547 for the Tories, 4 392 for the Liberals and 6 034 for the New Democrats.

These figures reveal a number of dynamics. Corporate donations

Table 2.2

Contributions received in excess of $100 by each registered political party and its associations and candidates 13 February 1975 to 18 January 1976

(based on returns filed to September 1, 1976)

	Progressive Conservative		Liberal		New Democrat	
	No.	$	No.	$	No.	$
Contributions by corporations						
Party	761	1 097 637	170	579 040	9	4 175
Riding associations	541	203 781	276	96 298	5	1 927
Candidates	2 447	834 050	940	309 173	37	9 658
Total	3 749	2 135 468	1 386	984 511	51	15 760
Contributions by unions						
Party	—	—	—	—	52	36 786
Riding associations	—	—	—	—	44	14 166
Candidates	—	—	—	—	129	45 928
Total	—	—	—	—	225	96 880
Contributions by persons						
Party	212	105 256	170	88 550	366	82 361
Riding associations	318	96 645	343	97 136	134	33 787
Candidates	1 670	462 432	885	256 285	398	91 145
Total	2 200	664 333	1 398	441 971	898	207 293
Grand total	5 949	2 799 801	2 784	1 426 483	1 174	319 933

Source: Ontario, Commission on Election Contributions and Expenses (1976).

Note: Figures are based on returns filed to 1 September 1976.

were still very important to the Progressive Conservative and Liberal parties, accounting for most of their total funding, yet the relative importance of this source of funding has declined. Given the support that the Act provides to individual donors and the encouragement that these parties have given to these donors, it seems fair to say that never again will these parties be criticized for receiving 90 percent of their funding from corporate contributors. Furthermore, because of the limitations on corporate donations, these parties must expand their fund-raising activities directed toward corporate donors if they wish to maintain strong levels of such donations. And this these parties have done – they more than doubled their numbers of corporate contributors over the first decade the Act was in effect.

Moreover, the three major parties have successfully broadened the base of their financial support by increasing the numbers of their individual contributors and, consequently, the proportion of funding

Table 2.3
Contributions received in excess of $100 by each registered political party and its associations and candidates, 1985

	Progressive Conservative		Liberal		New Democrat	
	No.	$	No.	$	No.	$
Contributions by corporations						
Party	2 084	1 677 162	1 629	1 505 193	12	9 150
Riding associations	1 066	388 794	388	132 710	16	5 875
Candidates	2 994	971 501	1 490	441 648	95	32 926
Total	6 144	3 037 457	3 507	2 079 551	123	47 951
Contributions by unions						
Party	—	—	—	—	88	86 513
Riding associations	4	2 000	—	—	112	47 424
Candidates	11	3 750	5	1 500	337	119 912
Total	15	5 750	5	1 500	537	253 849
Contributions by persons						
Party	3 362	936 934	1 759	643 335	4 779	814 485
Riding associations	1 037	269 060	463	110 831	35	8 901
Candidates	3 148	880 926	2 170	557 385	1 200	300 564
Total	7 547	2 086 920	4 392	1 311 551	6 034	1 123 950
Grand total	13 706	5 130 127	7 904	3 392 602	6 694	1 425 750

Source: Ontario, Commission on Election Finances (1986).

Note: Unfortunately 1985 was the last year in which the Commission made available these useful tables.

attributed to individual donors. One of the prime goals of the Camp Commission and the 1975 legislation was to promote more widespread popular funding of parties and thus greater public participation in the routine activities of parties. In relative terms, this goal has been achieved, yet questions do remain about the degree of public participation now found in the party system. Is it a significant step toward the democratization of this system in particular or of the political system in general?

In the first 10 years under the Act, all parties witnessed great increases in the number of major individual contributors donating more than $100. The Progressive Conservatives experienced a 343 percent increase in such individual donors, the Liberals a 314 percent increase and the NDP a 672 percent increase. Officials from all three parties recognize that individual contributors have become very important to the financial well-being of their parties, more so than was ever the case prior to 1975 or even in the years immediately following promulgation of the Act. This increasing role for individual contributors has been applauded by the Conservative and Liberal parties, who stress that the encouragement given to individuals to contribute has helped to democratize these parties, to enhance liaison between party élites and the "rank and file" and to eliminate the domination of party financing by a few wealthy interests.[3] Spokespersons for the NDP have also supported the increased involvement of individuals in that party's fundraising system, though these persons stressed that the NDP has had a mass-based contribution system from its inception, that union receipts never dominated party financing and that the party never had to worry about corporate contributions impugning the integrity of the party.[4]

The enhanced role of the individual contributor can be attributed to a number of the provisions of the Act and its related legislation. Officials from all three major parties have recognized that the tax credit provisions found in the Ontario *Income Tax Act* are a great incentive to individual donations. As a former Conservative cabinet minister commented, "The income tax credit is the thing that has really given the process the impetus. It's a pretty good selling point, particularly in the last half of the year" (Ontario, CECE 1982b, 128). Moreover, since the tax credit benefits the modest rather than the large donor, the system directs parties to seek donations not only from wealthy individuals but also from supporters of modest means, most of whom would never have been targeted for a contribution prior to 1975. Thus, the tax credit process has broadened the entire perspective of fund-raising.

A subsidiary effect of the tax credit process is that it encourages political actors not organized into parties and constituency associations to develop such organizations in order to benefit fully from the tax credit provisions. Registered candidates may dispense tax credit receipts for campaign contributions only during election campaign periods. Registered parties and constituency associations, however, may engage in year-round tax-creditable fund-raising, and therefore, these organizations have a far greater ability to finance their political activities than do independent political actors.

Furthermore, the increase in solicitation of contributions can be attributed directly to the contribution limitations found in the Act. The strict limitations on corporate, union and individual donations forced the parties to widen their bases of possible donors and to expand the means to secure such donations. This dynamic especially affected the Conservative and Liberal parties. In 1975, these organizations effectively lost their traditional form of financing – collecting a relatively small number of very large contributions. Under the new system, these parties had to solicit numerous contributions from all possible donors

in order to make up the shortfall caused by the elimination of unrestricted corporate fund-raising. The effect of this was significant increases
in the number of both corporate and individual contributors to these
parties.[5] This limitation on corporate contributions did not affect the
New Democrats but the limitation on union contributions did have a
similar effect on this party, leading it to stress the need to enlarge its
base of individual contributors.[6]

Along with a general increase in fund-raising, there have been
changes in the nature of fund-raising. While solicitation of corporations and individuals attending party events has continued, the need
to expand the number of donors, especially the number of individual
donors, has led all parties to develop a number of "modern" fund-
raising techniques. Two of the most significant have been direct mail
campaigns and fund-raising dinners. The Conservatives and the New
Democrats were quick to seize upon the opportunities associated with
direct mail solicitations to enhance their individual contribution figures, and they have maintained such campaigns to the present day. The
Liberal party, however, was slow to embrace this fund-raising technique because of its limited membership base in the late 1970s as well
as a general lack of central party organizational funding, but it too came
to engage in direct mail fund-raising by the mid-1980s.[7] The other major
technique has been the fund-raising dinner because a portion of the
ticket price constitutes a donation. The Act makes provision for such
fund-raising, and according to various party officials, this fund-
raising technique has become highly popular, especially among
constituency associations. These dinners have provided a relatively
easy and entertaining way to raise funds.[8]

The foregoing introduces a fascinating development resulting from
the reforms inaugurated by the *Election Finances Reform Act*. One of the
major effects of the Act was the revitalization of party constituency
associations. The Camp Commission found that, prior to 1975, riding
associations had been weak and ill organized (Ontario, Commission
on the Legislature 1974, 2). The reformed process of fund-raising established by the Act breathed operational life into the associations of all
major parties, making them, collectively, major actors within each party.
Historically, constituency associations had been dependent upon their
central party offices for the financing of constituency-level electoral
campaigns and other activities, but because the Act recognized constituency associations as legal entities capable of raising funds on their
own, the riding associations of all parties quickly became significant
fund-raisers in their own right. After only four years under the Act,
the combined constituency associations of all three major parties had

become quite wealthy: Progressive Conservative constituency associations had funding receipts of $823 640, or 46 percent of their central party's total funding; NDP associations had funding receipts of $718 058, or 59 percent of their central party's total funding; while Liberal associations had funding receipts of $349 087, or 68 percent of their central party's total funding level (Ontario, CECE 1980, 33).

In addition to the funds derived from the more open contribution system, constituency associations also benefited from the candidate reimbursement provisions of the Act. These subsidies, which amounted to an average of $6 060 per eligible candidate in 1975 and an average of $8 634 per eligible candidate in 1987, have greatly enhanced the financial strength of riding associations and thus the activities of these associations. In 1975, candidate reimbursements totalling $2 056 302 were divided among all eligible candidates. In 1987, candidate reimbursements totalled $3 125 780 (Ontario, CECE 1975; Ontario, Commission on Election Finances (CEF) 1988). These subsidy payments have been used for many purposes, from discharging campaign debts to establishing funds for future campaigns and financing general riding activities (Ontario, CECE 1982b, 136–39). Moreover, the subsidy has enhanced the ability of opposition parties, which usually have fewer financial resources than the governing party, to mount effective campaigns in ridings other than their traditional bases of support. In the mid-1980s, officials from both the Liberal and New Democratic parties affirmed this and stressed that the subsidy had been "important" in the organizational growth of their riding associations and a "crucial part" of the local campaigns waged by these associations (ibid., 138). It is not surprising that Tory officials echoed this sentiment in 1990.[9]

While the Act has been successful in accomplishing the objective of increasing the financial strength and consequent organizational power of riding associations, this has not occurred without problems. As constituency associations in all three major parties grew in wealth and power, tensions arose between the riding and central party organizations. These tensions were most prevalent within the Progressive Conservative and Liberal parties but were also present within the NDP. The basic tension stemmed from the central party's desire to tap into the wealth of its richest constituency associations to fund its year-round, provincewide activities, while most constituency associations wanted to retain their funds for their own local use. The result was internal party conflict between the centre and the ridings about the control and use of money. This tension was most pointed within the Liberal party in the early 1980s, when the central party organization was unable to raise sufficient funds to fully finance its permanent political activities

(Ontario, CECE 1982b, 169–70). The New Democrats also experienced such problems, especially since their central party had always been funded by the constituency associations (ibid., 172–73). In the late 1980s, even the Conservatives had to experience this unpleasant tension, for that party's central organization had to find funds to repay a $4 million debt while having to engage in routine party activities including election campaigns.[10]

The financial tensions led the parties to agree to an amendment to the Act, obtained in 1986, which entitled the central party organizations themselves to a campaign reimbursement. Therefore, by virtue of section 46(6) of the Act, every registered party is entitled to receive 5 cents per elector in all ridings in which the party polls more than 15 percent of the popular vote. In 1987, this provision enabled the Liberal party to receive roughly $303 000 in public funding, while the NDP received $253 000 and the Progressive Conservatives $232 000 (Ontario, CEF 1987b). This amendment is one of the major new initiatives to enhance the public funding of parties in general and the financial strength of central party organizations in particular.

The financial tension between central party organizations and their constituency associations, however, should not be exaggerated. Party officials are uniformly pleased with the enhanced financial and organizational health of constituency associations and the increased role these bodies can play in the political process. Moreover, the transitory financial problems central party organizations will experience at certain times should not distract from the recognition that under the current financing system, all major parties have, over the past 16 years, become wealthier, more capable of funding their activities and more capable of undertaking effective election campaigns. One of the Camp Commission's key objectives had been to provide recommendations designed to ensure that despite all the restrictions on contribution-making and disclosure, the major parties would still have access to sufficient funding to enable them to mount credible provincewide election campaigns. Spokespersons for the three major parties have asserted that this objective has been met.[11]

The contribution-making process, of course, cannot be evaluated apart from the disclosure process. Although limitations on contributions went far to eliminate the reality and perception of the corrupting influence of "big business" and "big labour" on the activities of parties and governments, these limitations needed to be augmented with strict provisions of disclosure.

The process of disclosure found in the Act and administered by the Commission has met these objectives. Officials from all major parties have commented on how open their financial affairs have become under the Act's requirement that all contributors giving $100 or more must be identified. This openness allows the parties to scrutinize each other and call the attention of the media and the general public to any "questionable" findings. It also encourages political actors to diversify their fund-raising while allowing them to defend themselves more rigorously from allegations of conflict of interest.[12]

Representatives from all three major parties have stressed that because of disclosure and the public/media review of the financial affairs of their parties, it was in the best public relations interests of their parties to ensure that the pattern of fund-raising undertaken by their organizations was "balanced" and "reasonable." These terms were then defined in relation to fund-raising and stressed a mix of financial support from individuals and corporations in the cases of the Conservative and Liberal parties or a mix of individual and labour support for the NDP. In all cases, the officials mentioned that to maintain popular respect, the parties had to demonstrate they were funded by a variety of social forces. Moreover, the social force *primus inter pares* was the general public, so all parties sought financial support from individuals, thereby attesting to the public appeal of their parties.[13]

The point about the defence of political actors against allegations of conflict of interest is also important. The disclosure of all major financial contributions has allowed parties, constituency associations and candidates to show publicly where their funding comes from and where it does not. Before disclosure, political actors were likely to be attacked for having undesirable funding patterns, leading to allegations of corruption. Furthermore, with a fund-raising system in which donors were guaranteed anonymity, political actors had limited ability to reply to such allegations. With disclosure, however, these actors can now explicitly name the sources of their funding and, because of the limitations on contributions, can effectively argue that their party or constituency association or candidate, or all three combined, cannot be swayed by donations (Ontario, CECE 1982b, 124–26).

With disclosure, then, the financing of parties became less mysterious, more diversified and a matter of public record open to informed analysis, criticism and rebuttal. Officials from all three major parties believe that this knowledge, combined with openness, has removed the taint from the process of party financing and has improved public confidence in the integrity of political parties.[14]

These effects have been the principal legacy of the entire Ontario party and campaign system over the past 16 years. Whereas prior to 1975 the system had been viewed as suspect, the reforms of 1975 changed the nature of the system for the better. These reforms, furthermore, have been applauded not only by the parties but also by interested academics, the media and, to a degree, the general public.[15] The current system of political financing in Ontario, while far from unproblematic, is less susceptible to the influence of wealthy interests and more open than ever to the involvement of ordinary citizens.

The Elements of Doubt

While the reformed Ontario party and campaign finance system has been effective in meeting the main goals set for it at its inception, the system has not been without problems and criticism. Some of these are of long-standing origin, others have emerged only recently; some remain problems for the system, others have been resolved through legislative amendment, though amendment has led to new criticism.

One major issue confronting the contribution-making process is the degree to which it has promoted public participation in the political process. Although the numbers of individual contributors to the major parties dramatically increased from the mid-1970s through the mid-1980s, this is not necessarily evidence of a major shift in the degree of popular participation in the activities of parties and their constituency associations. Although more individuals are now involved in the financial affairs of parties than prior to the passage of the Act, in relation to the electorate in the province, the number of persons making major contributions to political parties remains extremely small. In 1975, the total provincial electorate was 4 901 837, yet in 1976, the total number of individuals making contributions over $100 to political parties was but 2 435. In 1985, the total provincial electorate stood at 5 950 295, but in that year the total number of major contributors was only 18 288 (Ontario, CECE 1976, 13; Ontario, CEF 1986a, 19). Moreover, the question as to whether contribution-making constitutes serious participation and involvement in party politics must be addressed.

In dealing with this matter, Commission representatives from the three major parties unanimously agreed that contribution-making does not constitute political participation in the activities of parties and constituency associations. The simple giving of money is not the same as direct involvement in the running of a party apparatus and in the taking of a party's message to the general public. It is these latter actions that constitute political participation, and all three representatives admitted that their supporters are not nearly as participatory as they should be.[16]

This criticism respecting the Act's impact on democratic participation, however, does not undermine its success in promoting greater public involvement in giving to the major parties. As outlined above, the Act has worked well to diversify the type and broaden the scope of party financing. This was the main goal of the Act and this has been achieved. In expecting the legislation and its administration to greatly enhance public participation in the political process, thereby democratizing the entire process, the Camp Commission was simply guilty of naïvety.

Beyond these general issues, various analysts have identified a number of more technical problems concerning the working of the Act. One problem with the *Election Finances Reform Act* that still remains a concern is that the limits on allowed contributions under the Act make no allowance for inflation. Under the Act, these figures can only be altered to take account of inflation by statutory amendment. This has occurred once, in 1986, at which time the annual contribution limits were raised from $2 000 to $4 000 for each registered party and from $500 to $750 for any registered constituency association or candidate, with a maximum total limit of $3 000 directed to constituency associations (Ontario *Election Finances Act*, s. 19). This process of very intermittent amendment has been attacked by leading officials from all three major parties over the past 10 years because it causes contribution limitations to become overly restrictive and outdated. These analysts believe that the limitation figures should be indexed to the cost of living as measured by Statistics Canada's Consumer Price Index. In this manner, the value of permitted contributions would remain constant despite the effects of inflation and without the need for annual amendments to the Act. Although the Commission never endorsed indexation because it believed periodic amendment with legislative debate was sufficient and more desirable than automatic increases, current members of the Commission and its senior staff are in favour of indexation and of recommending to the government that the Act be so amended.[17]

Another problem concerns the timing of the release of campaign disclosure reports. Under the Act, all parties, constituency associations and candidates must file with the Commission financial statements showing campaign contributions and expenditures no later than six months after polling day. Certain academic analysts feel that the salutory effect of public knowledge of campaign contributions to political contestants would be maximized if such disclosure were to occur prior to an election.[18] In such a system, as followed in many American states, opposing parties and candidates, the media and ultimately the electorate would have the opportunity to review the financial affairs of all electoral participants and to draw any conclusions deemed fit prior to the casting of ballots.

Disclosure of this sort would provide the electorate with more information upon which to make a considered vote and would be an incentive to all political actors to ensure that their financial affairs not only conform to the law but are well within the bounds of reason as understood by the general public. The Commission, however, has refrained from endorsing pre-election disclosure on the grounds that administrative difficulties would be imposed upon both political actors and the Commission through the need to prepare and review such disclosure statements in the midst of an election campaign. Despite these objections, however, a number of members of the Commission, including New Democratic and Liberal representatives, support the concept of pre-election disclosure, so the matter may yet become a subject of future consideration and reform.[19]

Yet another problem raised by Progressive Conservative and Liberal party officials has centred upon the treatment of trade unions under the Act. The legislation and its attendant regulations permit parties to use paid voluntary labour without it being considered a contribution. In other words, the Act allows for people to take paid leaves of absence from their regular employment in order to work in election campaigns, without the value of this labour being considered a contribution, provided volunteers do not receive from their employer compensation in excess of what they would normally receive (ibid., s. 1). Over the past decade, officials from both the Progressive Conservative and Liberal parties have argued that this provides an undue advantage to the New Democrats, since they frequently receive the paid voluntary labour of numerous trade union officials during election campaigns.[20] Again, NDP members have challenged this criticism by stressing that all parties are free to make use of this provision; and, very likely, all parties do.[21] The ability of the NDP to secure the support of numerous trade union paid volunteers is simply evidence of this party's good rapport with trade unions and nothing more. As with the debate on trade union contributions to parties, a majority of the Commission members believe this provision reflects a historic compromise between corporate and union contribution-making rather than a surreptitious benefit to one party; with a New Democratic government in power, it is doubtful this approach will change.

One other concern of note respecting the contribution-making system has only recently been identified by staff with the Commission. According to Commission officials, the transfer payment provisions of the Act, allowing for the unlimited transfer of funds from central administrative offices of a party to its constituency associations and vice versa, are a serious loophole in the contribution limitations established by the

Act. Under the transfer provisions, contributors can donate to one branch of a party and stipulate that the donation be transferred to another branch so that a contributor, with the connivance of party officials, could indeed exceed the contribution limitations for specific donations.[22] Officials of the major parties have been reluctant to admit that such fraudulent actions occur, while they do say that intraparty transfers of funds affect only a small portion of party finances and that ultimately, once money has been given, it becomes party money. As such, a party's central office and its constituency associations are free to manoeuvre that funding as they deem fit.[23] Because it is difficult for the Commission to detect such contribution fraud and because there are valid reasons for the existence of the transfer provision, it seems unlikely that the potential for fraudulent behaviour could ever be eliminated unless the provision is abolished.[24] It is unlikely that the parties would support such an abolition.

The Starr Affair

While the above problems have attracted the attention of various actors and observers of the Ontario political finance system over the past 16 years, none have equalled the notoriety and significance of a series of events known as the Starr affair. While it is fair to say that the issues dealt with above have not excited public interest in the party and campaign finance system in this province, the same cannot be said of the events associated with the Starr affair. The provincial and national media have reported widely on this story; an Environics public opinion poll from August 1990 indicated that as a result of this scandal, 61 percent of Ontarians believed that the making of illegal political donations and other forms of violations of the contribution-making process established by the *Election Finances Act* were widespread; and finally, various political commentators have stressed that the Starr affair played a significant role in the defeat of the Liberal government in the general election of September 1990.[25]

As with most political scandals, the Starr affair gained public attention through a series of articles published in the media. In February 1989, the *Globe and Mail* reported that the National Council of Jewish Women (NCJW), a charitable organization under the direction of Patricia Starr, had made various political contributions contrary to the federal *Income Tax Act*, which prohibits such contributions from charities.[26] Subsequent reports alleged, among other accusations, that Ms. Starr had a close association with the Liberal government in Ontario, that she and the NCJW had given numerous donations to various Liberal MPPs, that some of these donations contravened the contribution limitations found in the Act, that certain of these contributions were directed through nominal donors in contravention of the Act, that at least one constituency association chief financial officer had engaged in "receipt splitting," a questionable activity under the Act, and that various constituency associations had filed deliberately incorrect financial statements with the Commission.[27]

By June 1989, the media allegations and the opposition parties' criticisms of the government's alleged unethical behaviour had reached such a crescendo that Premier Peterson established a judicial inquiry to investigate and report upon these various allegations of impropriety. This inquiry soon became embroiled in jurisdictional challenges to its competency, which eventually resulted in the Supreme Court of Canada ruling, in April 1990, that the inquiry's terms of reference were unconstitutional and a violation of federal criminal law powers.[28] Following this ruling, the police and the Election Finances Commission resumed their investigations. As a result, various criminal charges (fraud, conspiracy and uttering) were laid against Ms. Starr and other actors in the scandal, while the Commission preferred 75 charges against Ms. Starr and others for alleged violations of the *Election Finances Act*.[29]

Prior to the trial on the election finance charges, which was held in March 1991, the Commission dropped 42 of the 75 charges for want of sufficient evidence. This action resulted in Ms. Starr being the only individual required to face charges before the Provincial Division of the Ontario Court. At trial a further 22 charges were dismissed for insufficient evidence. Of the 11 counts that were tried, Ms. Starr was acquitted on three but convicted on eight counts of exceeding contribution limitations and of breaching the proper format for making contributions.

In passing sentence, the provincial court judge described Ms. Starr's conduct as "deliberate, willful, arrogant and reckless of the consequences." He continued: "in my view these are not minor matters. This statute is an important statute and persons engaging in political fundraising have a special responsibility to follow it." For violating this trust, Ms. Starr was fined $3 500. In the subsequent trial on the *Criminal Code* matters, she was convicted of fraud and breach of trust respecting misuse of charitable funds and sentenced to penal incarceration for six months (*Globe and Mail* 1991).

Since these charges were sub judice during the writing of this study, the officials interviewed were not asked to comment on issues and problems associated with particular charges. This study will thus offer no commentary on the specific matters brought before the courts. Despite this limitation, certain events and dynamics of the Starr affair can be used to evaluate the integrity of the party and campaign finance system.

By far the greatest problem with the political finance system revealed by the affair involved the regulation of contributions from a single source. Pursuant to section 20 of the Act, no person, corporation or trade union may contribute funds not actually belonging to the contributor. Through this provision, the drafters of the legislation sought to ensure that wealthy contributors could not evade the contribution limitations of the Act simply by routeing their funding through any number of nominal donors. The problem with such a provision, however, lies in its enforcement. How is the Commission to know that no second party has actually provided the funding for any given contribution? How is the Commission to be assured that contribution limitations are actually being obeyed and not systematically violated? At best, these questions highlight the difficulty confronted by the regulator; at worst, they indicate a flaw within the legislation open to perpetual abuse.

The Starr affair took this theoretical problem and made it a very real one. Questions were raised about whether donations made by persons associated with the NCJW actually derived from personal funds or the wealth of the organization. There were allegations that certain constituency associations engaged in receipt splitting (asking would-be contributors to redraft contributions in excess of the limitations by dividing them among nominal contributors). Finally, the media questioned whether alleged indictable violations were isolated or routine. If the Commission, through its investigations and indictments, actually cracked a major scandal, can it assure the public that similar past or present scandals have not gone unnoticed?

Commission members and officials admit that the Commission can never know for certain whether section 20 of the Act is being violated or not. As one leading Commission official said, this section of the Act "can never be definitively enforced" simply because the Commission is unable and unwilling to police and audit the actions of tens of thousands of contributors and thousands of party officials. The rigorous enforcement of this provision could only be accomplished "with an army of auditors, the election finance police force," the deployment of which would be prohibitively expensive as well as demoralizing to the vast majority of contributors and party officials who are honest and abide by the letter and the spirit of the Act.[30] Commission officials stress that honesty is the key to the integrity of the finance system. According to Donald MacDonald, the current chair of the Commission, the entire contribution-making process found in the Act is ultimately based upon the "honour system." Contributors are deemed to be acting in good faith unless proven otherwise. Only if the Commission becomes aware of questionable activities through its routine audits of financial statements will it engage in intensive investigations of the probity of particular financial activities.[31]

This approach, according to MacDonald, his staff and members of the Commission representing all three major parties, is eminently reasonable. All these officials have stressed that in its 16-year history, the Commission's experience has been that the vast majority of contributors and fund-raisers under the Act are law-abiding.[32] As MacDonald said, prior to the Starr affair there had been only a few investigations of deliberate contraventions of the Act, leading to only four charges and convictions. Furthermore, the chair and his staff commented that this limited number of in-depth investigations leading to charges was not evidence of slack law enforcement by the Commission. On the contrary, they considered the routine audit procedures established by the Act and its regulations very effective. All financial statements filed with the Commission, MacDonald has argued, must be reviewed by the chief financial officer filing the statement, an independent professional auditor and the Commission's auditors. Moreover, all such statements become public documents, open to review and scrutiny by the public, the media and political opponents.[33] While much can be done to improve the presentation format of this information, especially with regard to the provision of aggregated reports of individual and corporate contributions, the general effect of the review process, according to the chair, is that illegitimate financial activity is going to be uncovered: "Anybody who thinks they can violate the Act and get away with it is as naive as people who think they can plunk down a dollar and win the lottery" (*Toronto Star*, 12 August 1990, B1).

Echoing these sentiments, Commission officials commented that the agency's own internal audit function has always been quite effective in uncovering problems with financial returns, which are usually inadvertent, while having the potential to detect serious abuses. With regard to the deliberate violation of section 20, these officials proclaimed that crucial elements of the review and investigation process are public and media scrutiny and the resultant complaints regarding suspected illegalities. As one official forcefully argued, any violation of section 20 involves a conspiracy; the broader the violation, the greater the number of individuals involved in the conspiracy. Human nature being what it is, the greater the number of persons involved in a secret, the greater the likelihood of the secret not remaining one for long. And with publicity comes the investigative role of the Commission. In fact, the inability of the alleged conspirators in the Starr affair to maintain confidentiality was the key reason the scandal first became public knowledge.[34] Because they can review and audit financial activities against a backdrop of public scrutiny, Commission staff are confident they can detect abuses of the legislation, as was the case with the Starr affair, and that periods of relative quiescence are truly periods of time in which the law is being obeyed.

While the Commission believes that the Starr affair does not reveal any fundamental weaknesses in the Act or its administration, the general public and leading political figures do not concur. A clear majority of Ontarians believe that the contribution-making process is subject to widespread abuse. In relation to this belief, no doubt, various political leaders have stressed that the political financing system is in need of significant reform. In June 1989, Premier David Peterson announced that although he had previously believed in the integrity of the system, because of increasing revelations from the Starr affair he was "prepared to look at the laws and see if there are ways we can improve them because I think the integrity of those laws and the enforcement of those laws is extremely important" (*Globe and Mail*, 19 June 1989, A18). At the same time, then Opposition Leader Bob Rae announced that he was dissatisfied with the working of the system and that reform was "crucial" (ibid.).

Various reforms advocated by political actors and observers have included more severe penalties for those guilty of violating the Act; stricter reporting and audit provisions for parties, constituency associations and candidates; stricter limits on private contributions and more public funding of political parties; and an expanded public education role for the Commission. All of these proposals are interesting and have caused actors within the political financing system to reflect.

Most people agree that the schedule of penalties within the Act should be changed. Most actors want the level of fines substantially increased both to take account of inflation and to provide a stiffer disincentive to would-be lawbreakers.[35] Likewise, certain officials with major parties have called for more rigorous reporting and audit provisions for constituency associations and central party organizations.[36] Opinion on this proposal, however, is divided: some advocates of this approach have stressed the need to ensure more accurate reporting and scrutiny of financial transactions, while other actors and observers are sceptical and hesitant to increase the administrative burden already borne by chief financial officers and fund-raisers. Current Commission members, representing all three parties, have been quick to point out that the officials involved in constituency association work are all volunteers, that the volunteer ethos is integral to the viability of such associations, that the regulations under which these volunteers currently operate are already quite complex and that the imposition of even more complexity may discourage people from undertaking this important work. As more than one Commission party representative has argued, it is wrong to draft draconian regulations applicable to all party activists when only a tiny minority of these actors is at fault.[37]

Similar reasoning surrounds reform proposals aimed at increasing the limitations on private contributions while enhancing the degree of public funding for parties. Although Premier Bob Rae has spoken in favour of reform along these lines, no detailed suggestions have been rendered. It is interesting to note, however, that current Commission members, representing all parties including the NDP, are on record as opposing any reform that prohibits corporate or trade union contributions to political actors. Commission members have argued that the current contribution system is not in such a state of abuse as to warrant the drastic action of prohibiting major social institutions from supporting their favourite political parties.[38]

Opinion is divided, too, with regard to increased public funding. The issues here are very complex. New Democratic and Liberal members of the Commission support some form of increased public subsidies to parties as a means of reducing their dependence on private fund-raising and, therefore, of lessening the possibility of scandals such as the Starr affair occurring in the future.[39] Conservative members of the Commission, though, oppose this initiative.[40] All party members recognize, however, that this policy option entails complexities. The tough questions involve the determination of how much public funding to accord to parties as well as the eligibility of parties for such funding. The greater the amount of public funding provided to parties, the higher the proportion of party financing accounted for by the state and, therefore, the less involved is the general public in party financial support. Various analysts have claimed that this dynamic would harm parties by weakening the connection between them and the mass public, thereby vitiating one of the prime purposes of the Act, the encouragement of broad public involvement in party financing.[41] Moreover, increased public funding would likely necessitate the reconsideration of party access to such funding. Various smaller parties have long argued that the 15 percent standard of eligibility is too high for small parties and that it discriminates in favour of the older, established parties. Lowering this standard, however, leads to concerns that public funding would go to candidates with a low level of popular support. The state would then be in the position of promoting special interest candidates and perhaps perpetuating certain political actors who would not have the popular support to survive without such funding.[42] This policy issue is so complex that the Commission has not yet taken a definitive position on amending the public funding process.

Opinion is much more uniform on the issue of an increased public educational role for the Commission. Both party representatives with the Commission and staff have stated that this function is important and should be augmented in the future. It is hoped that through education directed at both the general public and party officials, the Commission can promote knowledge of the Act and its regulations, leading to greater understanding of the political financing system and to even greater obedience to the provisions of the legislation.[43] Although they consider the educational role important, senior Commission officials nevertheless contend that it and any other legislative or administrative reform will not necessarily lead to a well-run system of political financing. As MacDonald has argued, the integrity of the system depends upon the integrity of the individuals acting within the system. Thus, the continued success of the provincial party and campaign finance system is ultimately to be determined not by legislative and administrative pronouncements and reforms but by the values, attitudes and beliefs that motivate the actions of the people within the system.

One final aspect of the Starr affair deserves mention. The process of investigation by the Commission and the laying of charges highlighted a serious weakness in the Commission's administrative power. Under the Act, the office of the provincial attorney general must approve the laying of charges, and responsibility for prosecution rests with crown attorneys in the judicial district in which charges are laid. The problem with this structuring of lines of responsibility, in the view of certain Commission staff members, was that it impinges on the independence of the Commission.[44] Simply put, the Commission does not have full, independent authority to prefer charges and to oversee the carriage of its cases. The attorney general, moreover, is placed in an apparent conflict of interest situation in that he or she may have to rule on indicting either political foes or allies of the governing party. Indeed, it would be theoretically possible for the attorney general to have to rule on laying charges against him- or herself. The Starr affair saw some of these theoretical issues become practical problems. In this case, the office of the attorney general had to consent to indicting officials and supporters of the attorney general's own party. While Commission officials have been reluctant to discuss the operational relationship that developed between the agency and representatives of the attorney general, one Commission official remarked that the relationship "was not smooth."[45] Subsequently, MacDonald and other senior staff argued that in order to ensure the Commission's operational independence, it must have sovereign authority to lay charges as it deemed fit, and the carriage of such charges should be the responsibility of counsel retained by the Commission itself.[46] This will likely be high on the list of recommended legislative amendments the Commission submits to the government.

As a postscript to the Starr affair, it is to be noted that Donald MacDonald is pleased with the general results of Ms. Starr's trial on the election finance–related charges. In the opinion of the chair, the convictions illustrate to all concerned that the Act and its administration are important and that the Commission will enforce the Act through its prosecutorial powers when deliberate breaches are discovered. The deterrent effect of the Starr prosecution is thus not to be underestimated.[47]

THE EXPENDITURE LIMITATION SYSTEM

Although the Starr affair attracted both élite and mass attention to the nature and workings of the contribution-making process established by the *Election Finances Act*, the subject that has historically attracted most critical review has not been the contribution process but rather the expenditure limitation process created by the Act.

As outlined earlier, the *Election Finances Reform Act* of 1975 established a limited regime of campaign expenditure limitation. Under that Act, the only restrictions on such expenditures related to commercial advertising undertaken during the three weeks preceding the day prior to polling day. Apart from this limitation, parties, constituency associations and candidates were free to spend any amount of money they deemed necessary to promote their political causes.

Throughout the late 1970s and early 1980s, these narrow expenditure limitation provisions came to define the major point of dispute between the governing Progressive Conservative party and the opposition parties over the merit of the political financing system. Leading Liberal and New Democratic party officials attacked the Act's expenditure provisions as being woefully inadequate and as providing the Conservative party with undue electoral advantage because of its ability to raise greater funds than other parties. In 1982, former Liberal leader Stuart Smith was incensed: "The last election was purchased … Those saturation advertisements that the Conservatives ran represented the largest single media buy in Canadian media history. Even General Motors never bought that concentrated an amount of television for the introduction of its new products. That was absolutely obscene" (Ontario, CECE 1982b, 163–64).

Former New Democratic Party leader Michael Cassidy seconded

these sentiments. Also speaking in 1982, he said, "We (New Democrats) ran into the problem that exists in any democracy – where one party has got what amounts to unlimited access to campaign funds. The party closest to the people with the money has a built-in, if not insuperable advantage … It is certainly clear that in all three elections that I have been involved in since 1975, the financial advantage has played a great role in helping the Conservatives hang on to their position" (Ontario, CECE 1982b, 164).

The practical dynamic to which these men and their colleagues were reacting was that the governing Progressive Conservative party was consistently and quite dramatically outspending each opposition party in every election fought under the *Election Finances Reform Act*. In the general election of 1981, for example, total campaign expenditures for the Conservatives amounted to $7 412 934; for the Liberals, $3 664 086; and for the NDP, $2 038 297. Furthermore, the opposition parties were outraged at the amount of campaign spending undertaken by particular Tory candidates. In London South, Gordon Walker spent $77 881 on his winning campaign, Thomas Wells spent $65 141 on his victorious campaign in Scarborough North, and Larry Grossman, who had the single largest campaign expenditure, spent $90 552 on his win in the riding of St. Andrew–St. Patrick. By comparison, the average campaign expenditures of candidates for all three major parties during this election was $21 242; the average for all Tory candidates was $32 534. Although the New Democrats had no candidate whose expenditures came close to matching the calibre of Conservative "big spenders," it should be noted that two Liberals, namely Ian Scott in St. David and David Pretty in Oriole, spent $72 717 and $40 623 respectively in two losing campaigns. Both candidates significantly outspent their Conservative rivals (Ontario, CECE 1982a, 1982b).

The ultimate effect of such patterns of campaign spending, the opposition parties contended, was that the Progressive Conservative party was able to influence public opinion and gain electoral support simply because of its advertising and general campaign expenditure programs. Bernard Nayman, the New Democrat's provincial auditor, put the matter quite bluntly: "In this day and age, money means votes. Spending today, especially in the media, carries with it a lot of votes" (Ontario, CECE 1982b, 156–57). Leading officials of both opposition parties called for strict limitations on all campaign spending. Both parties stressed that the system of expenditure limitation found in the federal electoral legislation was wise and effective, and that the establishment of such a system in Ontario would promote the principles of fairness, openness and democracy found in the *Election Finances Reform Act* but only imperfectly realized through the existing expenditure provisions (ibid., 155, 157). About the Act, Stuart Smith caustically remarked: "By far the biggest problem is the fact that there is no limit on spending. It is like saying 'Apart from that Mrs. Lincoln, how did you enjoy the programme?' ... As long as people get away with the kind of obscene spending that has been going on in these elections, the *Act* is not achieving its intent. It is doing some good, but not achieving its intent" (Ontario, CECE 1982b, 156).

Not surprisingly, the Progressive Conservative party strongly objected to the positions advanced by the opposition. According to the Tories, the absence of comprehensive expenditure limitations was not detrimental to the Act, since the prime purpose of the legislation was not the equalization of electoral opportunity but rather the elimination of undue influence being exerted over parties, candidates and MPPs through the contribution-making process. Numerous Conservative officials feel that strong limitations on contributions, coupled with disclosure, eliminate the need for expenditure restrictions.[48]

Entrenched within this approach to campaign expenditures were two key ideas. One was that a party should be allowed to spend the funds it had legitimately raised subject to the limitation on advertising found in the Act. All Progressive Conservative party officials accepted the propriety and necessity of contribution limitations, yet they also believed that this limitation adequately addressed the problem of wealthy interests dominating political activities. Furthermore, if a party could raise more funds than its opponents, this was just an indication of that party's superior organizational skill as well as of its popularity. If that party wanted to spend its wealth in an election campaign on regulated commercial advertising as well as other means of promoting its political cause, so be it. The Conservatives simply perceived a general restriction on campaign expenditures as nothing but blatant discrimination against strong, well-organized parties in the name of an equality of condition designed to protect weak parties from capable competition.[49]

In contrast to opposition arguments, Conservatives believed campaign spending had no appreciable effect on the voting behaviour of electors. Conservative party officials would often proclaim that there was no strong correlation between the amount of money spent in a campaign and electoral success. The election returns, they asserted, provided numerous examples of candidates who outspent their opponents, yet lost.[50] If money spent determined electoral success, then the NDP should hardly ever have won a seat. That they did illustrated that electoral success was contingent upon matters beyond overwhelming wealth. Tories argued then, as they still do, that the determinants of electoral success were the strength of a party's legacy; the strength of its electoral platform; the credibility of its leader and its candidates; and the general ability of a party, its leader and its candidates to instil confidence in the electorate by providing them with a vision for the future. These elements, Tories have argued, and not the amount of money spent, determine who wins elections.[51]

While there is much merit in the Tory approach of stressing the importance of factors other than spending in determining voting behaviour, and while there was much evidence to suggest that there was no simple correlation between campaign expenditure and electoral success, the Conservatives eventually lost the battle over expenditure limitations. The Liberals and New Democrats strongly supported comprehensive limitations during electoral campaigns in order to equalize competition among parties; when these two parties had their chance to change the policy, they acted.

Their opportunity came in 1985 when the Progressive Conservative government led by Frank Miller was defeated on a nonconfidence motion and Liberal leader David Peterson was called upon to form a government. The Liberals had assured themselves of New Democratic support for their government through the unprecedented move of agreeing to an accord with the NDP whereby the new government pledged to undertake certain legislative reforms in return for a commitment of New Democratic legislative support for a period of two years. One of the provisions of the accord stipulated that the Liberal government was to amend the *Election Finances Reform Act* to establish a regime of strict election campaign expenditure limitations binding upon all parties, constituency associations and candidates (Spiers 1986, 164).

This commitment led to the amendment of the Act in 1986. Although this amending bill had a number of provisions, its dominant thrust was to provide for restrictions on campaign spending. Under the *Election Finances Act* of 1986, total campaign expenses incurred by a registered party or by any person, corporation, trade union, association or organization acting on behalf of that party during any campaign period must not exceed, in aggregate, the amount determined by multiplying 40 cents by the number of electors entitled to vote in all constituencies in which the given party is fielding candidates (Ontario *Election Finances Act*, s. 39(1)). With regard to local candidates and constituency associations, total allowable campaign expenditures incurred by the candidate, constituency association or any other person, corporation, trade union or other group acting on behalf of the candidate or constituency association must not exceed an aggregate dollar figure determined by multiplying two dollars by each of the first 15 000 eligible electors in the given electoral district, then one dollar by each elector over 15 000 but not exceeding 25 000, and 25 cents by each elector in excess of 25 000 (ibid., s. 39(2)). With respect to candidates in the six largest northern ridings, the Act provides for these candidates to spend up to an additional $5 000 above the given limit if they so desire (s. 39(3)).

This system of expenditure limitation has now been used in two provincial elections, with relatively favourable results. Because the most recent provincial election occurred in September 1990, financial data for that campaign are, as yet, unavailable; statistics from the 1987 general election, however, reveal that expenditure limitations are fulfilling their purpose. In this election, the three major parties were each entitled to spend roughly $2 400 000 on provincewide party campaigning. In practice, the Liberal party spent $2 351 759, the Progressive Conservatives $1 960 807 and the NDP $1 381 823. For constituency campaigns, the average allowable expenditure limit was roughly $45 000. In practice, most candidates experienced no problem in campaigning with this limit; the average candidate and association expenses for the Liberal party were $36 350, for the Conservatives $27 529 and for the NDP $18 772. Overall, total candidate and constituency association campaign spending for the Liberal party amounted to $4 339 939, for the New Democrats $2 242 581 and for the Tories $3 277 470. The grand totals of all campaign spending by these parties were, therefore, $6 691 698 for the Liberals, $5 238 277 for the Conservatives and $3 624 404 for the NDP (Ontario, CEF 1987a). In contrast, in the 1985 general election, which in terms of campaign spending was the most expensive election in Ontario history, total campaign spending by the Conservatives amounted to $13 074 207; by the Liberals, $5 639 063; and by the New Democrats, $4 863 021 (Ontario, CECE 1985).

The expenditure limitations in place during the 1987 provincial election demonstrably curtailed the escalation of election campaign spending. With limitations on such spending and with no party able to dramatically outspend any other, the issue of campaign manipulation through campaign expenditure has ceased to exist. This does not mean, however, that party, constituency association and candidate expenditures are now unproblematic. As Joseph Wearing (1990) has suggested, parties witnessed significant increases in their non-campaign spending between 1985 and 1987. In 1985, such expenditures for the Conservatives amounted to $2 592 791; for the Liberals, $827 969; and for the New Democrats, $374 700. In 1987, such expenditures for the Conservatives amounted to $4 141 113; for the Liberals, $7 931 624; and for the New Democrats, $4 616 692. Total party spending in 1985 was thus: Conservatives, $15 666 998; Liberals, $6 467 032; and New Democrats, $5 237 721. In 1987, it was Conservatives, $9 379 390; Liberals, $14 623 322; and New Democrats, $8 241 096 (ibid., 228–30). Two points here deserve comment. First, it is difficult to restrict only certain types of party spending and expect to see total party spending decline. Parties are adept at finding ways to promote their interests by circumventing regulations. Between 1985 and 1987, all parties increased non-campaign, hence unregulated, spending, the Liberals and New Democrats greatly increasing these expenditures. The effect of this spending on electoral outcome, moreover, is as questionable as that respecting campaign spending. Just as there is no unequivocal correlation between campaign expenditures and electoral success, neither is there any correlation between non-campaign expenditures and electoral success. Indeed, only a comprehensive limitation on total annual party, constituency association and candidate spending could effectively regulate and restrict general party expenditures. Second, the Act was designed only to limit spending during campaign periods, the periods when such spending was believed by the Liberals and New Democrats to be most influential. With regard to this objective, the Act has fulfilled its purpose.

There is discontent, however, with specific terms of the Act. The Act provides that various matters be exempt from being considered campaign expenses. Most of these exemptions, such as nomination costs, candidates' deposits, and auditors' and accounting fees, are noncontroversial. However, the Act exempts from limitation all "expenses incurred in relation to the administration of the political party or constituency association" (Ontario *Election Finances Act*, s. 1(1)(g)). In 1986, the Commission determined through its guideline-making process that this provision captured all party research and public opinion polling undertaken by parties and candidates during an election campaign (Ontario, CEF 1986b, G-24). The rationale for this move at the time was that such spending provided parties with the intelligence needed to conduct effective electoral campaigns. It was held, moreover, that this activity was of real concern only to central party offices, that all parties engaged in such activities equally, and that the level of spending for this research and polling was not excessive.[52]

Currently, however, Commission members representing the New Democrats and the Liberals question the desirability of this provision. The New Democrats historically opposed the exemption as being a serious loophole in the Act that enabled parties to engage in significant spending and provided them with a great opportunity to engage in party promotion under the guise of "research" and "public opinion." While the Liberal party has traditionally supported the exemption, Liberal representatives on the Commission have expressed reservations about it for the same reasons advanced by their New Democratic colleagues.[53] Representatives of the Conservatives, though, remain unimpressed by these criticisms; they argue that such spending is necessary and valuable in campaigns and should not be restricted by the state.[54] Because the Commission chair also supports the elimination of this exemption, it seems likely that the current balance of opinion on the Commission is in favour of this action.

A further exemption from the scope of the expenditure limitations, in contrast, has united all party representatives on the Commission in calling for reform. The Act does not regulate or restrict government advertising during campaign periods. While this matter had been a point of controversy between the governing party and the opposition parties in the early 1980s, it has not been a prominent issue lately, arguably because of restraint in government advertising during recent election campaigns.[55] Yet, the issue remains, and it has elicited critical commentary. Representatives from all three major parties feel that unrestricted government advertising during campaign periods does provide the governing party with a promotional opportunity not shared by opposition parties, thereby placing the former at an advantage. In an effort to eliminate this problem and to ensure that all parties compete as equals during election campaigns, party representatives with the Commission have advocated that the Act be amended to provide for restrictions as currently found in Manitoba and Saskatchewan, namely that government advertising during election campaigns be restricted to informational advertisement deemed necessary to the public interest.[56] Again, given the balance of opinion on the Commission on this issue and given the general reformist orientation of the New Democratic government, it seems likely that such a recommendation for reform would be favourably received by the government.

The final issue requiring analysis here is the one that will probably attract the most attention, critical comment and passion over the next few years. As on the federal stage, a system of campaign expenditure limitations applicable to parties and candidates and their supporters inevitably leads to concerns about special interest campaign advertising. These are concerns about whether this advertising violates the practice and theory of expenditure limitations, how it should be regulated, if at all, and whether such regulation constitutes an infringement of the freedom of expression as guaranteed under the *Canadian Charter of Rights and Freedoms*.

The practical attention devoted to this issue in recent years, how-ever, is not the result of perceived abuses relating to special interest advertising during the last two provincial elections fought under expend-iture limitations. Commission officials and party representatives unan-imously agree that this type of advertising played a very limited role in these election campaigns. While the Commission has not maintained any statistics on advocacy activities and spending, independent research augmented with educated estimations does corroborate this general opinion. In the 1990 election, for example, four major groups launched election advertising campaigns: a combination of teachers' federations; a combination of the Ontario Medical Association and five health care unions; the Canadian Auto Workers; and the National Citizens' Coalition. The teachers' group reportedly had planned expenditures of $250 000, while the medical group had budgeted $50 000. Both the Canadian Auto Workers and the National Citizens' Coalition have been reluctant to divulge the amount of their advertising spending, but in each case, it probably did not exceed $100 000.[57]

These figures pale in comparison with reported expenditures by special interest groups in the 1988 federal election. In that campaign, total special interest spending amounted to $4.5 million. Pro–free trade groups reportedly spent $3.4 million; anti–free trade groups spent $800 000.[58] Although such spending patterns have not been witnessed in Ontario, the debate sparked by the latest federal election regarding such expenditures has entered into the consciousness of leading polit-ical actors and observers of the Ontario electoral system, and this devel-opment has led to the establishment of certain strongly held and antagonistic positions.

Senior Commission officials believe that in order to fulfil the pur-pose and intent of expenditure limitations, all special interest expend-itures must be restricted. They advocate a basic policy that all spending by a special interest group must be authorized by a registered party or candidate; that all unauthorized spending should be prohibited; and that these groups should be unable to invoke any "good faith" defence per-taining to the expression of opinion on matters of general public inter-est.[59] Without such a regulatory approach, MacDonald has said that expenditure limitations become pointless, since parties and candidates can simply channel spending through "friendly" interest groups. Once one party or candidate takes this step, so the argument goes, others will follow, with the result being a Canadian replication of the laissez-faire system of special interest spending found in the United States that has turned American electoral politics into a process open only to the wealthy and in which wealth can determine electoral success.

Unrestricted special interest advertising is thus a threat to the very raison d'être of expenditure limitations.[60]

The regulation of special interest spending finds varying levels of support among Liberal and New Democratic Commission members. Liberal members support such restrictions for the reasons advanced by MacDonald, but NDP members are torn.[61] However, they do agree that unregulated special interest advertising has the potential to vitiate the principle and practice of expenditure limitations and that it enables wealthy interest groups, primarily business groups, to exert influence over public opinion during election campaigns. Moreover, NDP representatives believe that both élite and rank and file opinion within their party would probably support the prohibition of special interest advertising to promote the principle of equality of condition in campaign activity and to ensure that special interest advertising campaigns like those observed in the 1988 federal election or American elections could not come to exist and influence Ontario's electoral politics. These representatives fear that without regulation, the next provincial election will witness an unprecedented initiative by business groups to use all means at their disposal, including advertising, to attack the NDP and to instil fear in the hearts of Ontario electors. Although there have not been extensive special interest advertising campaigns in the last two elections, there is fear that this will not be the case next time. Despite these opinions, however, one NDP representative had reservations pertaining to the issue of freedom of expression involved in this area of policy consideration.[62]

Any attempt by the state to regulate or prohibit special interest campaign expenditures can result and has resulted in criticism and legal challenge on the grounds that this action constitutes a violation of the freedom of expression as guaranteed under the *Canadian Charter of Rights and Freedoms*. The argument here is that individuals and groups have an unfettered right under the Charter to express their points of view on political matters at any time, including election campaigns. Furthermore, the expression of public opinion is healthy in a pluralist democracy, so restrictions on this right must be carefully considered. To date, special interest advertising has not created problems serious enough to warrant limitations on this right, which could be "demonstrably justified in a free democratic society" (Hogg 1985, 718).

As witnessed on the federal stage in 1984, this logic was accepted by the Alberta Court of Queen's Bench in the case of *National Citizens' Coalition Inc. v. Canada (Attorney General)* in which the restriction on special interest expenditures was ruled unconstitutional under the Charter. In Ontario, Progressive Conservative party members generally hailed this decision as being sound and just, and as appropriately upholding the liberty of individuals and groups to express themselves, free from state intervention and control.[63] The civil libertarian aspect of this decision was so strong, in fact, that it attracted support from across the political spectrum, with some members of the NDP and the Liberal party expressing concern over legislative restrictions on such special interest expression.[64]

The degree of New Democratic and Liberal reservation over special interest expenditure restriction, however, should not be overestimated. As Commission representatives for these parties concede, general opinion within these parties favours state-imposed restrictions on these expenditures. Moreover, leading Commission officials, including the chair, strongly believe that state-imposed restrictions on special interest advertising can withstand judicial review. MacDonald contends that the Supreme Court of Canada would likely have upheld the 1983 amendment to the *Canada Elections Act* as constituting "reasonable limits" to the Charter on the grounds of maintaining equity and balance within the electoral process.[65] Because the chair and a majority of the Commission members consider this policy matter important and because the NDP favours regulation, it is to be expected that an initiative to amend the *Election Finances Act* by restricting special interest campaign expenditures to those authorized by registered parties will be high on the agendas of both the Commission and the government. Judicial review will presumably follow, perhaps by way of constitutional reference. The Supreme Court of Canada will ultimately be called upon to resolve the constitutional legitimacy of such expenditure limitations. Developments in Ontario will thus probably attract nationwide attention of all observers concerned with this issue.

REGULATION OF LEADERSHIP CAMPAIGNS

While the 1986 amendment to the party and campaign finance system is most noted for its provisions respecting the imposition of limitations on campaign expenditures, one other provision of the amendment deserves attention. With the *Election Finances Act* of 1986, Ontario became the first jurisdiction in Canada to impose financial disclosure provisions on the activities of party leadership contestants. The Act stipulates that all contestants must themselves register with the Commission prior to accepting any contribution for use in the leadership contest (Ontario *Election Finances Act*, s. 15(1)). A party holding a leadership convention must itself register this fact with the Commission, indicating the date the convention is called and the date of the leadership vote. The legislation furthermore stipulates that registered leadership candidates must maintain records of all income received and expenses incurred during the leadership campaign period, that contributions to these campaigns are not eligible for tax credits, that all contributors donating over $100 be identified and that all this information be filed with the Commission within six months after the contest so that it becomes a matter of public record (ibid., ss. 35(1), 43(4)). It is to be noted that the regulation of leadership contests involves only the public disclosure of total campaign receipts and expenses, and the naming of major contributors. The Act does not restrict the source of contributions or the total amount that any one contributor may donate, nor does it restrict the expenditures that any leadership contestant may incur during a leadership campaign.

The rationale for these provisions was founded upon the understanding that leadership campaigns were not totally the private affairs of the respective parties. Rather, such campaigns, especially those of the major parties, have important public overtones because those selected as leaders will become major actors on the political stage, perhaps as Leader of the Official Opposition or even Premier. At the very minimum, party leaders play a major role in shaping the nature of the parties they command, and they influence the course of public debate on the policy direction of the province. For these reasons, the Legislature believed it was important for the Ontario public, through the work of the Commission, to be made aware of the financial relationships between contestants, especially victorious contestants, and major individual, corporate and trade union backers. Furthermore, the Legislature believed that these disclosure provisions would induce leadership contestants to diversify their stock of contributors out of fear of being criticized for being too closely associated with a small set of financial interests. Diversification would ensure that leaders are beholden to no single interest or clique of interests, thus enhancing public confidence in the integrity of the political system.[66]

To date, only the Progressive Conservatives have undertaken the entire process; the Liberals have just begun. Moreover, because the required financial statements do not need to be filed with the Commission until six months following the close of the contest, the reports for the Conservative campaign, at the time of writing, were not available for analysis, so a review of the working of these legislative provisions is necessarily limited. A number of points, though, are worthy of attention. First, this system of disclosure is open to one of the same criticisms made of the general disclosure system found in the Act – that the disclosure emerges too late in the process. Preliminary disclosure should occur prior to the leadership vote. This proposal falls open

to the criticism that such pre-ballot disclosure would put serious administrative strains on the campaign organizations of leadership contestants.[67] The counterclaim, in turn, would be that administrative problems
would not be insurmountable and that pre-ballot disclosure is far more
valuable to leadership convention delegates, and ultimately the general
public, than disclosure six months after the fact.

Second, while Commission representatives from all three major
parties support the leadership disclosure provisions found in the Act,
not one of them expressed support for extending state regulation into
the process of leadership selection. Contribution and expenditure limitations for leadership contestants could be justified on the same grounds
as the general provisions respecting these matters, yet no party representative or Commission staff official supported such a move. The
party representatives uniformly contended that, apart from public concern respecting disclosure, the leadership selection process was an
internal party affair best left to the care and management of the parties
involved. As for concerns about possible conflicts of interest that may
arise through the contribution-making process or about problems that
may develop through excessive spending, the representatives all felt
that these matters can best be resolved through self-regulation and
party discipline.[68] Given this uniformity of opinion, it is unlikely that
the Act's provisions respecting leadership campaigns will be the focus
of reform in the near future.

CONCLUSION

The Ontario party and campaign finance system as established under
the *Election Finance Reform Act* of 1975 was a child of scandal. Fifteen
years after the promulgation of that legislation, the system found itself
enmeshed in another scandal. However, the evaluation of the system's
merit must not be based simply upon recent developments and problems. Full understanding and appreciation of the party and campaign
finance system in Ontario necessitate knowledge of the origins of the
system, the administrative and regulatory apparatus established to
implement the system, and the many dynamics that have marked the
working of this system over the past 16 years.

The political financing system currently found in Ontario was
developed to remedy specific problems associated with party and campaign financing, and to provide a behaviour system designed to fore-
stall future problems. The ultimate criteria for evaluating the worth of
this system then must be the following: Has it indeed fulfilled its objectives of opening the process of contribution-making, thereby circum-
scribing and limiting the influence of a few wealthy financial interests

over the activities of parties and candidates? Has it revitalized parties at all levels of organization by providing them with sufficient funding with which to undertake their activities? Was the system of expenditure limitation properly designed and administered to allow parties to compete effectively while eliminating the fear of wealth vitiating the fairness of electoral activity? Is the Commission capable of fairly and effectively overseeing the regulation of this entire system?

In reviewing these matters, one can not only gain a deep understanding of the Ontario system of political financing and its strengths and weaknesses, but also develop a heightened appreciation of the types of problems such systems confront, the variety of administrative responses available to deal with such problems, and the success and failure of the responses. As such, the Ontario experience can provide useful insight into the theory and practice of political financing, its reform and the related issues and problems.

Generally, yet most significantly, this study finds that the party and campaign finance system in Ontario has served the purposes for which it was established. The contribution limitations effectively regulate and restrict the amounts that any contributor may give, while the disclosure stipulations provide for public awareness of all major contributions. These provisions have been instrumental in eliminating the ability of small numbers of very wealthy interests to influence the activities of candidates and parties, and thus of MPPs and government, through confidential donations of large sums of money to these political actors. The prime objective of the Camp Commission – to eliminate the influence of "big money" through the contribution-making process – has thus been met. This objective, moreover, has been achieved in a manner definitely beneficial to political parties. The contribution limitations coupled with tax credit provisions have encouraged parties to seek out financing from a wide range of possible contributors while encouraging those interested in making modest donations to do so. The result has been an increase in the total number of contributors compared with the pre-1975 system, with individual contributors playing a greater role in the financing of parties than before 1975. The contribution-making system has thus had the effect of encouraging and broadening the base of popular financial support enjoyed by parties. This broadened base has, in turn, enabled parties to raise ample funding to finance their electoral and broader political activities.

Finally, the reformed contribution-making process has breathed life into constituency associations. Prior to 1975, these organizations had been at best marginal institutions, but under the Act, they have become important elements of all three of the major parties. Constituency associations have become active in ongoing fund-raising, local political undertakings and electoral campaigning. As a result of the Act's formal recognition of constituency associations, these are now legal entities requiring a permanent administrative structure, which provides them with the legal powers to engage in permanent fund-raising. This, of course, has enabled well-run riding associations to amass funds to promote local political activities, provide varying levels of support to central party organizations, and encourage citizens' involvement in the political process. Formal, legal recognition of local riding associations has thus demonstrated real and potential benefits to the political life of Ontario.

No analysis of the contribution-making process within Ontario is complete without devoting critical attention to the Starr affair. The events surrounding this scandal thrust the political financing system in this province into a crisis of legitimacy and highlighted the manner in which the contribution-making process can be, and allegedly has been, abused. A number of lessons can be learned from these developments. First, no contribution-making process or regulatory system can ever be guaranteed to be free from abuse. Second, the Starr affair demonstrates the effectiveness of the regulatory enforcement process within the system as much as it demonstrates how the system can be violated. The Act is always open to abuse, yet great difficulties confront those seeking to violate the Act and to escape detection and punishment. A whole host of audit and observation forces maintain both formal and informal scrutiny over those involved in the contribution-making process.

In addition to contribution limitations, the regulatory system in Ontario provides for campaign expenditure limits; in practice, these limits show further successes and problems in Ontario's political financing system. Ontario's experience with such limitations has been generally positive. Although there is still debate over whether these limitations are necessary, the record indicates that two of the three major parties in this province support such limitations, while the third can live with them. All major parties feel that the limitations do not harm their ability to take their message to the electorate and that they equalize the competitive strengths of the parties. Whether excessive campaign spending ever did constitute a threat to fair competitive elections in Ontario, campaign expenditure limitation does ensure that no party, now or in the future, could ever gain an electoral advantage because of money spent. Thus, the limitations fulfil their prime objective.

Special-interest campaign expenditure, however, remains an issue. Although there is no conclusive evidence linking either party or interest-group campaign expenditures to voting behaviour, numerous analysts fear that interest-group advertising can influence electors. Furthermore, since business groups have far greater resources to devote to special-interest advertising than do "social reform" groups, there is fear that the direction and substance of public debate may be skewed in favour of the interests of the wealthy corporate élite rather than of ordinary electors. The presence of special-interest campaign spending vitiates the spirit and practice of party and candidate limitations: through such activity, these actors may easily establish, or be compelled to establish, allied, ostensibly "independent" support groups to promote their partisan interests free from the spending restrictions imposed upon parties, constituency associations and candidates.

The result of this, so the argument runs, would be an escalation in the costs of political campaigning. This, in turn, leads to fears that effective electoral activity would require parties, constituency associations and candidates to have enormous amounts of funding; only the wealthy, or those supported by wealthy interests, could successfully engage in electoral politics. Whether or not this belief is well founded, its very presence in political discourse on the merit of the electoral system is corrosive to the very integrity of this system. Just as party, constituency association and candidate expenditure limitations were viewed as being necessary to dispel beliefs that success in electoral politics was contingent upon wealth deployed, so it is that concern for the principle of equity in electoral campaigning must lead to the extension of expenditure limitations to the activities of special-interest groups. Without such regulatory coverage, a gap does and will exist in the theory and practice of campaign expenditure limitations that will vitiate the purpose of the existing limitations and threaten public confidence in the moral worth of the electoral system overall. Restrictions on the campaign advertising activities of special-interest groups will affect their rights to freedom of expression under the Charter, and this is a matter of deep concern. However, the Charter does provide for limitations on rights in order to further social interests. The integrity of the electoral system is a social interest that merits such protection.

Overall, a review of the Ontario experience will lead to the consideration of matters ranging from the nature of administrative organization and the scope of regulatory coverage to the ethicality of such regulation. All this is simply the result of the state moving to administer a field of human activity that is complex, replete with conflicting opinions and values, and important to any individuals, parties and groups concerned with the integrity of the political system. In this sense, electoral reform is a project not only of the Royal Commission on

Electoral Reform and Party Financing but of all concerned individuals, parties and groups. And its success will depend on the ability of all these forces to develop wise, just and reasonable reforms. The task is great, but it is simply commensurate with the project.

ABBREVIATIONS

Alta. L.R. (2d)	Alberta Law Reports (Second Series)
c.	chapter
C.L.L.C.	Canadian Labour Law Reports
D.L.R. (4th)	Dominion Law Reports (Fourth Series)
Ont. C.A.	Ontario Court of Appeal
Ont. H.C.	Ontario High Court of Justice
R.S.C.	Revised Statutes of Canada
R.S.O.	Revised Statutes of Ontario
S.C.	Statutes of Canada
S.C.C.	Supreme Court of Canada
S.C.R.	Supreme Court Reports
S.O.	Statutes of Ontario
s(s).	section(s)
W.W.R.	Western Weekly Reports

NOTES

This study was completed in April 1991.

The author wishes to thank Leslie Seidle and the two assessors for their comments on this study. The author also wishes to acknowledge the assistance of numerous officials with the Ontario Election Finances Commission and Elections Ontario without whose help this study could not have been made a reality.

1. One of the scandals at this time came to be known as the "Fidinam Affair" (Surich 1975, 349).

2. Namely, Alberta and New Brunswick.

3. This information is based on personal interviews with Mackenzie and Maxwell.

4. Personal interview, Dickens.

5. Personal interviews, Mackenzie, Maxwell.

6. Personal interview, Dickens.

7. Personal interviews, Mackenzie, Maxwell, Dickens.

8. Ibid.

9. Personal interview, Mackenzie.

10. Ibid.

11. Personal interviews, Mackenzie, Maxwell, Dickens.

12. Ibid.

13. Ibid.

14. Ibid.

15. Ibid. Also, personal interviews, Bailie, White.

16. Personal interviews, Mackenzie, Maxwell, Dickens.

17. Ibid. Also, personal interviews with senior staff members, Commission on Election Finances.

18. Personal interviews, White, Baar.

19. Personal interviews, Dickens, Maxwell.

20. Personal interviews, Mackenzie, Maxwell.

21. Personal interview, Dickens.

22. Personal interview, MacDonald. Also, personal interviews with various senior staff officials.

23. Personal interviews, Mackenzie, Maxwell, Dickens.

24. Namely, the ability of a party to transfer funds to relatively poor constituency associations unable on their own to raise sufficient funds to enable them to conduct adequate election campaigns.

25. In general, see the *Globe and Mail* and the *Toronto Star* for June 1989. In particular, see the *Toronto Star*, "Peterson Mishandled Scandal, 51% Tell Poll," 29 August 1990, A1. See also the *Globe and Mail* and the *Toronto Star*, 7 September 1990.

26. "Charity Makes Political Donations Prohibited Under Income Tax Act," *Globe and Mail*, 15 February 1989, A1.

27. See "Starr Firm's Aid to Liberal Candidate over Limit," *Globe and Mail*, 9 June 1989, A1; "Cheques from Starr's Group to Member Were not Reported," *Globe and Mail*, 12 June 1989, A1; "A Fascinating Query: Did Starr Act Alone?" *Globe and Mail*, 14 June 1989, A1; "Trail Littered with Names since First Report," *Globe and Mail*, 26 June 1989, A14.

28. *Globe and Mail*, April 1990.

29. "Charges Laid over Election Spending," *Globe and Mail*, 19 June 1990, A1.

30. Personal interview, senior staff official.

31. Personal interview, MacDonald.

32. Personal interviews, MacDonald, Mackenzie, Maxwell, Dickens and senior staff officials.

33. Personal interview, MacDonald.

34. Personal interview, senior staff official.

35. Personal interviews, MacDonald, Mackenzie, Maxwell, Dickens and senior staff officials.

36. "Starr Political Donation Scandal Raises Doubts on Fund Raising Law," *Globe and Mail*, 19 June 1989, A18.

37. Personal interviews, Mackenzie, Maxwell, Dickens.

38. Ibid.

39. Personal interviews, Maxwell, Dickens.

40. Personal interview, Mackenzie.

41. Personal interviews, Bailie, Mackenzie.

42. Personal interviews, Bailie, White.

43. Personal interviews, MacDonald, Mackenzie, Maxwell, Dickens, Bailie and senior staff officials.

44. Personal interview, senior staff official.

45. Ibid.

46. Ibid.

47. Personal interview, MacDonald.

48. Personal interview, Mackenzie.

49. Ibid. See also, Ontario, Commission on Election Contributions and Expenses (1982b, 158–59).

50. Indeed, a review of the election returns for the 1981 provincial general election reveals that out of 125 contests, the candidate with the greatest campaign expenditures won 78 of these contests while losing in 47 others, for a success rate of 62 percent. In 22 of the contests in which the leading spender lost, the candidate outspent the winning candidate by more than 51 percent. In the 1985 provincial general election, the figures are even more thought provoking. Out of 125 contests, the candidate with the greatest campaign expenditures won only 64 of these contests, while losing 61, for a success rate of 51 percent. In this election there were 33 contests in which the leading spender lost while having outspent the winning candidate by more than 51 percent (Ontario, Commission on Election Contributions and Expenses 1981; Ontario, Commission on Election Finances 1986a).

51. Personal interview, Mackenzie.

52. Personal interview, senior staff official.

53. Personal interview, Maxwell.

54. Personal interview, Mackenzie.

55. Personal interview, White.

56. Personal interviews, Mackenzie, Maxwell, Dickens.

57. See "A Pasting for the Liberals," *Globe and Mail*, 17 August 1990, A4; and "Health Critics See Election Attention," *Globe and Mail*, 4 September 1990, A5.

58. The residual $300 000 was devoted to advocacy unrelated to the free trade controversy (Hiebert 1991).

59. Personal interviews, MacDonald, Bailie. These officials support the policy objectives and statutory language as found in the 1983 amendment to the *Canada Elections Act* in which s. 70.1(4) of the Act dealing with the "in good faith" defence was eliminated.

60. Ibid.

61. Personal interviews, Maxwell, Dickens.

62. Personal interview, Dickens.

63. Personal interview, Mackenzie.

64. Personal interviews, Maxwell, Dickens.

65. Personal interview, MacDonald.

66. Personal interviews, senior staff officials.

67. Personal interviews, Mackenzie, Maxwell, Dickens.

68. Ibid.

INTERVIEWS

Baar, Carl, Professor of Political Science, Brock University, November 1990.

Bailie, Warren R., Chief Election Officer of Ontario, October 1990.

Dickens, Penny, NDP representative on the Commission on Election Finances, October 1990.

MacDonald, Donald C., Chair, Commission on Election Finances, October 1990.

Mackenzie, Hugh, Progressive Conservative party representative on the Commission on Election Finances, October 1990.

Maxwell, Barrie Solandt, Liberal party representative on the Commission on Election Finances, October 1990.

White, Graham, Professor of Political Science, University of Toronto, November 1990.

REFERENCES

Canada. *Canada Elections Act*, R.S.C. 1985, c. E–2.

———. *Election Expenses Act*, S.C. 1973–74, c. 51.

———. *Income Tax Act*, S.C. 1970–71–72, c. 63.

Canada. Committee on Election Expenses. 1966. *Report*. Ottawa: Queen's Printer.

Canada. House of Commons. Special Committee on Election Expenses. 1971. *Report*. Ottawa: Queen's Printer.

Globe and Mail. 1989. "Starr Political Donation Scandal Raises Doubts on Fund Raising Law." 19 June, A18.

———. 1991. "Starr Fined $3500." 5 July.

Hiebert, Janet. 1991. "Interest Groups and Canadian Federal Elections." In *Interest Groups and Elections in Canada*, ed. F. Leslie Seidle. Vol. 2 of the research studies of the Royal Commission on Electoral Reform and Party Financing. Ottawa and Toronto: RCERPF/Dundurn.

Hogg, Peter. 1985. *Constitutional Law of Canada*. 2d ed. Toronto: Carswell.

Lavigne v. O.P.S.E.U. (1987), 87 C.L.L.C. 14,044 (Ont. H.C.); reversed (1989), 89 C.L.L.C. 14,011 (Ont. C.A.); affirmed (1991), 91 C.L.L.C. 14,029 (S.C.C.)

National Citizens' Coalition Inc./Coalition nationale des citoyens inc. v. Canada (Attorney General), 32 Alta. L.R. (2d) 249, [1984] 5 W.W.R. 436, 11 D.L.R. (4th) 482.

Ontario. *Business Corporations Act*, R.S.O. 1970, c. 53.

———. *Election Finances Act, 1986*, S.O. 1986, c. 33, ss. 1, 19, 20.

———. *Election Finances Reform Act (EFRA)*, S.O. 1975, c. 12, ss. 2–5, 10, 11, 13, 19, 20–24, 26, 28, 30–32, 35, 39, 45, 54.

———. *Income Tax Act*, R.S.O. 1970, c. 217.

Ontario. Commission on Election Contributions and Expenses (CECE). 1975. *Annual Report*. Toronto: CECE.

———. 1976. *Annual Report*. Toronto: CECE.

———. 1980. *Annual Report*. Toronto: CECE.

———. 1981. *Annual Report*. Toronto: CECE.

———. 1982a. *Annual Report.* Toronto: CECE.

———. 1982b. *Canadian Election Reform: Dialogue on Issues and Effects.* Toronto: CECE.

———. 1985. *Annual Report.* Toronto: CECE.

Ontario. Commission on Election Finances (CEF). 1986a. *Annual Report.* Toronto: CEF.

———. 1986b. *Guidelines for Chief Financial Officers.* Toronto: CEF.

———. 1987a. *Annual Report.* Toronto: CEF.

———. 1987b. "Statistical Report on Candidate and Campaign Reimbursements." Toronto: CEF.

———. 1988. *Annual Report.* Toronto: CEF.

Ontario. Commission on the Legislature. 1974. *Third Report.* Toronto: Queen's Printer.

Ontario. Legislative Assembly. 1972. *Journals of the Legislative Assembly.* Toronto: Queen's Printer.

Spiers, Rosemary. 1986. *Out of the Blue: The Fall of the Tory Dynasty in Ontario.* Toronto: Macmillan.

Starr v. Ontario (Commissioner of Inquiry) (1989), 62 D.L.R. (4th) 702 (Ont. Div. Ct.); affirmed (1990), 64 D.L.R. (4th) 285 (Ont. C.A.); reversed [1990] 1 S.C.R. 1366.

Surich, Jo. 1975. "Keeping Them Honest: Election Reform in Ontario." In *Government and Politics in Ontario,* ed. Donald C. MacDonald. Toronto: Macmillan.

Toronto Star. 1990. 12 August, B1.

Van Loon, Rick, and Michael Whittington. 1987. *The Canadian Political System: Environment, Structure and Process.* 4th ed. Toronto: McGraw-Hill Ryerson.

Wearing, Joseph. 1985. "Political Parties: Fish or Fowl?" In *Government and Politics of Ontario.* 3d ed., ed. Donald C. MacDonald. Scarborough: Nelson Canada.

———. 1988. *Strained Relations: Canadian Parties and Voters.* Toronto: McClelland and Stewart.

———. 1990. "Ontario's Political Parties: The Ground Shifts." In *The Government and Politics of Ontario.* 4th ed., ed. Graham White. Scarborough: Nelson Canada.

3

PAYING FOR THE POLITICS OF BRITISH COLUMBIA

Terry Morley

CONFORMING TO POLITICAL moods found elsewhere in Canada has never been an inclination much valued in British Columbia. Thus, it is not surprising that successive governments of the province have failed to grasp the spirit of reform that followed the federal *Report of the Committee on Election Expenses* (Canada, Committee 1966).

Instead British Columbia governments have maintained a regime that provides only modest regulation of party and election financing. The two major parties that operate within this regime are thereby able to develop and maintain very different patterns for raising funds, distributing those funds between branches of the party and spending them on various political activities. The different patterns are in part a function of a sharp ideological contrast between Social Credit and the New Democratic Party. But even more important, they result from the very different conceptions these two parties have of Canada. The Social Credit party has no formal ties to parties seeking federal office. The NDP sees Canada, and itself, as an integrated whole. The differences, which are pursued in this study, are reflected in means and modes of party finance.

The major reforms of party finance, which seem to owe their existence as much to the political scientist Khayyam Paltiel[1] as they do to sovereign legislatures and eager political parties, embody three fundamental principles. These are: (a) there should be a provision of public subsidy for partisan political activity; (b) there should be legislated limits on contributions and expenditures made for the purpose of assisting the capture of an elected public office; and (c) there should be public disclosure of contributions and expenditures made to and by political parties and candidates for public office.

The need for reform along these lines has been anticipated by many, including no less an authority on social and constitutional order than John Rawls. Professor Rawls argues that "political parties are to be made independent from private economic interests by allotting them sufficient tax revenues to play their part in the constitutional scheme" (Rawls 1971, 225–26). Three reasons for such a proposition emerge from the consideration of democratic theory put forth by Rawls.

The first is a concern for equality. Serious candidates for public office should have a more or less equal opportunity of gaining office and require more or less equal resources to undertake the pursuit. It is assumed that candidates endorsed by parties, or at least by established parties, are serious.

A second reason for reform arises from a traditional concern about the behaviour of public office-holders – the successful candidates. They are seen to properly serve the public good rather than to follow the behest of private interests. If it is assumed that he who pays the piper calls the tune, then it follows that the electoral piper should be supplied with public subventions rather than private donations. That would lessen any influence that powerful groups (business and labour groups for example) might have on politicians. It would also ensure that individuals could not obtain favours from governments by virtue of their contributions to campaign war chests. Such favours would include government contracts, patronage appointments and access to government decision making.

Third, there is a belief that adequate funding for the process of electoral office-seeking will stimulate political debate and that a wide and considerable debate on the issues of the day fits with broader notions of democratic mores which, in proclaimed democratic polities, are self-evidently in need of nurturing and strengthening.

Such views have undoubtedly inspired the various instruments for reform of electoral politics in Canada that have been developed at the federal level and in most of the provinces over the last 20 years. And although the instruments of reform are not found in the same abundance in British Columbia as in other places, arguments on the nature of constitutional democracy have not been without influence. British Columbia is different, but not so different.

The most important instruments of reform in Canada are found in different combinations in the different jurisdictions. The full catalogue contains the following eight:

1. Older reforms provide legislative injunctions prohibiting "corrupt practices such as the offering and acceptance of bribes, treating – notably with intoxicating liquors – and the conveyance of voters to the polling stations in particular circumstances" (Paltiel 1970, 111). Following the Pacific Scandal candidates were made responsible for the expenditure of campaign funds through the appointment of official agents. Contributions are, for the most part, required to be made through the official agents. And assisting the election of a candidate for a "valuable consideration" or for present or future employment is considered a corrupt practice (ibid., 113). All Canadian jurisdictions followed the federal government's lead in enacting these provisions in one form or another.

2. A scheme of tax credits allows those who contribute funds to registered political parties or to candidates for certain public offices to request, at the time of filing an income tax return, that a portion of the contribution be returned to them as a deduction of tax owing or in cash if they should owe no tax. Since the public treasury forgoes revenue through this scheme, it may be considered that such tax credits are a form of public subsidy. Nine jurisdictions, including the federal government, have adopted such a scheme.

3. Direct cash subsidies are provided from the public treasury to candidates for certain public offices and registered parties. Several formulas of eligibility are used in eight jurisdictions that provide such subventions.

4. Political advertising is regulated so that candidates for certain public offices and registered parties are more easily able to obtain broadcast time than are private advertisers. Some free time is made available. Broadcasters must provide additional paid time to candidates and parties on the basis of a formula that takes into account the number of legislative seats held by a party prior to the call of an election. In Manitoba and Saskatchewan, government advertising is regulated during the election campaign period.

5. Political organizations are required to become registered parties to take advantage of the benefits outlined above. They also acquire certain obligations outlined below.

6. The same eight jurisdictions that provide direct subsidies also impose some form of spending limit on registered parties and candidates for certain public offices. Four jurisdictions impose contribution limits, three of which, Ontario, Quebec and New Brunswick, also have spending limits. Ontario, Quebec and

Alberta limit contributions from out of province including transfers of funds from federal parties, and Quebec forbids parties and candidates from accepting donations from corporations, unions or anyone other than a Quebec elector.

7. Eight jurisdictions require some form of public disclosure of individual contributions, including those made by corporate or other collective entities. Nova Scotia requires reports only of total contributions. Public disclosure is also required for certain political expenditures, particularly those made by candidates and parties during election campaigns.

8. Ontario has a Commission on Election Finances [former title] with a general authority to oversee the process of the raising and spending of money for political purposes and with the power to impose penalties for noncompliance. In most other jurisdictions the chief electoral officer has a similar, if more restricted, authority, and generally operates with the public expectation that he or she will act independently of the government of the day in these matters. The courts in Canada may also grant relief from the breaching of the legislation, although in Ontario the Commission must give permission for certain prosecutions to proceed.

THE REGULATORY REGIME

In the light of the reforms outlined above, it makes sense to look first at what is missing from the regulatory regime in British Columbia before detailing what is actually in place. The British Columbia arrangement can be best understood in contrast to the arrangements that generally prevail in other Canadian jurisdictions. In British Columbia:

- No direct cash subsidies are provided from the public treasury to political parties or to candidates seeking election to the legislative assembly.
- No legislated limits exist on spending during election campaigns or between elections.
- No legislated limits have been set on contributions, nor is there a requirement to disclose individual contributions.
- No commission has been appointed with a mandate to oversee the processes of political finance.

Nevertheless, some rules are in place governing the spending and raising of moneys for the purpose of securing the election of candidates to the legislative assembly.[2] These are as follows:

1. The *Corrupt Practices Prevention Act*, in addition to prohibiting bribery and treating, required, three years before similar federal legislation, that candidates appoint official agents and that election expenses could be authorized only by the agent. A statement of expenses was required to be filed with returning officers, and a fine was provided for a failure to file. The filing of a false statement was declared to be a misdemeanour. In addition to this Act, three other pieces of legislation provided the rules for the election process after 1871.[3] The four acts were amalgamated in 1920 in the *Provincial Elections Act,* which provides the structure for the modern *Election Act.*

   More recently, a significant alteration to the legislated understanding of corruption in the raising of funds for political purposes in British Columbia was made by means of a 1961 amendment to the *Labour Relations Act.* This change prevented trade unions from using any portion of dues received by a check-off for political purposes. It went further and prohibited employers from checking off (deducting) dues from their employees to any trade union that would not give assurances in writing that no portion of the dues was being used for political purposes. This measure was quite obviously directed at the New Democratic Party, and it caused a considerable controversy in the province (Paltiel 1970, chap. 7). It was repealed in 1973 after the election of an NDP provincial government.

2. In 1979 the provincial income tax act was amended to provide tax credits for contributions made to recognized political parties and official candidates. This change followed the recommendations of the Royal Commission on Electoral Reform (BC Royal Commission 1978).[4] The formula is the same as that provided in the federal income tax act. A portion of the aggregate amount contributed by an individual taxpayer in one year to a "recognized political party" or to a "candidate" (as defined in the *Election Act*) can be deducted from tax otherwise payable, according to the following scheme:

   (a) 75 percent of the aggregate if the aggregate does not exceed $100;

   (b) $75 plus 50 percent of the amount by which the aggregate exceeds $100 if the aggregate exceeds $100 and does not exceed $550; or

   (c) the smaller of

       (i) $300 plus $33^1/_3$ percent of the amount by which the aggregate exceeds $550 or

       (ii) $500.

"Recognized political party" is defined in the Act as "a bona fide affiliation of electors comprised in a political organization that has as a prime purpose the fielding of candidates for election to the Legislative Assembly." There are provisions for the issuing of official receipts and for members of partnerships to claim portions of the amount contributed by the partnership.

3. Regulations similar to those imposed on broadcasters by the federal regulatory agency (the CRTC) concerning federal elections are also imposed for provincial elections, although British Columbia has no special rules to provide media access.

4. British Columbia has long recognized the existence of political parties. This is important to note since such recognition federally, and in most other provinces, has followed the reformist impulse aroused by Professor Paltiel and the Committee on Election Expenses.

As early as 1920 the BC *Provincial Elections Act* required not only candidates, but also "central committees of political parties" to file returns of election expenses. The key provisions in the present *Election Act* are found in section 176, which reads as follows:

(1) Within 60 days after polling day, the secretary and treasurer of the central committee of every political party, or other officers who acted in that capacity, shall transmit to the chief electoral officer a true return, in Form 29, or to the like effect, containing, as respects the political party, statements in detail of all
  (a) electoral expenses; and
  (b) disputed and unpaid claims of which the secretary or treasurer is aware.

(2) A political party within the meaning of this section is an affiliation of electors comprised in a political organization which has expended money in the support of any candidate in the election.

The *Constitution Act* (consolidated 14 November 1986) also attempts to define a "recognized political party" in section 1 as "an affiliation of electors comprised in a political organization whose prime purpose is the fielding of candidates for election to the Legislative Assembly."

It is true there is no formal scheme for the registration of political parties in British Columbia. Nonetheless party names are listed on the ballot at the direction of party leaders,[5] and the three similar definitions of party detailed above are available to assist the chief electoral officer in ensuring the appropriate political groups, and candidates for the legislative assembly associated with such groups, report expenditures as required by the *Election Act.*

Of course the chief electoral officer has considerable discretion in interpreting the rules and in determining how vigorously he will enforce the rules. Section 174 states that no person shall be "engaged or employed for payment or promise of payment" for "the purpose of promoting or procuring the election of a candidate at any election," and further that no person shall "pay or promise to pay any other person" for this purpose except as regards to:

(a) the personal expenses of the candidate;
(b) the expenses of printing and advertising, and the expenses of publishing, issuing and distributing addresses and notices;
(c) the expenses of stationery, messages, postage and telegrams;
(d) the expenses of public meetings;
(e) the expenses of a central committee room, and of not more than one committee room in each polling division;
(f) the expenses of transporting voters to and from polling places in the electoral district, but not from one electoral district to another electoral district;
(g) the expenses incurred by the employment of clerks and scrutineers.

No doubt this provision was intended to prevent candidates from buying votes by offering employment; however, this section has not been rigidly enforced. It is true that the exceptions would allow for certain employment, but in reality much of the work in modern elections performed by individuals drawing some form of salary or wage is, in a strict sense, under this interdict. It is not possible for a chief electoral officer to ignore this manifest reality.

It is a little more surprising that the requirement that the return of expenses required of candidates and central committees be sworn, or affirmed, before a commissioner for taking affidavits is not enforced. It is perhaps understandable that a by-election candidate for a fringe party (The Human Race Party) can insist that "God is my witness."[6] It is more significant that the New Democratic Party central committee return for another by-election was witnessed by a party caucus employee who was not a commissioner, and that the NDP's central committee return for the Point Grey and Nanaimo by-elections was made by way of an unwitnessed letter signed by a senior party official.[7]

But this does not mean that these returns are other than "true returns," and in any event the penalty for breaching the disclosure sections of the Act is a fine of "not less than $200 and not more than

$1 000." It does, nevertheless, raise some doubts about the reliability of the present system as a means of accurately disclosing campaign expenditures.

The returns of expenses are filed with the chief electoral officer and published with his or her report of the polling results, formerly available from the Queen's Printer and now obtainable from Crown Publications, a private company of former Queen's Printer employees that now owns the distribution rights for government publications.

Finally, it is important to note that an additional formal method of reporting campaign expenditures, along with administrative expenditures and the level of contributions (but not individual contributions), has been utilized by the Social Credit Party. Under the British Columbia *Society Act* the British Columbia Social Credit Party is a registered society. The incorporation number is S-0003562, and the party was first registered 29 April 1949 under the name British Columbia Social Credit League. The name was changed 31 March 1978.

There is no requirement that a political party register as a society, and most have not registered. The Social Credit decision to register in 1949 was a means of protecting the name and, since the party at that time had no seats and few prospects, an attempt to persuade the world, and themselves, that the Social Credit movement in British Columbia had a substantial form. No doubt the party has never sought deregistration because such a move would bring with it unfavourable publicity. In recent years members of other political groups without legislative representation have registered, likely with similar motives and desires, including members of the Reform Party of Canada who want their party to enter provincial politics.

Registered political parties are not required to disclose their financial statements under the legislation, but a party may choose to do so. If a political party or any society elects to report, then it must provide the Registrar of Companies, within 30 days after the annual general meeting, with a list of directors together with the financial statement presented to the annual general meeting. The statement must contain a statement of income and expenditure, a statement of the surplus or deficit, a statement of the source and application of funds, and a balance sheet for each reporting period, generally one year. The party must also file the auditor's statement.

The British Columbia Social Credit Party has chosen to report, and therefore the financial disclosure required under the *Society Act* is available for public consumption. Unfortunately the original file disappeared sometime in the early 1980s; and, despite a 1986 request from the Registrar of Companies for copies of annual reports and financial statements for the years 1950 to 1984 inclusive, these are not yet available.[8] The statements from 1985 are available in a temporary file.

Since Social Credit has elected to act as a reporting society, one reform that might appeal to a Social Credit government would be a requirement that all political parties register under the *Society Act.* Under the provisions of section 38(1) of the Act, it would be possible for the Registrar to order that the parties be reporting societies. It may be, however, that for other reasons the Social Credit Party will reconsider its policy of registering as a society. A recent nomination battle in the electoral district of Burnaby–Edmonds was decided by a single vote, and the losing candidate appealed to the Supreme Court of British Columbia to have the nomination set aside. (Although the courts have generally been reluctant to interfere with the internal operations of political parties in Canada, they frequently are asked to settle internal disputes within registered societies.) The judge set aside the nomination and required the Social Credit Party to hold another nomination meeting. No doubt this decision will give officers in all political parties some pause in pursuing the society registration option and may make compulsory registration less attractive to a Social Credit government.

THE BRITISH COLUMBIA PARTY SYSTEM

The resistance in British Columbia to the reformist movement that followed from the Report of the Committee on Election Expenses, the peculiarities of the formal arrangements found in the province and the prospects for change are all necessarily understood as an aspect of the party system that has developed. The party system in turn reflects fundamental divisions in the province and long-held beliefs. Therefore it is helpful, before examining in detail the financial observances of the parties, to sketch the context in which the parties operate. Not only does British Columbia have a rather different regulatory regime for the financing of elections and political parties than other Canadian jurisdictions (except, possibly, Newfoundland), but British Columbia politics are conducted with rules and constraints not found elsewhere in the country.

From the time that the party system became solidified in the early years of this century until 1933, the Liberal and Conservative parties dominated British Columbia politics, taking turns forming the government. Although a handful of labour and socialist MLAs were elected, they did not play major roles in the political life of the province. In 1933, with the collapse of the Conservative regime under Simon Fraser Tolmie, the newly launched Co-operative Commonwealth Federation (CCF) managed to come second with 31.5 percent of the popular vote, capturing 7 seats. The Liberals with 41.7 percent had a comfortable majority with 34 seats and others, mostly Conservatives running under other designations, managed 6 seats.

The advent of a socialist party that enjoyed significant popular support meant the breakup of the old two-party alternation in government. The wartime sentiment for partisan cooperation pushed the Liberals and Conservatives into coalition. The fact that in 1941 the CCF received more votes than any other party (33.4 percent compared with 32.9 percent for the Liberals) and 14 seats helped to set the new coalition in electoral cement. In the postwar years it was believed that some combination of free enterprise political forces was necessary to keep the socialists from power.

Nevertheless, strains between the coalition partners who continued to be enemies in the federal arena led to a breakup of the arrangement in 1951. A general disenchantment with all those who had kept the coalition together for more years than many in the province would have wished, combined with a newly introduced transferable-vote, alternative-ballot electoral system, enabled W.A.C. Bennett, a Conservative MLA who left his party after losing a leadership challenge, to make the Social Credit Party into the new instrument for keeping the CCF out of government.

Bennett stayed as premier for 20 years, winning six more successive elections. The CCF (after 1961, transformed as the NDP) managed about a third of the popular vote during the period, but Social Credit generally received another 10 percent beyond that and always a majority of seats. The Liberals and Conservatives and a few independents might obtain 20–25 percent of the popular vote, but this did not translate into more than a handful of seats. Social Credit was secure as the only viable alternative to the CCF-NDP and W.A.C. Bennett never forgot to warn the electorate about the evils of socialism when he spoke in the legislative assembly and on the hustings.

In 1972, Bennett's Social Credit Party finally lost an election. The NDP, with 39.6 percent of the popular vote, was rewarded with 38 of the 55 seats. Social Credit, with 31.2 percent of the vote, won 10 seats, and the Liberals and Conservatives, with 29.1 percent of the vote, split 7 seats between them.

The wonders and vagaries of the first-past-the-post electoral system (W.A.C. Bennett abolished the alternative ballot after the 1953 run-off election) were not lost on those citizens of the province made unhappy by the prospect of socialism and the reality of NDP initiatives. Believing themselves to be a majority, they cast about for some new instrument that would ensure the defeat of Dave Barrett's NDP government.

As it happened, the instrument turned out to be a refurbished Social Credit Party. It seemed for a while that the Liberals, or some new group combining Liberals and Conservatives into a "majority movement," would inevitably replace Social Credit as the alternative to the NDP. But Social Credit had the preponderance of resources. It had a cadre of experienced organizers, more seats in the legislative assembly than any other political group, and a leader who owned the well-known Bennett name by virtue of being W.A.C. Bennett's son. It also enjoyed the fruits of a pervasive rumour that a secret fund controlled by the Bennetts was available to assist in any restoration.

In late 1975 Dave Barrett, the NDP premier, called an election. The NDP received 39.2 percent of the vote: almost an identical showing to the one that had made them the government three years earlier. But Social Credit got 49.3 percent and won 35 seats, a clear majority. (The NDP won 18 seats with the Liberals and Conservatives each capturing 1 seat.) The Liberals and Conservatives only managed 11.1 percent of the popular vote. With Social Credit again the instrument of the anti-socialist–free enterprise sensibility, the popular vote obtained by third parties continued to shrink in the next three elections, and after 1979 only Social Credit and NDP MLAs were found in the assembly. The return of the two-party system had been accomplished with a vengeance.

There is a difference, therefore, between the values that drive this party system and those that are central to other party systems in Canada, including those central to the federal party system in British Columbia. As Donald Blake and his UBC colleagues have shown, there is a "separation of federal and provincial party systems in the province [that] has evolved to such an extent that nearly half those who possess a party identification are attached to different parties in federal and provincial politics" (Blake 1985, 168). Alan Cairns and Daniel Wong explain this in the following terms:

> The divergence of federal and provincial party systems in British Columbia was neither accidental nor inevitable. It results primarily from the differential consequences attached to left-wing strength in the federal and provincial arenas, and from the different party strategies those consequences elicit. These strategies have never been responses to the brute fact of CCF/NDP strength *per se*; rather, they derive from the interaction between the institutional incentives which parliamentary government holds out for majority government, and the real and manipulated fears in a divided society over the prospect of a left-wing government. (Cairns and Wong 1985, 300)

These incentives and fears not only create an ambiguity that complicates BC politics[9] but also create a set of conditions that bind some British Columbians to ideas current in other places in Canada (and elsewhere) and compel others to move in the opposite direction. In these ways is the province divided and those divisions inform public policy, including policies to regulate the pattern of party financing and election campaigning. The actions of the players in British Columbia politics in regard to these questions can only be understood and explained in this context.

THE BRITISH COLUMBIA NEW DEMOCRATS

There is but one New Democratic Party in British Columbia, and the modes of provincial and federal activity are never permitted to diverge. Any person joining the British Columbia New Democrats is also considered to be a member of the New Democratic Party of Canada. Those who toil in the service of the party must work in the interests of candidates both for the legislature and for Parliament. It is seen as right and proper so to do. The idea is one social democracy under two leaders.

However, social democratic interests do sometimes diverge, and there are always two leadership interests. The resulting tension is exacerbated by the constitutional roles played by federal and provincial governments and by the formation of an NDP government in the province. It is a tension recognized by those employed by the party in Vancouver and in Ottawa.

The paradox of sustaining unity in diversity has inspired a formula for revenue-sharing in the British Columbia NDP that is equalled only by the federal-provincial fiscal transfer system found in this country. It is still true that the idea of what was once called the new Jerusalem – now paraded as a better deal for ordinary people – motivates the raising of funds. But the form of the fund-raising is moulded by this paradox even as it is driven by the system of tax credits.

Because moneys raised through the 1974 federal tax-credit rebates are available to the provincial organization, a significant increase in election spending has been made possible. In the 1972 provincial election the NDP reported a total expenditure of $490 767. This was divided between the central campaign which spent $190 867 and the 55 candidates who spent $299 900. In the election that followed in late 1975, these figures more than doubled. The 55 candidates reported expenditures of $607 516 and the central campaign $342 481, for a total of $949 997. Table 3.1 shows the NDP returns for election expenditures for the last five elections, and they clearly reflect the party's greater ability to raise funds after 1974 and the 1979 provincial tax-credit scheme.

Table 3.1
Reported provincial general election expenditures, New Democratic Party, British Columbia section, 1972–86
(dollars)

	1972	1975	1979	1983	1986
Candidates' expenditures	299 900	607 516	720 005	1 289 131	1 626 322
Central committee expenditures	190 867	342 481	382 575	965 300	1 416 767
Total expenditures	490 767	949 997	1 102 580	2 254 431	3 043 089

Source: British Columbia Chief Electoral Officer, Statement of Votes for provincial general elections held in 1972, 1975, 1979, 1983 and 1986.

Fund-raising Strategies

The British Columbia New Democrats require funds to fight federal and provincial general elections and by-elections, and to sustain the party's administrative apparatus. Although there is a distinction drawn between these two sorts of activities imposed by the reporting requirements of the *Election Act* and reflected by separate administrative and election budgets (the latter includes funds set aside for pre-election campaigning), party managers believe that a healthy administrative structure provides considerable assistance in successfully contesting the elections.

It should be noted that a certain portion of the cost of maintaining a viable organization between elections is borne by the public treasury. MLAs receive a little more than $40 000 a year, paid monthly to pay the expenses of an office which, if funds are available, can include some staff. In fact, constituency associations will sometimes provide additional funds to pay the expenses and even a small salary for party activists who volunteer to help. In theory the office is nonpartisan and the party name is not to be displayed. Certainly the staff spend much of their time in a nonpartisan fashion assisting the MLAs' constituents who bring problems to be solved. But inevitably they spend some portion of their time on partisan chores – arranging meetings, organizing fund-raising, maintaining membership lists and preparing for the next election campaign.

MPs are also provided with offices and a much more generous staff allowance, although the guidelines for controlling partisan activities are much more elaborate and stringent. Yet the line between partisanship and nonpartisanship is not a clear one, and there is no doubt that these offices help both parties sustain an administrative structure between elections. As well, staff members employed out of public funds by the legislative caucus generally spend a portion of their time, sometimes a large portion, on partisan activity. They are, after all, hired in part because of their party affiliation.

Although public moneys are used for partisan purposes in this manner, the bulk of the funds used to sustain the administrative apparatus and to fight the election campaigns is raised from contributions. For many years these contributions were gathered by volunteers during the annual membership drives. The practice in democratic socialist parties throughout the world has been to charge a membership fee as part of conceiving membership as a privilege with obligations which, if they are not adhered to, can lead to the loss of that membership. Before 1970 the British Columbia New Democrats imposed a fee of at least $10 for individuals, with lesser fees for certain categories of people – youth, unemployed and those on welfare. For a time there were family membership rates.

It became apparent that there were two problems with this system. The principle of exclusivity now based on a membership fee rather than on adherence to a doctrine did not fit well with the cultural ideas of believers in equality, living in a liberal democratic society. Party members were not comfortable refusing membership to those who had little money. Even when the minimum fee was $10, it was felt that a considerable number of individuals might find it difficult to pay that amount. Equally important was the realization that, at the other end of the scale, relatively well-off party members would feel that they had done their regular duty by paying the membership fee and would give additional funds only during election campaigns. There was a widespread belief that for these reasons the membership drives were not raising sufficient funds.

After 1970 the provincial party levied a $25 fee on constituency associations for every member claimed. The constituency association could keep moneys raised beyond the $25 fee and could also allow people to be members who paid less than $25. Two problems were associated with this scheme. First, the provincial party was unable to get the benefit of donations from wealthier and more generous members of the NDP. Second, in certain nomination battles, notably an unsuccessful attempt in 1979 to take the nomination from a sitting MLA, questions were raised about the practice of association executives signing up $1 members to help stack the nomination meeting.

In 1987 the party's governing body between conventions, the Provincial Council, appointed a task force to develop a new revenue-sharing scheme that would encourage donations throughout the year and in nonelection years (BC New Democratic Party 1987). That scheme got rid of all distinctions between membership moneys and other donations and adopted the principle that "a buck is a buck." Thus "a member who gives *any* [my emphasis] tax-receiptable money shall have their membership extended by 12 months." This allowed a new formula to be developed for splitting contributions between the different levels of the party. It also promoted a more complex arrangement for fund-raising.

A fund-raising manual developed by provincial office staff sets out the model for constituency associations (BC New Democratic Party n.d.). It was developed for election campaigns but is also designed so that it can be used between elections. Constituency associations and other fund-raising groups are urged to treat fund-raising as a special kind of campaign requiring discipline and skills. The first step is to put together a carefully selected team. Those in charge are urged to "be quite ruthless in choosing only those individuals with the particular range of skills needed." Since this is a "direct-ask" strategy, the skills include high energy levels, the ability to communicate in a confident manner and a natural optimism. There are three components to the direct-ask strategy.

1. A direct mail letter to be sent in the first few days of a campaign to motivate potential donors and to introduce the follow-up telemarketing appeal. Much good advice is dispensed on the principles of direct mail, with a clear injunction that the letter should ask for a specific amount for a specific purpose. To defend this view, the manual cites a study of New York panhandlers that showed that those "who asked for a specific amount or for a specific purpose ('so that I can get on the subway') were more likely to get something than those who asked for vague 'spare change.'"

2. A telemarketing drive using a phone bank is described. (Sympathetic law firms with several lines and many telephone sets are often asked to let their offices be used at night for this purpose.) A sample pitch is provided and the fund-raisers are told to use couriers to pick up the cheque once a donation is agreed to. "Under no circumstances should the contact be left with the promise that he or she will mail the cheque."

3. Home visits by the couriers constitute the third element of the fund-raising campaign and provide an opportunity to enrol members in the party and to obtain workers for the election campaign.

The efforts of the constituencies are vital for the provincial party. In 1989, the last year that complete figures are available, the New

Democratic Party of British Columbia reported a total tax-receiptable income of $3 123 465. Fund-raising costs were $367 076, just under 12 percent of the gross income, leaving a net of $2 756 389. The revenue-sharing breakdown of this amount is provided in table 3.2. It should be noted that the fund-raising costs were all incurred for direct mail campaigns which raised almost 40 percent of the total revenues.

The provincial section share obtained from constituency quotas was $1 565 972. This provided a hefty 88.2 percent of the provincial section's total income of $1 776 350. By contrast $32 499 came through affiliation fees from union locals, amounting to 1.8 percent of the total income. The provincial section itself, by taking a 15 percent agency fee on direct mail sent from provincial office, received $160 395 or 9 percent of the total income, with 55–70 percent of these provincial direct mail

Table 3.2
New Democratic Party, British Columbia section, revenue sharing, 1 January to 31 December 1989
(dollars)

Total tax-receiptable income	3 123 464.88
Fund-raising costs	(367 075.84)
	2 756 389.04
Revenue-sharing distribution:	
Federal party	412 996.97
Constituency quotas	1 565 972.01
British Columbia section	160 394.52
Central by-election	111 144.66
Conference fees	310.00
Provincial ridings: regular	328 678.66
by-election donations	104 542.37
by-election appeal	24 126.40
nomination windows	11 654.40
1990 undistributed	4 180.00
Federal ridings: regular	6 534.38
special windows	22 100.57
International solidarity	881.45
Women candidates fund	1 352.35
Young New Democrats	1 520.30
	2 756 389.04

Source: New Democratic Party of British Columbia, Treasurer's report and financial statements for the year ended 31 December 1989.

proceeds being credited to the constituency where the donor resides or holds membership. The party in British Columbia now collects almost 40 percent of its revenues from direct mail (Brown and Rubin interviews 1990).

In an election year the British Columbia New Democrats receive other forms of income. Working through the party's labyrinthine financial arrangements requires patience, and the party itself provides no guide to the passage of revenue and expenditure. What follows is based on figures available in the financial statements for the year ending 31 December 1986.

Table 3.3 summarizes these complex arrangements. In 1986, the year of the last British Columbia election, the party in British Columbia raised a total of $3 677 966. Of this amount, labour organizations, generally national and international unions and labour centrals such as

Table 3.3
New Democratic Party, British Columbia section, revenues and expenditures in election year 1986

	$	%
Revenues		
Tax-receiptable revenue	3 469 180	
Labour contributions	208 786	5.7
Total fund-raising revenues	3 677 966	
Less:		
Fund-raising costs	244 845	6.6
Federal party share	499 323	14.5
Retained by provincial constituencies	1 329 205	
Retained by other party groups	3 706	
Net revenue retained by provincial party from fund-raising	1 600 887	
Plus:		
Local union affiliation fees	25 109	
Interest and miscellaneous	15 580	
Constituency quotas for 1986 election	500 001	
Organizer co-op	184 000	
Total revenue available to provincial party	2 325 577	
Expenditures		
Administrative costs	1 438 392	
Election expenditures	1 428 429	
Total expenditures	2 866 821	
Deficit	(541 244)	

Source: New Democratic Party, British Columbia section financial statements, 31 December 1986.

the BC Federation of Labour, contributed $208 786, which is almost 5.7 percent of the total. The remaining $3 469 180 was raised almost entirely from tax-receiptable contributions. The cost of fund-raising was $244 845 (6.6 percent) of the gross tax-receiptable contributions, leaving net tax-receiptable contributions of $3 224 335 which, when added to the union contribution, gave a net revenue figure of $3 433 121. The sum of $499 323 (14.5 percent) of the net tax-receiptable proceeds was transferred to the federal party, $1 329 205 (38.7 percent) was retained in the constituency associations, $358 297 (10.4 percent) was credited to the provincial election fund, and $3 706 was transferred to various small groups who did some fund-raising.

In addition, the provincial section received $25 109 in local union affiliation fees and $15 580 in interest and miscellaneous fees, for a total net income of $1 283 279 available to be spent on regular party administration. In the event the provincial section had administrative costs of $1 438 392, leaving a deficit of $155 113.

The election fund for 1986 had notional revenue of $1 042 298. The sum of $358 297 was designated for the fund from the revenues retained by the provincial office. Another $500 001 was provided by the constituencies for quotas levied, and the remaining $184 000 came from the organizer co-op.

The organizer co-op is coordinated by the federal office of the NDP. Individuals with campaign experience, often young people able to travel at short notice, are put on a list of organizers. In federal elections these organizers usually work in their own areas, although some of them are moved to key ridings where the party believes it has a good chance of holding a seat or, more likely, of gaining one. The co-op idea was designed for provincial elections when these experienced organizers from across the country can be concentrated in the province where the election has been called.[10]

When a provincial election is called, the provincial campaign managers identify individuals on the list who they feel have the appropriate mix of skills needed to make a contribution. The provincial party assigns them to different constituencies or, occasionally, to other tasks. In British Columbia they are paid a modest salary plus expenses by the local campaign or, in a few cases, by the provincial party. The federal party picks up the travel costs and other incidental expenses, which become a contribution to the provincial campaign.

In 1986 the New Democratic Party of British Columbia reported expenditures of $1 416 767 to the chief electoral officer. Their own records show post-election expenses of $11 662 for a total expenditure of $1 428 429. The shortfall between election revenues and expenditures was $386 131. Added to the administrative deficit of $155 113, this left an excess of expenditure over revenue for the year of $541 244. This in turn had to be combined with the deficit at the beginning of the year of $458 192, leaving a new total deficit position of $999 436. The obvious need to dramatically turn around this million dollar deficit before a fresh election call has been the central focus of the British Columbia New Democratic Party's financial strategy since 1986 and provided the inspiration for the new system of revenue sharing.

Revenue Sharing in the NDP

The British Columbia New Democrats raised large sums of money during the 1980s. Since 1982 they never raised less than $2 million and have twice managed to raise more than $4 million. But the party has also spent large sums of money and found itself short of cash, owing money to the bank and continuing to run in a deficit position. There are two important reasons for this.

First is the not uncommon reality that it is easier to enlarge a staff than to cut it back. Because the British Columbia New Democratic Party runs candidates in federal and provincial elections, and increasingly in municipal contests, there is never much time between elections or between pre-election periods for the machinery to be given a rest. Moreover, the members of a party with its roots in extraparliamentary organization feel that political activism is not something to be invented at election time and then forgotten. The party's administrative apparatus is expected to be available to assist in a wide variety of projects. In any event, the next election in British Columbia is never seen to be very far down the road. To maintain such a constant level of activity is expensive.

Second, the principle of sharing revenue with the different levels of the party has meant that, in a cash-short situation, large debts owed from one level to another inevitably build up. Those who have a primary identification with one of the levels attempt to conserve (some would say hoard) cash, the better to fight whatever particular political battle, federal or provincial or municipal, most attracts them. In this circumstance the debt to another level of the party does not seem to be the same thing as "real" debt and has often been ignored.

To overcome these two problems, senior party officials have developed a new system that makes use of provincial office control of the federal and provincial tax receipts.[11] The idea has been to design a system of splitting the funds that has built-in incentives for constituencies to raise money now so that they may keep more cash later when the election comes around. As part of this initiative they have also attempted to curb the spending of the federal party.

The first step has been to establish a tax rate for the constituencies. In 1988 there was one "tax," called a quota, to provide the revenue for the provincial party's administrative budget. With the anticipation of a 1990 election, two "taxes" were levied, with a "surtax" thrown in for good measure.

The first tax for 1990 was the administrative quota, determined by taking the three-year average revenue from each redistributed provincial constituency and calculating the percentage of the total revenue from all the constituencies that the individual constituency had raised. A budget expenditure figure has been set by the provincial council at $933 000, and each constituency owes its previously calculated percentage of that figure. An election budget revenue figure from the constituencies has also been set at $800 000, and each constituency owes its previously calculated percentage of that figure as well.

Figures from the constituency of Saanich South provide an example of this formula. The three-year average revenue from Saanich South was calculated to be $37 016. The total three-year average revenue for all the constituencies was $2 649 327, giving Saanich South a tax rate of 1.397 percent. That means its administrative quota is $13 035.34 and its election quota is $11 177.48, based on the budget figures above.

How does Saanich South go about paying its taxes? First it sets out to pay the administrative quota. If a donor gives Saanich South $100, then $70 goes toward the quota. Saanich South never sees the cash, but its account with the provincial party is reduced by that sum. Of the remainder, $15 goes to the federal party, and the constituency keeps $15. That is in phase one. Phase two begins when a constituency has paid down 50 percent of its administrative quota. At that point only $55 goes to pay down the quota, and the constituency can, if it wishes, get $30 in cash. It should also be noted that if the donor gives money to the federal riding association, then that association keeps $15. However, in phase one the provincial constituency where the donor resides, or is a member, still is credited with $70 against the quota and in phase two with $55. If the donor gives the $100 through a provincial direct mailing or to the provincial office, then the provincial party keeps the $15, but the donor's constituency gets the credit against the quota.

Once the administrative quota is paid off, the constituency can turn its attention to paying the election quota. No doubt in a perfect world the constituencies would continue to raise funds with 15 percent continuing to go to the federal party and the rest going to pay down election quotas. But this would mean that the constituencies would not have any cash and little incentive to go on tax-receipted direct-ask fund-raising drives. This situation has caused the provincial party to create "fund-raising windows."

There are pre-election windows and an election window. When there is a pre-election window, the money raised is shared as follows. As always, 15 percent is paid to the federal party. Then 25 percent goes to the provincial party, and 30 percent goes to pay down the election quota for the constituency. And the remaining 30 percent is remitted to the constituency "**in cash.**" (The bold-face in quotes is an important exhortation found in the 1990 New Democratic Party of British Columbia Budget Documents.) There is an automatic 10-day nomination window from the date of the nomination. In 1990 there were four other scheduled pre-election windows for the provincial constituencies.

Once the election is called there is an election window in which 60 percent of the contribution flows to the constituency, but is only paid in cash after the whole quota has been paid. The remaining 40 percent is the provincial party's share. There is one additional wrinkle. The original $800 000 budget did not cover all the pre-election expenses. So another $142 000 was required, to be raised as a kind of surtax, which accounts for the 25 percent that goes to the provincial party. If that "surtax" had not been levied, the constituency would have received 55 percent credit toward its election quota. In a sense it still does, but the quota got bigger if not better.

Finally there is a phase three for payment of quotas. In terms of cash, the provincial office continues to hold 55 percent of the moneys with 15 percent remitted to the federal party and 30 percent kept by the constituency or other source of the funds. At year end, the retained moneys were to be distributed in the same proportions as each source – provincial constituency, federal riding, youth section, municipal parties and provincial party – raised throughout the year. As well, municipal parties[12] are given an election window every three years before the municipal election date, when they can retain a 60 percent share of funds they collect instead of the normal 15 percent. Provincial constituencies and federal ridings where there is a by-election to be fought also get pre-election and election windows. Since it is considered that direct mail contributions go into the pot first to pay down constituency quotas, the year-end share retained by constituencies is now 70 percent, with 15 percent remitted to the federal party and 15 percent provided to the provincial office.

Constituency Responses to Revenue Sharing

Not all constituency activists, and not all MLAs, were pleased with the new revenue-sharing scheme. There had always been resentment in the constituencies about all forms of revenue sharing and this new scheme, which favoured the cash needs of the provincial party and the federal party over their own needs, raised concerns in many constituencies about their ability to raise sufficient cash to be able to fight an election.

Some constituencies, often with the support of their MLAs, have adopted a counterstrategy to deal with the problem as they perceive it. They make no real effort to pay down either quota. Although membership renewals and donations from provincial direct mailings will in fact ensure that some of the administrative quota is paid, the constituency just lets that happen. Instead, they try to raise as much money as possible that is not tax-receiptable, through auctions, picnics, dinners and similar events, all of which can be retained in the constituency. When the election is called, they use these funds and, more often than not, money borrowed from the bank on the personal guarantees of the key activists, to pay off all quota money owed to the provincial office. They anticipate that intense fund-raising during an election, when the constituency retains 60 percent of the tax-receiptable funds collected, will give them a better chance to raise sufficient funds to pay for the local campaign and to pay back any bank debt. As of 17 October 1990, 33 of the 75 provincial constituencies had paid down less than $500 of their election quota (22 had paid nothing). Some of these would simply be weak areas, still disorganized, but most of them would likely be resisting to some extent the provincial party policy on revenue sharing.[13]

Nelson–Creston is one provincial constituency that has accepted the revenue-sharing scheme and has been busily paying down its quotas. But, like many other constituencies, it also conducts an active fundraising program designed to obtain non-receiptable moneys, none of which need to be sent off to Vancouver or Ottawa. The different projects are interesting. They include a ball game followed by an auction, a firewood sale, a book sale and an art auction held in the well-to-do Vancouver district of Point Grey. In addition the constituency has well-developed plans for obtaining tax-receiptable donations that include requests for contributions from those who have left the area for well-paying jobs elsewhere ("the diaspora") and who retain personal ties to the candidate; a campaign directed at small business; a list of individuals likely to make donations of more than $500 and a plan of what to say to them; a strategy for persuading local unions to give directly to the campaign rather than through the provincial office; and a dinner with the provincial leader during his election tour. Nelson–Creston, where $26 815 was reported spent by the NDP in the 1986 election, expects to raise more than $50 000 net for the constituency from these various activities.[14] The better organized constituencies have similar fund-raising plans that include salmon barbecues, garage sales and dinners featuring various ethnic foods.

Federal-Provincial Relations

The New Democratic Party finances much of its federal general election campaigns by "taxing" the provincial parties through a federal election quota. The quota is set by the federal council (the governing body of the federal party between conventions), and it is based on the perceived ability of the different provincial sections to raise the funds. The money goes to the central campaign fund. It is, in a very real sense, a classic transfer payment from the NDP's "have" provinces – British Columbia, Alberta, Saskatchewan, Manitoba and Ontario – who pay 95 percent of the total quota, to the NDP's "have-not" provinces east of the Ottawa river, who are supposed to pay 5 percent, but in reality are never able to pay any more than token amounts.[15]

In the last federal election in 1988, the amount to be raised through the quota from all the provincial parties was set at $2.2 million. British Columbia's share was $585 000 (26.5 percent), exactly the same as Ontario's. (Saskatchewan's share was 22.7 percent, Manitoba's 14.7 percent and Alberta's 4 percent.)

But at the end of 1987, the British Columbia party still had a deficit of $700 000 and no more borrowing power, in part because in 1987 the British Columbia section had taken advantage of a federal 2-for-1 debt-reduction plan and borrowed $300 000 to pay back a $600 000 debt in revenue-sharing arrears. The provincial party therefore used an idea from the Liberals who had, they believed, required constituencies to assign 50 percent of the federal government rebate to candidates in 1984. Being of a more thoroughgoing disposition than the Liberals, the British Columbia New Democratic Party required federal constituency associations to assign 100 percent of the rebate to the provincial party. As a senior party official put it:

> We required 100 percent and we did so to avoid the problems that the Liberal party got itself into, which is that while the federal Liberal party is in debt to the tune of 6 million or 7 million dollars ... at the constituency levels ... there are large amounts of money just sitting there that the federal party can't get its hands on. To avoid that situation of prosperity at the margins and crippling debt at the centre we developed [this] system. (Brown interview 1990)

Several federal candidates, including a number of MPs, complained bitterly but to no avail. With the assignments as security, the provincial party was then able to go to the bank and borrow the money to pay the quota. The rebates reported by the chief electoral officer totalled $558 127, which paid most of the $585 000 provincial quota (Stanbury 1991, chap. 6). In addition, the provincial party required federal ridings to pay election quotas of $260 000. The provincial party also spent an additional $209 746 coordinating the federal campaign in British Columbia. This was reported as a deficit of $311 291 in 1988 because at the time of the preparation of the financial statements only $223 455 had been received. A further $334 688 was reported in the party's 1989 statements as a surplus on the federal election. So, in fact, the provincial party made a small profit of $23 397 on the 1988 federal election. A breakdown of revenue and expenditures for this election is found in table 3.4. There is a small discrepancy of $16 in the amount reported by the chief electoral officer and the amount reported by the party treasurer.

The payment of large election quotas is not the only source of financial tension between the federal party and the provincial sections, including British Columbia. The control of direct-mail pieces, the federal share of moneys raised for provincial elections and federal party expenditures have all caused considerable strife. At meetings of the federal party finance committee, the five "have" sections are often frustrated by the alliance between the federal office and the five "have-not" sections. To form a common front, the key officials from Ontario and the western provinces met in Wascana, Saskatchewan, in April 1989 and drafted a statement affectionately known as the "Wascana Slough Accord" (New Democratic Party 1989).

In 1989 the provincial party in British Columbia mailed 18 direct-mail packages, 8 to targeted groups[16] and 10 to the party membership. The federal party mailed an additional 7 packages.[17] By 1989 two things were apparent. One was that party members were becoming angry about what many saw as excessive appeals. The second was that, because the funds raised by federal direct mail were not shared by the federal party with provincial sections, the federal program would inevitably siphon off funds that might otherwise be raised for the forthcoming provincial election. The other provinces had similar problems. Saskatchewan was particularly enraged by the mailing of a federal package into the province at the start of the 1988 election campaign, thereby making it very difficult for the Saskatchewan section to raise sufficient funds to pay its large federal election quota.

The Wascana group agreed that the federal program must be curtailed. The Saskatchewan party went further by insisting that if more than two federal packages came in 1989, it would withhold monthly

Table 3.4
New Democratic Party, British Columbia section, statement of revenue and
expenditures, 1988 federal election
(dollars)

Revenue	
Federal riding quotas	260 000
Election Act rebates	223 455
Total	483 455
Expenditure	
Federal election quota	585 000
Fund-raising coordinator	45 332
Travel	2 845
Staff travel	5 637
News monitoring	5 264
Clerical staff	16 348
Telephone	14 086
Postage	13 507
Messenger service	1 693
Stationery and supplies	9 731
Literature	36 088
Signs	10 799
Data processing	28 355
Workshops	5 173
Election planning committee	3 470
Miscellaneous	11 438
Total	794 291
Excess of expenditure over revenue	311 291
Surplus reported in 1989	334 688
Profit	23 397

Sources: New Democratic Party, British Columbia section financial statements, 31 December 1988,
exhibit "D", and New Democratic Party of British Columbia, Treasurer's report and financial
statements for the year ended 31 December 1989.

revenue-sharing cheques. The British Columbia party sought an assurance, and believes it has received that assurance, that there would be
no federal direct mail during the provincial general election. But the
larger question of coordinating the direct-mail efforts continues to be
a matter of negotiation. Provincial grievances have been partly redressed
by a recent decision that 15 percent of federal direct-mail revenues will
be remitted to the province in which they are raised (Howard interview 1991).

Another provincial grievance arises from the fact that the
15 percent federal "tax" on all moneys raised by constituencies, provincial parties, youth groups and any other entities that are sources of

tax-receiptable funds, applies to the large sums raised to fight provincial elections. The "tax" on provincial election funds has been particularly difficult for the Ontario party. The Wascana discussion paper states the problem feelingly:

> In Ontario provincial elections all monies are receipted locally at the constituency level rather than centrally by the provincial party.
>
> Because election contributions do not flow through the provincial party, the Ontario NDP does not generate the revenues from which to divert 15% of all election contributions to the federal party. Nor is it aware of the scope of the ... obligation ... until after the provincial election when the constituencies file their returns with the electoral office.[18]
>
> At that point the federal party does an accounting on Ontario's provincial election revenues and presents the section with a bill for a windfall 15% share. Unfortunately this money has already been spent by constituencies, is uncollectable by the provincial party and is therefore unavailable for payment to the federal party.
>
> And just to ensure that no provincial funds slip into federal coffers, Ontario legislation makes it illegal to make payments to a federal party from provincially receipted monies. Such payments can only be made from federally receipted funds raised in Ontario.
>
> The prospect of launching a federally receipted fundraising campaign, either during or after a provincial election, for the purpose of meeting a sudden speed up in federal revenue sharing is simply wishful thinking and points to a critical flaw in our federal-provincial revenue sharing arrangements. (New Democratic Party 1989)

The British Columbia party does not face any legal barrier to using provincially receipted funds to pay moneys to the federal party, as do Ontario and Alberta. However, British Columbia party officials are nonetheless concerned that the federal party will plan expenditures based on windfall revenues that are mostly uncollectable and, worse, that the revenues collected from British Columbia on this basis will not only hinder the British Columbia party's own cash needs for a provincial election but will mean that the British Columbia party pays an undue proportion of cash to the federal party, compared with the other provincial sections.

All these concerns, shared more or less by the five wealthiest provincial sections, demonstrate the inevitable complications of designing laws to regulate election financing in a federal state in which some provincial parties are integrated with federal parties and others are quite independent.

Summary

Those who contribute to the New Democratic Party in British Columbia are given a joint federal and provincial tax receipt to maximize the tax credit to them. As W.T. Stanbury points out, this is done to maximize the total value of tax credits available to the individual. Stanbury reports that in British Columbia Roger Howard, the party treasurer, uses a computer algorithm to divide each individual's contributions to the party so as to maximize the value of the total federal plus provincial tax credits to the person (Stanbury 1991, chap. 6). For example, in a simple case, if individuals give $200 to the party they will receive a federal receipt for $100 and a provincial receipt for $100. Party officials are conscious that to issue a federal receipt for the full $200 and then to issue another provincial receipt for the full $200 would be fraudulent, and consequently this has never been the practice (Howard interview).

The provincial party, referred to in certain documents as the provincial section, does not permit constituencies or other groups in the party to issue receipts. It has used its control of the receipt to insist that the cash flow through the provincial office. A revenue-sharing formula of considerable complexity determines the division of the cash, with the largest share being kept in the hands of the provincial party. However, the provincial party cannot prevent the federal party from running its own fund-raising programs, invariably direct-mail programs, issuing a federal receipt and keeping all or most of the proceeds.

The sums raised through tax-receiptable contributions are divided between the different levels of the party according to the formula. Stanbury reports that in 1988, a federal election year, 43.7 percent of the total received were federally receipted; in 1989 and 1990 the fraction of BC sectional revenue that was federally receipted dropped to 27.1 percent and 29.6 percent respectively (Stanbury 1991, chap. 6). The provincial party's fund-raising efforts have been driven by this reality of revenue sharing, by the large deficit that followed upon the 1986 provincial election, by the need to sustain an administrative structure capable of providing a range of services and by the desire to build a cash surplus to be available for the next provincial general election that had been anticipated for 1990 and will now occur in 1991.

The measure of the success of this program is shown in table 3.5 through a comparison, made over the last five years, of the total revenue figures, the total income available to the provincial section after the revenue sharing, the total expenditures made by the provincial section including the net expenditures on elections and on the provincial pre-election campaign, yielding a bottom line surplus or deficit.

Table 3.5

Revenues available and expenditures made by the New Democratic Party, British Columbia section

(dollars)

	1985	1986	1987	1988	1989[d]
Total revenue	2 415 356	3 677 966	2 703 417	4 098 044	2 756 389
Provincial section income	1 856 344	1 528 124	1 875 836[a]	2 416 650[b]	2 167 419
Provincial section expenditure	1 578 308	2 069 368	1 576 751	2 158 319[c]	1 603 513
Deficit	(458 192)	(999 436)	(700 351)	(442 020)	
Surplus					121 886

Sources: Audited statements of New Democratic Party, British Columbia section for the years 1985, 1986, 1987 and 1988, and the Treasurer's report for the year 1989.

[a]This includes an accounting adjustment for the previous year of $182 361.
[b]This includes an accounting adjustment for the previous year of $175 951.
[c]This includes the net expenditure on the federal election of $311 291.
[d]These are not the audited figures and might change.

A final complication relates to services in kind contributed to the party. For the most part these are provided by the unions who free up staff members so that they can work full time in election campaigns. Most of these are assigned to constituencies, but one or two are sometimes seconded to the central campaign staff. Often the constituency will pay their expenses. The unions continue to pay the staff so assigned their regular salaries, and some unions will also pick up the living expenses and pay travel costs for staff organizers from out of province. In the 1986 election there were 25 to 30 union staffers seconded for all or part of the campaign. Union staff members have also been assigned to work in by-elections and, of course, in federal elections.

In some constituencies local unions provide secretarial services and office supplies and equipment. Also, some small businesses[19] and sympathetic professionals will provide photocopying, stationery or access to telephone banks for fund-raising. A few trade bills may be paid off by unions or other sympathizers. It is very difficult to provide an accurate account of services in kind, except for the secondment of union staffers, since no records are kept.

THE BRITISH COLUMBIA SOCIAL CREDIT PARTY

The British Columbia Social Credit Party does not suffer any strains with its federal counterpart, for it has no federal counterpart. It is true that in the past Social Credit MPs were elected to serve in Ottawa and that a few of them came from British Columbia with the blessing of

W.A.C. Bennett. But Bennett had little time for federal politics, and after the defeat of the Social Credit government in Alberta in 1970 the national party was captured by anti-Semitic extremists, causing the provincial "Socreds," as they are commonly called, to have nothing whatsoever to do with the tiny group that still owned the Social Credit name on the fringes of federal politics.

The motivating political idea of the British Columbia Socreds is to draw support from federal Conservatives and federal Liberals so that an electoral majority may be gathered to ensure the defeat of the NDP. To this end, the party makes it a point of principle never to become involved in any institutional way with federal politics. In a sense, despite the handful of Social Credit MPs elected in the 1950s and 1960s, and despite fraternal feelings for the Social Credit Party of Alberta when it held power, the British Columbia Social Credit Party has always seen itself, at least since the days of its own accession to government office, as a purely British Columbian phenomenon. The lack of ties to a federal organization is not a matter for regret.

Without these ties, the process of getting and spending money is considerably simplified. There are three distinct periods of fundraising activity together with campaign expenditure patterns that reflect the styles of W.A.C. Bennett, William R. Bennett and William Vander Zalm, the three long-serving leaders of the British Columbia Social Credit Party from 1952 through to 1991. Yet there has been no dramatic break with the habits of the past in the contemporary party. Certainly there has been no break with the rules of the past as preserved by Social Credit governments except for the introduction of the provincial tax-credit scheme.

The Legacy of W.A.C. Bennett

W.A.C. Bennett cut his political teeth in the Conservative party. He was elected a Conservative MLA in 1941, and in 1948 he resigned his provincial seat to run unsuccessfully as a Conservative candidate for Parliament. He re-entered the provincial house in 1949 as a Conservative, albeit a disgruntled one. No doubt his election experiences influenced his views on the two traditional rules of party finance. The first was to make sure that there were sufficient funds in the kitty to be able to wage a vigorous campaign. The second was to make sure that the candidate – or the party leader – was seen to be insulated from the raising of those funds. The contradiction between these basic rules was not lost on W.A.C. Bennett.

When Bennett was premier he made it clear to his ministers and to the backbench MLAs that they were responsible for doing what was necessary to win re-election, and that included welcoming financial contributions. At the same time, when he set out to raise money from the well-heeled business community that had greeted the Social Credit victory with some scepticism (and some relief at the avoidance of the alternative), he asked his friend, Einar Gunderson, to establish a fund to provide the necessary insulation. Gunderson, a prominent Vancouver chartered accountant, had served as Bennett's first Minister of Finance but was forced to leave the post because he was unable to retain a seat in the legislature. Bennett then served as his own Minister of Finance with Gunderson as his adviser.

Gunderson and Bennett established the Free Enterprise Educational Fund to solicit funds from business. The fund was designed to be entirely separate from the party. Gunderson, and any colleagues he might choose to associate with the work of the fund, would decide what to do with the cash. For the most part it would be used to pay the major expenses of the central campaign – media time and advertising expertise. Moneys would also be made available for local campaigns in selected constituencies. The establishment of a separate fund gave W.A.C. Bennett the opportunity to state publicly that he had no idea about who contributed what and also the opportunity to state clearly and privately what priorities he had for using the funds.[20]

The Son Shines: Bill Bennett Takes Charge

In the beginning, William R. (Bill) Bennett was not disposed to tamper with the political shrines built by his father. Until 1979, six years after he became Social Credit leader, he continued to let party finances be directed by Dan Campbell, who had served his father as a senior cabinet minister. Campbell and Grace McCarthy, who had also served in the senior Bennett's cabinet, were widely credited with providing the organizational savvy that allowed Social Credit to survive the election loss of 1972. The antipathy to the NDP government in many business circles made it relatively easy to raise funds for the 1975 election. But by the election of 1979, the Socreds seemed less attractive, in part because Campbell had helped orchestrate a campaign of phoney letters to the editor and planted news stories of dubious provenance which came to light as the "dirty tricks" scandal. Bill Bennett's government only narrowly survived the 1979 election, and he soon cast around for new advisers and a new fund-raising strategy. No doubt this change was further inspired by the fact that stories of large cash expenditures by Campbell during the election campaign caused the party to issue a revised set of figures after the first set was denounced as inaccurate.

Since the Socreds now counted many active federal Conservatives and federal Liberals in their number – and in their caucus – it seemed advisable to make renewed efforts to persuade members of the business community who traditionally favoured those two parties to consider giving money to Social Credit. It also seemed obvious that a finance campaign team composed of individuals well known in the Vancouver business community would have the best chance of successfully undertaking this task.

Michael Burns, a well-known Vancouver businessman, was appointed to coordinate these efforts in 1980. A number of professionals and business people joined the team,[21] including Michael Warren, a prominent lawyer with the Vancouver firm of Owen Bird. In 1981 Bennett recruited a number of new faces to assist him, including two political professionals from Ontario's "Big Blue Machine," Patrick Kinsella, who became his principal secretary, and Jerry Lampert, who took a senior position with the party. They worked closely with the Burns volunteers to develop direct-mail campaigns and other techniques for raising funds from a generally sympathetic business class. Essentially they transmitted what they had learned in Ontario, mostly from senior staff of political consulting firms working for Republican candidates in the United States, to the innocent West Coast of Canada.

On 27 June 1984, British Columbia Social Credit Funding Ltd. was incorporated. Three directors were named: Michael Burns, Vancouver businessman Richard Stewart and Leslie Peterson, a lawyer who had served as a senior minister in W.A.C. Bennett's cabinet and is now, among other things, Chancellor of the University of British Columbia. The Free Enterprise Educational Fund was reincarnated with a new suit of clothes.

Burns and his canvassers worked in the following manner. The various business and professional communities were assigned to different members of the group. One person might take on the mining companies, another the large corporations belonging to the Council on Forest Industries, another would be responsible for the chartered accounting firms, and a lawyer or two would canvass the downtown Vancouver law firms. A letter was often sent to "soften up" the prospect. One example is the letter from Michael Warren to many British Columbia law firms on 10 December 1985, asking for "an annual donation of $150 per letterhead lawyer" on the basis that law firms benefit from "increased industrial activity generated by a free enterprise system." The heart of the operation was a follow-up face-to-face contact between a team member and a prospect whom the member would know personally, on the theory that it is always harder to say "no" to a friend.

In addition to the corporate side of fund-raising, the Socreds developed a sophisticated direct-mail operation. In 1981 it was a brand-new idea for the party. Jerry Lampert describes how it was established:

It had been something we'd been using back east for the federal
Conservatives and the Ontario Conservatives ... We had the help of
some knowledgeable people from back there ... It began with a solicitation letter to the party membership – 50 000 plus individuals – that
had a very good response ... And then we got into what they call in
the game prospecting where you buy lists ... based on the demo-
graphics of the kind of voter you expect to be supporting the party and
you build a bank of donors. The interesting thing on that side is you
really do appeal to the small contributor so that [in the] first series of
direct mail ... the average contribution was, say, around $26. That
program proved very successful and has been built on and built on
to the point where there are close to 100 000 donors in the file which
is quite remarkable. (Lampert interview 1990)

It is worth noting that the provincial tax credit legislation now
made it possible for the Social Credit Party to persuade these noncor-
porate donors that they could give even more money to the party than
they would have considered doing if the legislation had not been in
place. And it put the Socreds, in terms of small givers, on a not-quite-
level playing field with the NDP.[22]

Back on the corporate side, Michael Burns developed a special
group of donors called the "Top Twenty." The name had an élitist ring,
and indeed it was the business and professional élites who were invited
to join. But in fact there were about 60 individuals involved, and the Top
Twenty referred to the 20 swing ridings in the province that the Socreds
believed would, in a polarized climate, determine which party would
form the government. The members of the Top Twenty were told that
their more substantial contributions were crucial to ensure that these
seats were won by Social Credit.

The Top Twenty club members paid $4 000 to $5 000 a year to belong.
Most of them helped raise additional funds from friends, some of whom
would join the club and in turn raise money from their friends. In return,
the premier and key ministers would come to speak and, more important, the premier and the ministers would make themselves accessible
if a member of the Top Twenty was anxious to have a seasonable word
or two.

Not all the ministers were keen about such special access or about
a group so closely associated with key operatives in the premier's office.
When Bill Bennett stepped down in 1986, the Top Twenty became an
issue in the leadership race. First, Grace McCarthy, a long-time cabinet
minister under both father and son and a leading candidate to succeed
Bill Bennett, refused to speak before the group. She "didn't think it

would be right" (McCarthy interview 1990). Then Bill Vander Zalm, also a leading candidate, who had quit the cabinet and the legislature in 1983, declaring his colleagues to be "gutless wonders," followed suit. The Top Twenty club did not survive Vander Zalm's capture of the leadership.

Michael Burns's position as chief fund-raiser was also a casualty. The team he built gave way to Vander Zalm's own draft choices. On 12 September 1986 Burns sent a letter to members of the Top Twenty and another to his canvassers announcing his resignation. The election was called on 24 September for 22 October. David Poole, soon to become the premier's principal secretary, was named the campaign manager with an overall responsibility for fund-raising. Peter Toigo, the premier's friend and owner of a restaurant chain, became involved in the corporate fund-raising, much to the dismay of those who had done the job for several years.

From 1987 on, the Social Credit fund-raising strategy was largely driven by Premier Vander Zalm's political crises. It is not necessary to detail them here except to state that there were many periods of siege mentality in the premier's office. There is abundant evidence that business leaders and Vancouver professionals became disenchanted with Vander Zalm and general agreement that this disenchantment had a significant effect on corporate giving.

The response of the premier's office was to put more effort into the direct-mail campaigns. Brian Battison, a party staff member who had experience with direct mail while working for the Democratic party in the United States, organized the packages and wrote most of the copy. British Columbia Social Credit Funding Ltd., with two new directors, Peter Webster, a member of a prominent Canadian family, and Evan Wolfe, a car dealer who had been Bill Bennett's Minister of Finance, received the funds. Webster signed many of the letters, but others came from Vander Zalm himself.

It would seem that the results of the direct-mail packages were gratifying, although it is impossible to obtain any figures. Those who guard the fund take the view that, since the law does not require disclosure of its balance, then a policy of nondisclosure is a law-abiding policy. It doesn't seem likely that the party fund-raisers would continue to rely on direct-mail packages if they had not proven to be successful, and it does seem likely that a controversial figure such as Premier Vander Zalm would have had success in raising money in this way from his many fervent admirers.

The letters themselves suggested that the sky was falling, and that sentiment led some members of the press to speculate that the Social

Credit Party might not have sufficient funds to fight the next election. But a falling sky, which can only be kept in its place by a favourable answer to the appeal, is very much central to the whole technique of direct mail. Probably the direct-mail appeals have made up any loss in corporate donations and have produced sufficient funds to fight a general election. In 1986 the Social Credit Party was able to run the campaign without borrowing money. There is evidence from interviews that the party could do the same in the next provincial campaign.

It is interesting to note that Michael Burns, Michael Warren and some other members of the Burns fund-raising team have quietly taken up again the chore of directly approaching business and professional prospects for donations to the Social Credit fund. A more modest version of the Top Twenty has been instituted as well. The 1989 donor recognition program lists four levels of contributor: the Sustaining Donor gives $25 a year or more; Legacy Partners contribute $100 to $499 and are invited to a reception at the Social Credit annual convention; Benefactors contribute $500 to $999 and "receive a higher level of recognition" than do less generous donors; and the Premier's Circle donors, who contribute over $1 000 a year, receive a quarterly report from the Premier and are "invited to an annual reception with the Premier and other Senior Elected Officials."[23] The premier's own political difficulties in 1989 and 1990 make it very difficult to determine the success of this fund-raising initiative.

The Pattern of Spending

Although it is not possible to accurately determine the amount of money raised and held by British Columbia Social Credit Funding Ltd., it is possible to follow the party's spending pattern. To maintain the party administration and to fight general elections and by-elections, the Social Credit Party receives regular and special subventions from British Columbia Social Credit Funding Ltd. The party directors draw up a budget and present it to the fund directors; once it is approved, the regular draws are forthcoming. Funds needed for by-elections and general elections are also requested by the Social Credit Party board and then forwarded when approved by the fund directors (Lampert interview 1990).

There is no doubt that the fund directors will approve these requests, and other special requests, if they have the blessing of the premier. The premier is a member of the Social Credit board, and its officers consult with him on these budgetary requests. The income then received by the party is also disclosed in the annual statements filed with the Registrar of Companies under the *Society Act*. The reported income figures are not particularly helpful since they do not reflect the revenue actually raised and held by the funding company, and surpluses are moved between different accounts with deficits made up by funding company subventions. In addition, general election and by-election expenses are reported to the chief electoral officer.

Social Credit expenditures for five years are listed in table 3.6. In addition to these expenditures the Social Credit Party has fought six by-elections since the 1986 general election. The party's reported by-election expenditures are listed in table 3.7. NDP-reported expenditures are included for comparison. For Social Credit, the Alberni, Nanaimo and Point Grey by-election party expenditures are included in the 1989 expenditure figure. For the NDP, the provincial party expenditures in all the by-elections are included in the NDP's 1988 audited statements, and they have been included in figures already given. The NDP was successful in all six by-elections.

Like the NDP, Social Credit receives services in kind that are used primarily to help fight election campaigns. Most of these services are donated at the constituency level. In 1986 those responsible for the central campaign made a point of paying cash to their suppliers. Depending on the timing of their own elections, the Saskatchewan and Alberta Conservatives will send a handful of organizers who continue to be paid from their home provinces. More important are what have been called "massive amounts of contributions in kind not accounted for in the most part," available in many constituency campaigns from local businesses who make available secretarial services and send supplies and equipment – everything from paper to a photocopier. Some of these

Table 3.6
Social Credit expenditures 1985–89
(dollars)

1985	596 168
1986	1 322 539
1987	3 150 8301*
1988	632 054
1989	891 607

Sources: British Columbia Registry Office, Victoria, BC, and 1986 Statement of Votes, Chief Electoral Officer of BC.

*Includes $1 817 226 for the central election campaign, the same figure reported to the chief electoral officer. Also for the 1986 election, Social Credit candidates reported combined expenses of $2 294 140, making the total election expenditure reported $4 111 366. In 1983 the party reported to the chief electoral officer central campaign expenses of $1 800 364 and in the annual statement, expenses of $1 793 095, a discrepancy of $6 603.

Table 3.7
Provincial by-election expenditures, June 1988 to December 1989
(dollars)

		Social Credit	NDP
Boundary Similkameen			
(election: 8 June 1988)	Candidate	147 851	48 522
	Party	0	18 983
	Total	147 851	67 505
Alberni			
(election: 19 November 1989)	Candidate	37 887	12 710
	Party	7 985	15 610
	Total	45 872	28 320
Nanaimo			
(election: 15 March 1989)	Candidate	42 216	37 000
	Party	25 745	18 578
	Total	67 961	55 578
Point Grey			
(election: 15 March 1989)	Candidate	106 971	71 591
	Party	30 187	20 560
	Total	137 158	92 151
Cariboo			
(election: 20 September 1989)	Candidate	67 636	41 091
	Party	146 238	42 679
	Total	213 874	83 770
Oak Bay–Gordon Head			
(election: 13 December 1989)	Candidate	68 697	59 362
	Party	77 557	29 328
	Total	146 254	88 690

Sources: Reports on by-elections held in 1988 and 1989 from the British Columbia Chief Electoral Officer.

contributions come in the form of discounted services. So, for example, if the constituency needs to rent a vehicle or two for the campaign it can often do so at a much reduced price.

Social Credit constituency campaigns have generally become more elaborate and sophisticated over the last decade. When W.A.C. Bennett was in control, candidates in marginal seats would often receive financial assistance from Gunderson's educational fund, and many constituencies came to expect that cash would arrive once the election was called. When Kinsella and Lampert and their associates took over the political direction of the party under Bill Bennett, they were determined to wean the constituencies from this dependence. For one thing, they knew that the cost of a modern campaign making extensive use of television advertising would quickly eat up the cash previously sent to local campaigns. In 1983 they kept the subventions to a minimum $2 000 or so, and by 1986 almost all the constituencies had learned that they were on their own.

Sitting MLAs in particular, after talks with Bennett and his staff, recognized that they would need to make certain that they had sufficient funds in a campaign kitty if they wanted to be as certain as possible of re-election. Most new candidates got the same message. This led most constituencies to develop a fund-raising program based on the provincial efforts.

A team of fund-raisers would be appointed by the constituency executive. In constituencies with one MLA, or with two, this would almost always be done at the urging of the elected member(s). The fund-raisers, mostly local businessmen (with some businesswomen and professionals) would divide up the list of contacts so that they could all be approached individually. An experienced fund-raising coordinator would attempt to instil a spirit of friendly rivalry among his or her canvassers. As with the provincial campaign, the canvassers would mostly approach people known to them, and as a consequence these campaigns began to have a quite high rate of return. Those involved with the central campaign and local fund-raisers agree that most constituencies have now built a healthy fund sufficient to allow their candidate to wage a full-scale campaign in the next election.

Many of the local fund-raisers have been trained by the professionals at the centre. One advantage that Social Credit constituency fund-raisers have over their counterparts in the NDP is control of the tax receipt. The provincial party issues tax receipts, but it has also authorized constituencies to use the receipt for their own fund-raising. Generally in the Social Credit Party, those who collect the cash, keep the cash. The provincial party keeps the money it raises, the constituencies the money they raise. The only revenue sharing is in terms of memberships, where the money is split 50–50.

Many constituencies have set up formal funds in which the directors or trustees are independent of the association. The device of an independent fund is modelled on British Columbia Social Credit Funding Ltd. (although most are not incorporated) and is done for similar reasons. First, the amount of money held by the fund can be kept secret, and it is hoped that this will prevent party members and contributors from becoming complacent and closing their wallets. Second, the distribution of the funds is more easily controlled by the MLA or the candidate and the few key individuals who do most of the fund-raising. This means that they can direct moneys to the projects they consider the most important. Finally it is felt, or at least hoped, that an independent fund provides a way of insulating the candidate from having any detailed knowledge about the contributions to the fund.

Concerns about the operation of these independent funds have become public. These concerns follow a controversy over a retirement gift of an automobile to MLA Bill Reid by his constituency.

Reid, then a staunch supporter of Premier Vander Zalm, was the cabinet minister responsible for the distribution of lottery funds. In 1989, when it was revealed that he gave, unasked, a large grant to a society concerned with persons with disabilities for the purpose of developing a recycling program in his constituency – and with the proviso that the society buy the recycling materials from a company controlled by two of his close friends – Reid was forced to resign. The NDP opposition, in full cry, demanded that Reid be charged with a criminal offence; and, when officials of the attorney general's ministry decided that there was not sufficient evidence to secure a likely conviction, the NDP justice critic proceeded with a private prosecution.

The "Reid affair" continued to be much in the news and was proving embarrassing for a government intent on holding an election sometime in 1990. In the summer of 1990, Reid announced that he would not seek to run again. He seemed bitter about having to make this decision. In October his "retirement" present was revealed in the newspapers, and the question was asked why the constituency would agree to spend some $15 000 on an automobile just before an expected election call.

The answer, of course, is that the constituency did not in fact control the funds. Instead a special campaign fund had been established which, as usual, was controlled by individuals close to the MLA. Despite denials, it seems clear that some of the funds used to buy the car were raised as tax-receiptable donations.[24] As one senior Social Credit official pointed out, it is also quite possible for a group holding these trust funds to decide that it does not like a nominated candidate and then withhold the funds from his or her election campaign.

The British Columbia Social Credit Party has been beset for many years by charges, generally veiled charges, of financial impropriety. Editorial writers were fond of arguing that Einar Gunderson should not sit on any government-appointed agencies as long as he controlled the Free Enterprise Educational Fund (Sherman 1966, 305). Bill Bennett had to live with the "dirty tricks" scandal that ended the career of Dan

Campbell, who had been his chief fund-raiser, and Bill Vander Zalm has had more than his share of trouble in this regard. Mason and Baldrey (1989) describe many of these charges, which include an RCMP investigation into the relationship between the premier and his friend Peter Toigo, after it had been suggested by members of a Crown corporation board of directors that a charge of influence peddling might be warranted. More recently the premier was embarrassed by the disclosure that a cabinet minister, Elwood Veitch, had received a $1 000 donation from the realtor who handled the sale of Fantasy Gardens for the Vander Zalms. Unfortunately the realtor was facing charges of theft laid by her former partners. Veitch returned the donation.

In this atmosphere it is not surprising that it is occasionally suggested in the media, and by others, that contributions are given in the expectation of favours to be received. The fact that discretionary spending on highway contracts is often increased in election years is seen as a potential device for obtaining contributions. In 1986, for example, in Cariboo, a vast constituency served by the long-time Minister of Highways, the area manager had some $30 million available for day-labour contracts that were not subject to a bidding process.

At the same time, those involved with the central fund-raising campaign have been instructed to consider it a warning bell when a donation of more than $10 000 is offered. Large donations are turned down for fear that the government and the party will be compromised. In 1986 Vander Zalm told his campaign team to make sure that they did not spend more money than in 1983. In the end they spent only $17 226 more than he wanted (Poole interview 1990).

But rumours are largely inspired by the absence of rules requiring the disclosure of political contributions. This is unfortunate because there is no evidence to suggest that the Social Credit Party attempts to hide its actual cash expenditures. The reports provided the chief electoral officer and made under the *Society Act* seem quite accurate, with the exception of the initial failure to report Dan Campbell's cash expenditures in 1979. But, as with the other parties, they do not reflect the contribution value of services in kind.

Finally, a note on the 1986 Social Credit leadership convention, which chose William Vander Zalm. The money to fund the campaigns of the 11 candidates was raised without any use of the tax-credit scheme. All those involved with the campaigns are very close-mouthed about amounts raised and spent, but knowledgeable observers estimate that expenditures were something in the order of $3 million. Almost everyone acknowledges that Grace McCarthy spent the most, with estimates ranging up to $1 million. In interviews it was suggested that Brian Smith and Bud Smith spent around $500 000 each. The other million or so was spent by the other candidates with the eventual winner, Vander Zalm, seen as spending less than half the amount that each of the Smiths is believed to have dispensed. Most of the campaigns ended up in debt, and a number of fund-raising events had to be held to make certain that the candidates were not left with debts they could not personally meet. Grace McCarthy and Bill Vander Zalm did not need to hold these fund-raisers.

THE ALSO-RANS

In 1972 the Liberals reported that their central campaign had spent $223 754 and that Liberal candidates had spent $191 268 for a total expenditure of $415 022. In 1986 the total expenditure reported was $238 201. The central party spent just a little over $24 000, only a fraction more than in 1983, but a somewhat more impressive sum than the zero funds reported in 1979. Still, without any seats in the assembly since 1979, the Liberals seem to be a spent force. John Turner's election in 1984 in Vancouver Quadra encouraged some Liberals to dream of a comeback inspired by a magical return of Turner charisma, but that was not to be.

The expenditures for all parties in the 1986 provincial election, including the Liberals and other small parties, are listed in table 3.8. In

Table 3.8
Reported expenditures in 1986 provincial general election for recognized parties and candidates of those parties

	$	%
Social Credit	4 111 366	54.0
New Democrats	3 043 088	40.0
Liberals	238 201	5.4
Progressive Conservatives	45 799	
Libertas BC	20 945	
Communist Party of Canada	18 719	
Green Party	5 970	
Western Canada Concept	2 358	
People's Front	2 170	
Libertarian	927	
New Republican	0	

Source: British Columbia Chief Electoral Officer, Statement of Votes for the provincial general election held in 1986.

addition, six independent candidates reported expenditures totalling $13 188. One of them running in Skeena spent $11 984 and received 793 votes. An expensive hobby.

CONCLUSION

The contrast between the Social Credit Party and the New Democratic Party is stark as regards party finance and much else as well. But the differences are not as great as they once were or seemed to be. Social Credit does not enjoy unlimited wealth, and the NDP is not strapped for funds even though it may have problems with cash. It is true that in 1986 the Socreds outspent the NDP by more than $1 million, counting both candidate and central campaign expenditures. But then the Socreds attracted more voters to their cause. It cost them $4.31 a vote. The NDP paid $3.69 for each of its votes. By contrast the provincial treasury spent more on both parties for each registered voter: $5.36 per voter, according to the chief electoral officer's report.

The distribution of central campaign expenditures would also seem to be similar for both parties. A breakdown of the 1986 NDP expenditures shows that advertising accounts for 62 percent of the central campaign's expenditures. The next most expensive items are staff costs at just over 18 percent of the total. Everything else, including surveys and the leader's tour, accounts for the remaining 20 percent. Social Credit also spends the bulk of its central campaign funds on advertising. The Socreds spend a greater proportion of their total on surveys and less on staff than does the NDP. Of course the party in power gains some organizational advantage from having ready access to public service and other resources of government (Lampert interview 1990).

The NDP spends more money between elections than the Socreds spend. In addition to staffing costs, the NDP spends considerable sums on executive and council meetings, policy committees and internal newspapers and newsletters. Social Credit spends more modest administrative sums, and, according to senior party officials, their expenditures are more oriented to election preparation.

If we take both parties' administrative expenditures from 1985 to 1989, add to these the total expenditures in the 1986 election plus the substantial sums spent in the six by-elections not posted in the annual statements, and exclude all the NDP expenditures on the 1988 federal election, then during the five-and-a-half-year period the NDP outspent Social Credit. The NDP total is $11 602 201, compared with $9 582 421 spent by Social Credit. Table 3.9 provides the breakdown.

It is impossible to compare total revenues over a similar period because British Columbia Social Credit Funding Ltd. and the various

Table 3.9

A comparison of expenditures made by the Social Credit Party and the New Democratic Party, British Columbia section, 1985–89

(dollars)

	Social Credit	NDP
1985 Administrative expenditures	596 198	1 578 308
1986 Administrative expenditures	1 322 539	1 683 237
1987 Administrative expenditures	1 333 604	1 576 751
1988 Administrative expenditures	632 054	1 847 028
1989 Administrative expenditures	891 607	1 603 513
1986 Central campaign	1 817 226	1 416 766
1986 Candidates' expenditures	2 294 140	1 626 322
1987/88 by-election Expenditures not included above	695 053	270 276
Total expenditures	9 582 421	11 602 201

Sources: Reports of the British Columbia Chief Electoral Officer, 1986, 1987 and 1988, Social Credit financial statements filed pursuant to the *Society Act* 1985 to 1989, and New Democratic Party of British Columbia financial statements from 1985 to 1989.

constituency funds need not, and will not, provide details of their holdings. Still, it is unlikely that Social Credit would be able to raise much more money than the NDP. It must be remembered that a substantial portion of funds raised by the New Democrats is transferred to the federal party or used for federal election purposes. As well it seems unlikely that either party has a great advantage in obtaining services in kind. The NDP imports more organizers paid for by angels from afar. But the Socreds have more than a few angels on their side and would seem to be more successful in obtaining supplies, discounted and free, for their local campaigns. However, NDP local campaigns have also known some generous suppliers. The playing field is pretty level.

The two parties are in some important sense taking part in very different games. Not so much ideological games, although in terms of their attitudes to the reform of party and election finance they own different histories and wear different policies. An NDP government will require complete disclosure of all financial transactions that political parties conduct. It will also impose contribution limits and spending limits and will seriously consider direct public subsidies.[25] Social Credit will seriously consider spending limits but will never require the disclosure of contributions. Even the Social Credit government's own commissioner, Judge Eckardt, couldn't persuade the party that the disclosure of all contributions over $100 was the quid pro quo for tax credit legislation.[26]

However, the important differences are historical and structural. The NDP has always looked to Ottawa, even from faraway Vancouver. Socialism can know no boundaries, not even the mythic boundaries of the Canadian federation.

Social Credit, which has never looked to Ottawa, fears that the Rocky Mountains are not tall enough to keep out strangers. The party can know nothing more important than its own need to be the guardian of British Columbia's virtue, which is why resistance to the fashions of Ottawa and Toronto is seen as nothing less than a patriotic duty. It is a welcome duty if it helps maintain a political system that has kept the old faith and preserved the new entrepreneurs.

Party finance in British Columbia, and electoral reform, are all bound up in two different visions of the centre – and of the periphery. Is it not always so in Canada?

ABBREVIATIONS

am.	amended
c.	chapter
R.S.B.C	Revised Statutes of British Columbia
s.	section
S.B.C	Statutes of British Columbia

NOTES

This study was completed on 26 March 1991. A number of significant changes in the political life of the province have occurred since this date. William Vander Zalm resigned as premier and as leader of the Social Credit Party on 2 April. He was succeeded as premier by Rita Johnston, who became leader of the Social Credit Party in July, after a narrow convention victory over Grace McCarthy. In the general election held on 17 October, Social Credit won only 7 of the 75 seats. The New Democratic Party, with 51 seats, formed a majority government in early November. The Liberal Party, after winning 17 seats, now forms the official Opposition.

1. Professor Paltiel was the research director of the federal Committee on Election Expenses. Through his scholarly and popular writings, including Paltiel (1970), he was instrumental in keeping the issues of party and election campaign financing on the political agenda.

2. The full text of the rules and provisions set down here can be found in three acts: the *Election Act* (consolidated 13 March 1990); the British Columbia *Constitution Act* (consolidated 14 November 1986); and the British Columbia *Income Tax Act*.

3. These were: the *Election Regulation Act, 1871;* the *Qualification and Registration of Voters Act, 1871;* and the *Trial of Controverted Elections Act, 1871.*

4. The Commission was established primarily to recommend changes to the electoral district boundaries. The sole commissioner, provincial court Judge Larry Eckardt, also made several other recommendations, including this provincial tax credit legislation.

5. One of the quirks of the BC system for the production of ballot forms and papers is that the candidate of the government party is listed first on the ballot, followed by the candidate of the party whose leader is the recognized Opposition leader in the last assembly, followed by the other candidates in alphabetical order. This W.A.C. Bennett invention survived the premiership of David Barrett and is still contained in the *Election Act* (86).

6. 12 February 1990, *Return of Candidates Election Expenses and Affidavit of Candidate and Official Agent* filed with the Chief Electoral Officer, British Columbia, by Louis Lesosky following a by-election in the electoral district of Oak Bay–Gordon Head held on 13 December 1989.

7. 15 November 1989, *Return of Candidates Election Expenses and Affidavit of Candidate and Official Agent* filed with the Chief Electoral Officer, British Columbia, by Hans Brown, Secretary, and Roger Howard, Treasurer, following a by-election in the electoral district of Cariboo held on 20 December 1989, and 11 May 1989 letter to Jeanette Gogo c/o Harry Goldberg, Chief Electoral Officer, signed by Lin Rubin, Director of Administration, New Democrats of BC, filed with the Chief Electoral Officer, British Columbia. Roger Howard, the party's treasurer for more than 18 years, has confirmed that he did not notice until recently the requirement that the return be witnessed by a commissioner.

8. Letter to British Columbia Social Credit Party from M.A. Jorre de St. Jorre, Registrar of Companies, dated 21 January 1986 in the British Columbia Social Credit Party temporary file at the Registry of Companies, Victoria, British Columbia.

9. Elkins (1985) is an eloquent essay on ambiguity and complexity in the politics of British Columbia.

10. Social Credit organizers are aware of this practice and hope that it will be possible to call an election that overlaps with the election period in some other province, preferably in Saskatchewan or Manitoba.

11. The key players have been Hans Brown, the party's provincial secretary (chief executive officer), who has laboured to make the budget process more realistic; Lin Rubin, the director of administration, who acts as a comptroller for the party; and Roger Howard, the provincial treasurer since 1972 (not a full-time job) and a University of British Columbia professor of physics, who has developed the computer programs that translate the complex rules of revenue sharing into exact dollar amounts.

12. In several BC municipalities the New Democrats run candidates identified as NDP candidates, and the organizations formed for this purpose by NDP members are municipal parties. Like federal ridings or the youth section, they can act as the source of tax-receipted funds and retain the source's 15 percent share.

13. In the interviews I conducted on this point it was apparent that the provincial office staff had been successful in persuading most constituencies without MLAs to enter into the spirit of the revenue sharing, but that a number of the strongest constituencies in terms of NDP voting support with MLAs continued to be hostile toward the new policy.

14. Nelson–Creston draft fund-raising plan dated 18 June 1990.

15. In April 1989 the five "have-not" sections had only paid $9 050 of their $115 000 assessment. See New Democratic Party (1989, 6).

16. The groups whose membership the NDP sends appeals to include Greenpeace, the United Nations Association, the CBC Radio Guide subscribers, the John Howard Society, Energy Probe and similar activist-oriented constituencies.

17. This information is contained in the discussion paper prepared by the British Columbia provincial office following the meeting at Wascana (New Democratic Party 1989).

18. "Commission" is meant instead of "office."

19. The British Columbia NDP has a formal policy of refusing to accept "directly or indirectly any corporate donations except those from small businesses who support the principles and policies of the NDP: all such small business donations to be approved by the Provincial Executive." There are differences of opinion within the NDP about what constitutes a small business.

20. The Free Enterprise Education Fund is described in more detail in Mitchell (1983, 364–65). I have confirmed its existence by interview.

21. "A number" is vague, but an accurate reflection of the Social Credit political culture. No one can remember exactly how many individuals took part. Perhaps 10 to 20 were involved, but some only in a peripheral fashion, and it is unclear when certain individuals became involved and when they ceased to be active. In the NDP a fund-raising group has a membership. Lists are kept and a formal, if not real, hierarchy is identified. The "right" doesn't like to do business in such a structured fashion.

22. The NDP in BC still had an advantage because it could provide a joint receipt as described above that would provide a greater tax credit for donations over $100. For very large donations, the contributor could get $1 000 back instead of $500, a not insignificant difference.

23. See "Get Involved, Stay Involved," published by British Columbia Social Credit Funding Ltd.

24. This use of campaign funds is not dissimilar to the "golden parachute" which permits "members of the US Congress who were in office on January 8, 1980 to keep campaign contributions for personal use after leaving office." This "grandfather clause" is described in Sabato (1989), which urges that the practice be ended as it cannot seem to be other than an improper conversion of funds intended for one purpose and used for another not foreseen by campaign contributors. See especially pp. 68, 69.

25. Leadership contests in the NDP are strictly regulated. In the 1984 contest in British Columbia, candidates were not permitted to spend more than $20 000. The provincial party sponsored a leadership candidates' tour around the province, but the cost of the tour for each candidate was paid for out of the $20 000. Full disclosure of contributions and expenditures was required. These were published in the party's monthly newspaper, the *Democrat*. A nomination process requiring candidates to have more than a handful of supporters prepared to sign nomination papers was used to prevent fringe candidacies. These same rules applied for the 1987 convention following the resignation of Robert Skelly as leader. As it happened, Michael Harcourt was elected to the post without opposition. He paid the expenses of a pre-convention tour from donations given to his leadership campaign and provided a statement of contributions and expenditures to the party newspaper.

26. In addition to recommending tax credit legislation, Judge Eckardt in his 1978 report called for disclosure of all contributions over $100. He was ignored. See BC Royal Commission (1978).

INTERVIEWS

I am grateful to the following individuals for granting interviews. In certain instances some of those named below have asked me not to use specific quotes. A few individuals asked that I not indicate that they spoke to me on these matters, and of course they are not listed here.

Brown, Hans, Provincial Secretary and Campaign Manager, New Democratic Party of British Columbia

Howard, Roger, Provincial Treasurer, New Democratic Party of British Columbia

Jones, Cate, Fundraising Co-ordinator, New Democratic Party of British Columbia

Lampert, Jerry, former Principal Secretary to the Premier of British Columbia

McCarthy, Grace, MLA, former cabinet minister and former president, British Columbia Social Credit Party

Poole, David, former Principal Secretary and Deputy Minister to the Premier of British Columbia

Rubin, Lin, Director of Administration, New Democratic Party of British Columbia

Warren, Michael, Partner, Owen Bird, Barristers and Solicitors, and fundraiser for the British Columbia Social Credit Party

BIBLIOGRAPHY

Blake, Donald E., ed. 1985. *Two Political Worlds: Parties and Voting in British Columbia*. Vancouver: University of British Columbia Press.

British Columbia. *An Act to Amend the Labour Relations Act*, S.B.C. 1961, c. 31.

———. *Constitution Act*, R.S.B.C. 1979, c. 62, s. 1.

———. *Corrupt Practices Prevention Act*, R.S.B.C. 1871, c. 158.

———. *Election Act*, R.S.B.C. 1979, c. 103, s. 176.

———. *Election Regulation Act, 1871*, R.S.B.C. 1871, c. 157.

———. *Income Tax Act*, R.S.B.C. 1979, c. 190.

———. *Labour Relations Act*, R.S.B.C. 1960, c. 205; am. S.B.C. 1961, c. 31.

———. *Labour Relations Act Amendment Act*, S.B.C. 1961, c. 31.

———. *Provincial Elections Act*, R.S.B.C. 1920, c. 27.

———. *Qualification and Registration of Voters Act, 1871*, R.S.B.C. 1871, c. 156.

———. *Society Act*, R.S.B.C. 1979, c. 390.

———. *Trial of Controverted Elections Act, 1871*, R.S.B.C. 1871, c. 167.

British Columbia. Royal Commission on Electoral Reform. 1978. *Report*. Victoria: Queen's Printer.

British Columbia New Democratic Party. 1987. *Report of the Revenue Sharing Task Force to Provincial Council*. Vancouver.

———. n.d. *Direct Ask Fundraising Manual*. Vancouver.

Cairns, Alan C., and Daniel Wong. 1985. "Socialism, Federalism and the BC Party System 1933–1983." In *Party Politics in Canada*. 5th ed., ed. Hugh G. Thorburn. Scarborough: Prentice-Hall Canada.

Canada. Committee on Election Expenses. 1966. *Report*. Ottawa: Queen's Printer.

Elkins, David J. 1985. "British Columbia as a State of Mind." In *Two Political Worlds: Parties and Voting in British Columbia*, ed. Donald E. Blake. Vancouver: University of British Columbia Press.

Globe and Mail. Various dates.

Mason, Gary, and Keith Baldrey. 1989. *Fantasyland: Inside the Reign of Bill Vander Zalm.* Toronto: McGraw-Hill Ryerson.

Mitchell, David J. 1983. *W.A.C. Bennett and the Rise of British Columbia.* Vancouver: Douglas and McIntyre.

New Democratic Party. 1989. "Discussion Paper, Federal Party Finances." Vancouver.

Paltiel, Khayyam. 1970. *Political Party Financing in Canada.* Toronto: McGraw-Hill.

Rawls, John. 1971. *A Theory of Justice.* Cambridge: Harvard University Press.

Sabato, Larry. 1989. *Paying for Elections.* New York: Priority Press Publications.

Sherman, Paddy. 1966. *Bennett.* Toronto: McClelland and Stewart.

Stanbury, W.T. 1991. *Money in Politics: Financing Federal Parties and Candidates in Canada.* Vol. 1 of the research studies of the Royal Commission on Electoral Reform and Party Financing. Ottawa and Toronto: RCERPF/Dundurn.

Vancouver Sun. Various dates.

4

THE EVOLUTION OF POLITICAL FINANCING REGULATION IN NEW BRUNSWICK

Hugh Mellon

POLITICAL ACTIVITY IN New Brunswick has often been viewed as a vigorously fought contest where reliance on patronage and close commercial-political connections is widespread. Writing in the early 1960s, Thorburn observed that "politics at the provincial level is largely a battle of the ins *versus* the outs for patronage plums" (1961, 163). Since then this traditional expectation has become less valid. More recent commentators such as Young and Bickerton have questioned the continuing importance of partisan competition and elections within Maritime politics (Young 1986; Bickerton 1989, 461–63). Such authors point to socio-economic and federal-provincial ties as subjects deserving of further study, and their work suggests important avenues for research. Analysis of party and campaign financing provides a bridge between the study of electoral rivalry and the new emphasis on the interrelationship of politics and economics in contemporary settings.

Societal evolution, the declining importance of patronage in the contemporary economy and public demands for increased openness have all contributed to a changing political environment. One aspect of this environment that has been transformed is the regulatory regime relating to the financing of partisan activity and campaign expenditures. In New Brunswick, the legislative centrepiece of the regime is the *Political Process Financing Act*, which was passed late in the second term (1974–78) of Premier Richard Hatfield's government. This Act, although amended several times, remains largely intact. It sets out a range of controls on party fund-raising and spending. It also provides a system whereby political parties receive a significant level of public funding. Overall, it appears there has been widespread acceptance of and compliance with the resulting regulatory regime. Given New Brunswick's experience of more than a decade under this system, it is both timely and constructive to reflect upon events and trends in this province as similar topics are being debated at the national level.

This study, which is divided into four sections, first examines the background to the introduction of the *Political Process Financing Act* in the provincial Legislative Assembly. Attention is given to the various provincial committees and studies that dealt with matters of electoral and party reform.

The second section examines the debate in the Legislative Assembly arising from the proposed regulatory legislation and outlines the *Political Process Financing Act*'s main provisions.

The third section looks at the experiences and trends following the Act's implementation. Key amendments to the Act over the 1978–90 period are reviewed.

The final section provides an overall assessment of the evolution in financing trends and regulatory efforts. It also examines remaining regulatory issues and potential developments.

BACKGROUND AND BUILD-UP, 1966–78

Two sets of factors lay behind the introduction and passage of the *Political Process Financing Act* in 1978. The first set involved the gradual modernization of New Brunswick's electoral laws and their administration, which dates from the mid-1960s. There was also a set of factors particular to the 1977–78 period, which preceded the Act's introduction and passage. Taken together, they provide a general picture of what was behind the 1978 legislative initiative and the public debates that ensued.

Reform of provincial electoral laws grew as an issue after a minor controversy over a 1963 electoral recount in Saint John. In an effort to prevent a recurrence of such a difficulty, Liberal Premier Louis J. Robichaud (1960–70) commissioned J.E. Michaud to inquire into provincial electoral practices and make recommendations. This was still an era when voters could use home-made or party-sponsored ballot papers. Michaud reported that "it did not take me long to realise that the Elections Act was defective in many respects" (1966, 3). He diagnosed two problems: the markedly different voting provisions at elections for various levels of government, and the short period of employment for those running the provincial electoral system. Both voters and election administrators were vulnerable to confusion and a lack of suitable information. Michaud sensed that traditionalists might disagree, but he opted to argue for harmonization of provincial electoral administration with practices at the federal level: "I believe that the different systems of voting lead to confusion, and in my opinion, should be made uniform at all elections, and I do so recommend" (ibid., 4).

Michaud's recommendations covered a wide variety of matters. In addition to supporting adoption of a uniform ballot, he called for adjustment of electoral districts, the permanent appointment of the chief electoral officer and returning officers and notation of a candidate's party allegiance on the ballots. To allow for such notation there would be a system of "recognized parties" encompassing the parties of the premier, opposition leader and any party with an official name that put forth 10 candidates. Michaud also advocated establishment of urban constituencies for cities and towns of a certain size. At that time New Brunswick operated with a system dominated by large, multi-member county ridings.

Counties and local loyalties were for many years important features of provincial politics. Indeed, from Thorburn's perspective, "localism, shading into small-scale regionalism, is the dominant characteristic of the New Brunswick electorate" (1961, 50). Political changes in the 1960s, however, began to undercut these local ties. The Robichaud government's "Equal Opportunity"[1] initiative dramatically altered relations between the local and provincial levels of government. The county level was dismantled, and the provincial government assumed complete responsibility for services such as education, social welfare and hospitals. Redistribution, uniformity and efficiency replaced localism and regional diversity (Young 1987, 95–99).

The Equal Opportunity program "can also be understood ... as clearing the internal environment of the provincial state" (Young 1987, 93). Intraprovincial barriers to provincewide modernization were being reduced. This was part of an ongoing transformation in the character of government in New Brunswick and of the provincial approach to the promotion of economic development. In the past, provincial and local party networks had provided economic benefits to their loyalists in the form of government jobs, appointments and contracts. State structures, meanwhile, were weak and decentralized. Changes after the Second World War brought major adjustments. Young's assessment of this period led him to assert that "the patronage system gradually withered at its roots, particularly in urban areas" (Young 1984, 1). After decades of general acceptance of widespread patronage and of efforts "aimed at protecting domestic firms from upper-Canadian aggression" (ibid.), state structures were strengthened and centralized while outside firms and investment were avidly sought.

Reforms of the 1960s

Premier Robichaud and his government used some of Michaud's suggestions in legislation passed before the 1967 provincial election. The resulting legislation provided for a standardized ballot, a permanent provincial chief electoral officer and some constituency redistribution. The constituency handiwork may have helped the government electorally, but it also "augmented the unhealthy ethnic split between the North and the South which already existed" (Stanley 1984, 166). The northern and eastern regions of New Brunswick are home to a sizable Acadian, French-speaking population, while the southern and western portions of the province are largely English-speaking.

The procedures for setting constituency boundaries and for declaring potential conflicts of interest on the part of candidates were also important issues. "While the Conservatives failed to convince the Liberals to adopt single-member ridings or to appoint an electoral-boundaries review committee with representatives from government and opposition, they did persuade them that the proposed qualifications for candidates running for election were too restrictive" (Stanley 1984, 166). It was decided that only elected candidates need be concerned with conflict of interest regulations.

The reforms of the 1960s helped set the stage for the debates of the 1970s. Steps such as the appointment of a chief electoral officer indicated restraint upon the traditional partisan conventions. A number of existing practices were overturned and the distribution of provincial ridings became the subject of intensified political attention. Electoral reform remained a governmental concern after the defeat of the Robichaud government in 1970 by Richard Hatfield and the Progressive Conservatives. Hatfield supported the idea of moving to a complete set of single-member electoral districts. However, his government delayed taking action for several years (Childs 1973).

The Early 1970s

During the early 1970s, both parties recognized the value of further discussion concerning electoral administration and financing issues. As a result of this shared perception, Premier Hatfield and Opposition Leader Robert Higgins agreed on the appointment of a Select Committee on the New Brunswick *Elections Act* in June of 1973. The Committee, composed of both Progressive Conservative and Liberal MLAs, heard public submissions and made a thorough study of matters pertaining to electoral rolls, financing issues and overall election administration. They consulted with outside experts such as the federal Chief Electoral Officer Jean-Marc Hamel and various electoral officials from Nova

Scotia, British Columbia and the neighbouring state of Maine (New Bruns. Select Committee 1974, 4).

In October 1973, Premier Hatfield finally moved on the idea of single-member districts. He appointed a Commission, made up of private citizens and headed by G. Edwin Graham, a prominent executive with New Brunswick Telephone Company, Limited. This Boundaries Commission was to divide up the existing multi-member constituencies and create a provincewide system of single-member ridings. The members of the Commission produced a draft map of constituency boundaries and then solicited public input. Following widespread hearings, Graham and his colleagues presented a revised set of riding proposals to the government early in 1974, as the first stage of their work. Still to come were their final reflections on elections and legislative representation.

Both committees received a significant number of submissions from across New Brunswick. The Select Committee of MLAs, for example, "received a total of 72 submissions presented ... by individuals and/or organizations" (New Bruns. Select Committee 1974, 1). Issues such as voting procedures, campaign conduct and expenditure limits were raised during the hearings. It is worthwhile examining the work of the two committees and their contribution to the debates about electoral operations and party behaviour. Such debates took place not only among committee members, but also within the senior ranks of both the governing Progressive Conservatives and the opposition Liberals.

Recommendations of the Select Committee
The Select Committee produced a thoughtful report containing 29 recommendations. The recommendations ranged from rejection of a permanent voters list to proposals covering recounts and mail voting, legal recognition of political parties and controls on election expenses. It is to these last two items that our attention now turns.

On the question of the legal status of political parties the Select Committee's position was expressed this way:

> The Committee recommends that provincial parties and constituency associations be required to become legal entities capable of suing and being sued in the Civil Courts, and of being held liable and responsible for abuses and violations of any regulatory legislation. A legal, registered entity and specific named individuals should be identifiable to accept responsibility in order to improve and maintain public confidence in the system. (New Bruns. Select Committee 1974, 12)

Note the reference to the state of public confidence in the party system. Committee members were clearly concerned with upgrading both openness and public confidence in the political system.

The Select Committee also chose to support the introduction of regulations on party fund-raising and expenditure practices. Calls for such a response had come from both private individuals and various groups during the Committee's hearings. Groups as diverse as the New Brunswick Federation of Labour, the Young Liberals of l'Université de Moncton, the Greater Moncton Chamber of Commerce and the New Brunswick Progressive Conservative Association all called for at least some degree of regulation.[2]

Fund-raising was always an ongoing challenge for parties in the less wealthy parts of Canada.

> In poorer provinces, leaders or their agents could try to raise money in Toronto or Montreal at fundraising dinners, or appeal to sister parties elsewhere for help. But they inevitably had to look within their own provinces for the bulk of the funds to run their party, and that search inevitably drove fundraisers and ministers to scrutinize lists of those doing business with the government. (Simpson 1988, 188)

Patronage and kickback types of transactions had been widespread over the years as governments sought to build up funds while in power, to tide them over their potential subsequent years in opposition.

By the early 1970s such practices were becoming troublesome. Committee members were sensing the potential for widespread public discontent. Furthermore, economic and social modernization was leaving a diminished sphere of matters for partisan distribution. In addition to Equal Opportunity, the Robichaud government had instituted collective bargaining for public servants. The subsequent rise of provincial public sector unionism helped constrain political firings or dismissals after the 1970 election (Fitzpatrick 1978, 129). Public sector operations and the hiring and firing of permanent civil servants were now becoming more bureaucratized.

In the view of the Select Committee members, changes were needed to prevent public criticism as well as to provide their parties with a firmer financial footing.

> We recognize and support the premise that private financing alone has failed to meet the requirements of modern parties and candidates. As noted, it has created to a degree some mistrust and loss of confidence in our political system. The Committee recommends the adoption of

legislation which would provide a minimum degree of public assistance coupled with adequate disclosure and reporting regulations which would eliminate from the system any suspicion of abuses. (New Bruns. Select Committee 1974, 13)

The Committee called for disclosure of contributions over $100, tax credits for donors, campaign expenditure reimbursement, limits on candidate and party expenditures, and post-election filing of party and candidate financial reports (New Bruns. Select Committee 1974, 13–16). It also urged "the establishment of adequate legislation for strict control and enforcement by way of severe penalties for infractions" (ibid., 16).

The reports of both the Boundaries Commission and the Select Committee on the Elections Act were rapidly dealt with by the Hatfield government. In February 1974, a proposed constituencies map bearing the general imprint of the Commission's handiwork was introduced into the Legislative Assembly. After debate and minor adjustment a constituencies map was approved.

Elections Act *Amendments*
In May 1974, there was debate and the subsequent passage of amendments to New Brunswick's *Elections Act*. In this case, the degree to which the government accepted the Select Committee's recommendations was a major point of debate. Senior opposition spokesperson and former Select Committee member Norbert Theriault proclaimed that "once again, the government has built a skeleton of intentions in order to make the people believe they are making fundamental reforms when, in reality, there is nothing of a substantive nature in this bill" (New Bruns. Leg. Ass. 31 May 1974, 1675).[3] Opposition Leader Higgins branded the bill "a first-class fizzle" (ibid., 1679). At issue was the government's rejection of the Select Committee's recommendations relating to expenditure limits and public disclosure of donations. The Committee had endorsed limits on election expenditures for both political parties and individual candidates (New Bruns. Select Committee 1974, 15–16). With reference to disclosure:

The Committee recommend[ed] that parties and candidates be required to file extensive financial reports within a reasonable time following an election. The reports should include an indication of the sources and amounts of campaign funds as well as the name of the donors for all contributions in excess of $100. (New Bruns. Select Committee 1974, 16)

Instead of including expenditure limits and broad public disclosure requirements, the government's legislative package was more
modest. Provision was made for the registration of political parties
and their agents. The chief electoral officer was assigned responsibility for maintaining the resulting registry, and the parties were to be
responsible for informing him or her of personnel changes among their
chief party agents and electoral district agents. Provisions were also
included for the mandatory reporting of election expenses by chief
agents, electoral district agents and candidates, with the chief electoral
officer reviewing the reported expenditures and publishing them in
summary form. However, there would be no legislated limits on expenditure or donation levels. Premier Hatfield defended this decision by
pointing to what he argued were administrative difficulties encountered in Quebec and the United States with regulations similar to those
envisioned by the Select Committee.

> The Honourable member [Theriault] makes a great thing about the
> recommendation with regard to finances and disclosure. He says they
> are fundamental to improving the image of our political system, and
> I agree with this and have agreed with it for some time. The problem
> is to find a meaningful and effective way to handle it.
>
> The recommendation of the [Select Committee] report with regard
> to disclosure and financing was basically the one that was passed by
> the federal government and by the political jurisdiction of the province
> of Quebec, and in their efforts to try to improve the situation, they
> didn't really impress anybody. There are still the same charges and
> countercharges being made in the province of Quebec even after their
> four years of experience with this type of legislation.
>
> You also gave the impression that the government of the United
> States took the position that they should go for ultimate disclosure
> and that that cleaned up their whole situation, but I don't think their
> situation has ever been worse since they took that action.
>
> I feel that to take half a step or one that is not well considered will
> have a far worse effect if it doesn't meet the problem; therefore, the
> government's position is that we will not make cosmetic changes in
> legislation just to react to a situation for the sake of appearance. (New
> Bruns. Leg. Ass. 31 May 1974, 1683)

It might be noted that the Ontario Commission on the Legislature,
chaired by Hatfield confidant Dalton Camp, took a similar stance against
spending limits and in favour of wider disclosure (1974, 42).
Moving to simple publication of expenses was a limited step, reflect-

ing the government's caution in supporting political reforms as well as the reluctance of "grassroots" and "backroom" organizers to move rapidly into relatively uncharted waters. The extent of political reform in New Brunswick in the 1960s and 1970s was difficult for some to adapt to. Hatfield and his government were making significant structural changes to the central machinery of government in the early 1970s (Leger 1983, 18), and legislation was passed setting out tighter procedural controls over public purchasing and Crown construction contracts (Starr 1987, 73).[4] Hatfield had shown himself to be a moderate reformer on several fronts, yet there was evidence that elements within his party were reluctant to give up past practices. Victory in the 1970 provincial election gave rise to demands for the customary patronage rewards. Some wanted jobs (Jonah 1971), while others wanted to replenish party coffers after a decade in opposition (Simpson 1988, 185–90). As leader, Hatfield had to take these views into consideration. He and his government opted for limited change in the field of political party regulation, but did not close the door completely on discussion of possible future reforms. It is noteworthy that, while defending his government's legislation, Hatfield endorsed full public funding of political parties as "the ultimate answer" (New Bruns. Leg. Ass. 31 May 1974, 1684).

The Election of 1974

Despite opposition protests, the government's proposed amendments were passed and implemented in time for the provincial election in the fall of 1974. This was a novel election, coming as it did after changes in constituency boundaries and amendments to the administrative and regulatory protocols governing the conduct of elections. The transitory character of the election intensified as political observers awaited the final report of the Boundaries Commission. The redrawing of constituencies had been simply their first task; their final report was to provide their reflections on the essentials of legislative representation. While selected individual changes may seem minor with hindsight, the whole atmosphere was marked by awareness of change and the passing of customary practices. This was summed up in the following passage from an editorial in the Saint John *Telegraph-Journal* entitled "A Different Election" – "N.B. Election '74 may turn out, in the long run, not only to have a new set of rules but to be the only one of its kind" (1974b).

The election was actively contested, and the Progressive Conservatives and the Liberals spent almost $1 million each. The reported expenditures of the Progressive Conservatives, Liberals and New Democrats are set out in table 4.1. Given the closed and generally

Table 4.1
Reported expenditures by party, 1974 provincial election campaign
(dollars)

	Chief agents	Electoral district agents	Candidates	Total
Progressive Conservatives	228 060	661 234	40 472	929 766
Liberals	344 415	597 249	22 670	964 334
New Democrats	17 787	4 183	5 450	23 420

Source: New Brunswick, Chief Electoral Officer (1974, 26). Both le Parti Acadien and the Canada Party, short-lived protest parties, also fielded candidates, but their reporting of election spending was fragmentary.

Note: Figures are rounded to the nearest dollar.

unregulated character of the campaign process before 1974, it is difficult to ascertain whether these expenditure levels corresponded to the then prevailing pattern of party and candidate spending. Whatever the case, some strategists and activists within the two major parties were concerned that the expenditures might seem unnecessarily high to members of the general public. In fact, during the campaign, Premier Hatfield himself had criticized Liberal party campaign spending levels.[5] This seems somewhat surprising, given the similarity in the spending levels reported by both parties.

Hatfield and the Progressive Conservatives triumphed in the election. Their campaign stressed such issues as the Bricklin automobile, the proposed Point Lepreau nuclear power plant, the value of a second term to consolidate the government's achievements and optimistic pride in New Brunswick's economic potential. The Premier pointed repeatedly to the possible benefits presented by public support of the Bricklin project (Starr 1987, 83–84).

The Boundaries Commission Report, 1975
Electoral reform continued to be an issue after the 1974 election. In the following year the final report of the Boundaries Commission was presented to the government. The report stressed support for a multi-party system, a plurality electoral system, decennial redistributions by independent commissions, reduced population variances among seats, public education about politics and improved salaries for elected members. The deep roots of traditional perspectives on the character of legislative representation can be seen in the following passage from the Commission's report: "The effectiveness of the representation depends on whether the representatives are on the government or opposition

side of the House and whether or not a member is in Cabinet" (New Bruns. Representation and Electoral Districts Boundaries Commission 1975, 3). The quality of representation was understood as being determined by access to the levers of power. Debate and public involvement were subservient to the aim of winning power.

Controversy and Criticism

During the mid-1970s a series of controversies and court actions helped keep political party financing and behaviour an important issue. Taken together, these are the second set of factors contributing to the movement toward the adoption in 1978 of party financing controls. By 1977 the Hatfield government was tarnished by several publicized Progressive Conservative Party fund-raising scandals (Simpson 1988, 185–94; Starr 1987, 66–117) and by accusations of ineptitude resulting from the collapse of the Bricklin automobile venture (Starr 1987, 85–101). Liberal leader Robert Higgins responded to these events in March 1977 by calling for a royal commission on party financing. Furthermore, he suggested that there had been government interference in RCMP inquiries into Progressive Conservative financing matters (ibid., 107). Higgins then went on to announce that he would resign if his accusation of interference was disproven. Hatfield rejected the call for a royal commission, but did institute a judicial inquiry to investigate the interference allegation.

In late January 1978, provincial Chief Justice Charles J.A. Hughes unveiled his report on the allegations made by Higgins. The Chief Justice found that there had been no clear interference, but the political atmosphere remained tense. Higgins and another prominent Liberal MLA, John Turnbull, resigned their seats. Higgins also stepped down as Liberal leader. This outcome certainly did not satisfy everyone. In an editorial entitled "Bob Exits, Head High" the *Telegraph-Journal* of Saint John observed:

> Now, the Chief Justice has found that there was no obstruction of the RCMP by the provincial Department of Justice. But that is the finding of a judicial inquiry after long, involved and at times uncertain evidence flawed or shaded "by differences in perception, frailty of human memory and certain inconsistencies." (*Telegraph-Journal* 1978a)

The day the Hughes Report was made public, Premier Hatfield announced his intention to present a legislative proposal relating to party fund-raising and spending (*Telegraph-Journal* 1978b). He and the government began moving on a variety of fronts to dispel the troubling clouds of controversy and criticism (Starr 1987, 113). Former Justice Minister Baxter launched legal action against the CBC over its initial coverage of the allegations of governmental interference into police inquiries. Early in the 1978 session of the Legislative Assembly, the government provided "43 volumes of documents concerning the bankrupt Bricklin (Canada) Ltd. sports car venture" (De Merchant 1978).[6] Discussions over issues such as controlling conflicts of interest and access to information gained heightened governmental priority.

The government delivered its Throne Speech on Tuesday, 14 March 1978. Among the commitments was an announcement of plans to introduce controls over party financing and campaign spending. Commentators and political activists from across New Brunswick awaited the government's proposals with anticipation and curiosity.

Meanwhile, Premier Hatfield was concerned that the preparation of the proposed legislation be looked after by individuals knowledgeable about the realities of political parties and campaigns. In light of the reservations he had expressed in 1974, there was a need for the proposals to do more than sound impressive. Practicality and effectiveness were required.

Introducing Legislation

During the late 1977 and early 1978 period Premier Hatfield approached two knowledgeable and thoughtful Progressive Conservative activists, Harry Scott and Bruce Hatfield,[7] to work on party and election spending issues and to make recommendations. Both were members of the same law firm. Through the winter and spring Scott and Bruce Hatfield worked long hours researching and refining ideas. They examined rules in a variety of other jurisdictions, most particularly Quebec. In their deliberations they were often joined by the premier for extended debates, and under his general guidance Scott and Bruce Hatfield became the architects of what was to become the *Political Process Financing Act*.

The Progressive Conservative caucus received their ideas and proposals in early April 1978. By June the proposed legislation was ready for debate in the Legislative Assembly. These debates are discussed in the next section, but mention should first be made of several key points regarding the period preceding mid-1978. First, serious electoral reform was not undertaken until the mid-1960s, when Robichaud's Liberal and Hatfield's Progressive Conservative governments tackled the job. Second, the strategy of administrative reform and centralization initiated by Robichaud's Equal Opportunity program and maintained by Hatfield served to erode the degree of reliance upon local patronage networks and partisan privileges. The times were changing, and if potential public upset were to be prevented, the behaviour of the major parties needed alteration. The third key point is that concerns were being raised within the senior ranks of the Progressive Conservatives and the Liberals about the possibility of difficulties stemming from political party financing scandals and perceived party misbehaviour. The final point to be noted is that 1978 was a pivotal year for the Hatfield government. It had been embroiled in difficulties arising from investigations of Progressive Conservative fund-raising, the fallout from the Bricklin collapse and the difficulties encountered by any government after eight long years in office. The Hatfield government was attempting to weather the political storm brought upon by the criticisms of the recently resigned Liberal leader, Higgins, and the fallout from the resultant inquiry by Justice Hughes. A major feature of the government's response was the introduction of legislation relating to party and election campaign financing.

THE *POLITICAL PROCESS FINANCING ACT* OF 1978
Premier Richard Hatfield rose in the New Brunswick Legislative Assembly on 6 June 1978 on second reading of Bill No. 60 (Political Process Financing) with these words:

> This legislation is the fulfilment of a promise I first made during the 1974 provincial election campaign, and it is one of a continuing series of reforms the government has initiated since taking office to make the political system in New Brunswick more democratic, more responsible, more rational and less susceptible to undue influence than it was in the past. (New Bruns. Leg. Ass. 6 June 1978, 4263–64)

The proposed legislation accompanying this grand declaration was broad-ranging and comprehensive. In a variety of respects it built on the earlier work of the Select Committee of MLAs. Expenditure limits and disclosure of contributors would now be put into place, with provision made for regulation of party fund-raising and campaign expenditures as well as initiation of a system of limited public funding of political parties. There was no question that the legislation as drafted represented a serious response to the issues. The Saint John *Telegraph-Journal* declared: "The current reform bill looks like a sincere attempt to correct some of the problems and to get the financing of political activity on a businesslike basis" (*Telegraph-Journal* 1978c). Perhaps the best measure of the bill's serious intentions was the limited number of partisan jibes or recriminations in the subsequent legislative debate. Suggestions for improvement were made and discussed seriously, and the low level of partisan "sound and fury" was noteworthy.

Before dealing with the debate generated by the proposed bill let us review its key provisions. While introducing the bill's contents Premier Hatfield outlined the "four broad principles that shaped [its] ... development" (New Bruns. Leg. Ass. 6 June 1978, 4265–69). These principles included support for disclosure of political contributions with a system of limits on contributions; partial public funding of the political parties in keeping with their fundamental role within the political process; disclosure of political expenditures made by parties; and restraints on expenditures made by candidates and parties during election contests. Enforcement was to be the ultimate responsibility of the newly created provincial Supervisor of Political Financing. The Supervisor was to be assisted in this task by an advisory committee composed of party representatives.

In section 37(2), the bill stipulated that individuals, corporations and trade unions could make donations only "to a registered political party, registered district association or registered independent candidate." Provisions for registration were set out in the *Elections Act*, and insistence on registration in the 1974 *Elections Act* amendments eased potential control and surveillance difficulties. All donations over $100 would now have to be disclosed. To foil anyone attempting to avoid detection through multiple small contributions, the disclosure provisions were made clear. Section 58(1)(i) stipulated that all corporation and trade union contributions would have to be reported as well as "the name and full address of each individual who has made contributions totalling more than one hundred dollars to the party and the total amount of his contributions to the party." Receipts for such donations were to be issued, and records kept by the party. Tax deductibility was not a feature of the legislative proposals. There was to be a donation ceiling of $6 000 from any one source in election years and $3 000 in other years.

Registered political parties would now collect an annual payment in proportion to the number of votes received by their candidates at the immediately preceding provincial general election. The reimbursement rate was to be $1 per vote obtained, with the Supervisor of Political Financing overseeing the payment process. It was envisioned by the government that parties would need to meet the standard of having members elected to the Legislative Assembly if they were to obtain reimbursement at the full $1 per vote level. There were also provisions for a reimbursement to election candidates who received 20 percent of the votes cast in their constituency.

Also included in the bill was a set of controls on the record-keeping and expenditures of registered political parties, registered electoral district associations and independent candidates. The parties were now to have auditors who would assist with the submission of regular financial reports to the Supervisor of Political Financing. Among other things, these reports were to include complete lists of all contributions of over $100, including the names of the contributors, this figure being the threshold for disclosure. The reports were also to contain summary records of all contributions received from individuals whose total donation was under $100. Registered district associations and registered independent candidates also had to maintain donation and expenditure records. If dissatisfied, the Supervisor of Political Financing could select an auditor to review their records.

The *Political Process Financing Act* called for the registered political parties to provide the Supervisor with two financial returns each year. The first return would cover the first six months of the year and the second would cover the remaining months. Returns were to be submitted within three months of the end of the period they applied to. If an election was called, the deadline for submission of financial returns would be extended for an additional 90 days. The financial returns for registered independent candidates had to be submitted within 90 days of the election. Material submitted by the registered parties and candidates was to be made available to the public within three months of its receipt.

Registered parties were to report on their existing holdings and assets within a set time. No secret financial stockpiles were allowed.

The regulatory regime also included limits on campaign expenditures that were similar in conception to those recommended in the Select Committee's report. Election campaign spending was to be reined in and controlled. Premier Hatfield's position that "the spending limits have been based on the number of electors the parties and candidates must reach" (New Bruns. Leg. Ass. 6 June 1978, 4268) reflected an approach he had rejected four years earlier. Limits were to be applied in both by-elections and general elections. The expenditure limits were to be based upon a set amount per elector. For by-elections, the amount per voter was slightly higher. Despite the per-voter figures, there were also allowable minimum and maximum levels per candidate, which helped guarantee a basic level of expenditures in a province where constituencies varied considerably in terms of population.

The Supervisor of Political Financing

The Supervisor of Political Financing was given the important job of making sure that people and parties complied. An Office of the

Supervisor was to be maintained, and documents filed under the legislated requirements were to be made available to the public. The Supervisor's office was to provide guidelines to interested parties or individuals concerning the legislation's provisions. It was also charged with responding to interpretation requests. Furthermore, it was the Supervisor's responsibility to detect noncompliance and encourage corrective action.

Provision was made for the appointment of an Advisory Committee to assist the Supervisor. Each party with members in the Legislative Assembly would have two representatives on the Committee. The Supervisor and the Chief Electoral Officer of New Brunswick were members as well, with the Supervisor serving as the chairperson. Generally speaking, this Committee was to be called together when the Supervisor wished to gather feedback and advice from those with direct practical campaign and party experience.

Given the importance of the Supervisor's position, it is not surprising that the method of selecting this person should have become a point of contention. Liberal leader Joe Daigle, Higgins' successor, objected to the government's proposal that the Supervisor be appointed by the Lieutenant-Governor in Council on the basis of a Legislative Assembly recommendation. Daigle called for the establishment of a higher standard than a majority-vote recommendation. The government responded by emphasizing the age-old reliance on majoritarian types of provisions. In the end, Daigle yielded on this point, although he requested that the government confer with the legislative opposition on the choice (New Bruns. Leg. Ass. 27 June 1978, 6341).

Public Payments and Tax Credits

The government did revise some of its original proposals, however. The idea that only parties with elected members would receive an annual allowance was widely opposed as unnecessary favouritism to the Liberals and Progressive Conservatives. Hatfield, recognizing the problems inherent in the provision, moved to include the NDP.

> Since Bill 60 has been introduced, we have noted with interest the widespread criticism of the limitations on the annual allowance. It has been urged that if supporters of the Liberal and Conservative parties can, in effect, vote $1 for the support of their party, then supporters of other established parties should do the same. (New Bruns. Leg. Ass. 27 June 1978, 6341–42)

To accommodate this criticism the government made the annual allowance payable not only to parties with elected members, "but also to all registered parties that had at least 10 candidates in the last general election" (New Bruns. Leg. Ass. 27 June 1978, 6343).

Tax deductibility also provoked widespread discussion. The government had not included deductibility in its legislation because, as Premier Hatfield commented, "when we were drafting this legislation we looked more closely at the tax credit system and found it had some serious problems which convinced us to avoid it, at least for the time being" (New Bruns. Leg. Ass. 27 June 1978, 6348). The government's position was that tax deductibility and public payments to parties could be viewed as alternative policy tools in that both involved funding of party activities and were both ultimately "a drain on provincial revenues" (ibid.). Public payments based on votes were viewed as more reflective of majority preferences and easier to administer. Deductibility was portrayed by the Premier as being more reflective of the preferences of richer citizens (ibid.). Liberal leader Daigle proposed a reduced per vote rate of funding, and the application of the amount reduced to creation of a tax credit system (ibid., 6351). Notwithstanding such proposals, the government remained insistent that tax deductibility would not be added to the legislation. Daigle also questioned the level set for the expenditure limits, but this was not a major source of controversy.

General Approval of the Act

Within the province the legislation was greeted with general, if cautious, support. The bill seemed a thoughtful response to a complex and occasionally troubling set of issues. Newspaper editorials voiced these sentiments. The already quoted Saint John *Telegraph-Journal's* overall editorial response was positive and it was not alone in such a view. The *Moncton Times* applauded the bill for whatever impetus it might give to increased public participation and reduced dominance of political life by lawyers.

> It thus may well be that the greatest benefits to eventually emerge from the Political Process Financing Act will not be so much the direct limits on spending and political contributions and so on, but the indirect encouragement to greater participation in the political process by the grassroots. (*Moncton Times* 1978)

Save for the shift in the provisions covering public funding to the parties, the bill went ahead generally as envisioned by the government. Premier Hatfield selected Samuel "Sam" Field, a chartered accountant from Fredericton, to serve as Supervisor of Political Financing. Field had not been active in partisan circles. He had had previous public sector experience as a general manager of the province's Community Improvement Corporation. In selecting Field the Premier engaged in the consultative spirit requested in the Legislative Assembly. Field was a strong choice. In addition to his professional training and public sector experience, he had built up a private sector track record with a construction firm in the Fredericton area. It was agreed that he should keep this job and that the Supervisor's position would be part time. Reaction to the Field appointment was good and the *Telegraph-Journal* reported that Liberal leader Daigle said Field's "career was impressive" (*Telegraph-Journal* 1978d).

From the day of his appointment, Field oversaw the preparation of the office of the Supervisor and the working out of administrative details. This process went quickly, and by 13 September 1978 all sections of the *Political Process Financing Act* were proclaimed. As events unfolded, it was fortunate the legislation was expedited, because a provincial election was called for 23 October 1978.

In the next section our attention turns to the Act's impact and provincial experience with it over the 1978–90 period. The Act as passed in 1978 was generally well-received as observers perceived it to be a sound legislative effort. People appeared supportive and committed to making it work. Evidence of this was the generally constructive tone of Assembly debate and the choice of Sam Field as Supervisor.

EXPERIENCE WITH THE LEGISLATION

It did not take long for the *Political Process Financing Act* to begin altering activities and perceptions. In fact, the very first annual report of the Supervisor of Political Financing suggested that the Act may well have contributed to an immediate reduction in the costs of campaigning.

> While it is perhaps too early to pass judgement on the effectiveness of the *Political Process Financing Act*, the implementation of controls over election period spending appears to have resulted in a significant reduction in the amounts spent in the 1978 campaign as compared to the last general election held in 1974. Total spending by parties and candidates in the 1978 general election amounted to $1 493 794. Reporting requirements in 1974 were much less stringent. However, based on the information available, a total of $1 929 883 was reported as having been spent by the parties and candidates to contest the 1974 election. This represents a decrease of $436 089. (New Bruns. Supervisor 1979, 6)

Such a "decrease" becomes even more striking when the 1978 figures are adjusted to correspond to 1974 price levels. When this calculation was performed by the Office of the Political Financing Supervisor for its first annual report the result was "a reduction of some $1 158 000 or a decrease of 44%" (New Bruns. Supervisor 1979, 6).

The evidence of significant restraint found in the 1978 campaign has carried over to the subsequent elections of 1982 and 1987. The total level of party and candidate campaign period spending for all provincial elections since the 1974 *Elections Act* amendments is outlined in table 4.2. While there have been increases in actual dollar spending, adjusting the figures to constant 1978 dollars reveals a pattern consistent with the 1978 experience.

The fact that total campaign period spending, as measured in constant dollars, in both the 1982 and 1987 elections was below the level reached in 1978 is interesting. Given the limited number of cases, however, further analysis should be undertaken cautiously. A number of points should be noted about the "pattern" of campaign expenditures. First is the already mentioned concern in Progressive Conservative and Liberal circles about public perceptions of the 1974 campaign spending levels. Liberal leader Daigle reiterated this view during the debate over the *Political Process Financing Act*'s introduction.

> If you check the figures across the North American continent, including the United States, you will see that in 1974 – and I don't have all the figures here but I checked them – we spent much more, much more than for any other election that was held in the last 10 years on a per voter basis. (New Bruns. Leg. Ass. 27 June 1978, 6375)

Analysis of all these expenditures would obviously be a major task. The most detailed public study of the topic was done in the early 1980s by Mark Pedersen, then a graduate student at Queen's University. He concluded that provincial parties were exercising greater care over their expenditures and observed that their strategists were opting to direct an increased share of expenditures to mass media advertising (Pedersen 1982), hoping to reach target audiences more effectively.

An additional point that deserves mention is the impact of public financing for the parties. This funding enabled opposition parties to express their views year round and allowed them to move some organizational expenses from the election campaign period.

Although efforts to transfer actual campaign-oriented spending to a pre-campaign period are a possibility, there are several potential restraints. First, unlike many other regulatory regimes, New Brunswick's

Table 4.2
Campaign period spending
(dollars)

| Election year | Total election period spending by parties and candidates, 1974–87 | |
	Actual	1978 constant
1974	1 929 882	2 651 399
1978	1 493 794	1 493 794
1982	2 117 990	1 411 372
1987	2 636 389	1 427 572

Source: Adapted from Schedule 3, "Comparison of Election Period Spending both in Actual Dollars and in Constant 1978 Dollars, General Elections of 1974, 1978, 1982 and 1987" in the Supervisor's *Annual Report* for the period 1 April 1987 to 31 March 1988, 17.

Note: Figures are rounded to the nearest dollar.

Act calls for registered parties to submit financial reports covering contributions and expenditures reports twice a year, thus promoting diffusion of such information. Second, the Act also provides for year-round controls on media expenditures. Aside from the costs involved in mailings and in publicizing public meetings, there are limits on the amount that registered parties or registered district associations/registered independent candidates may spend ($25 000 and $200 respectively).

The 1987 election spending reports reveal some degree of spending restraint overall. Both candidates and parties spent significantly less than they were allowed. Expressed as a percentage under the party spending limit of $494 763, the Liberals, PCs and NDP were, respectively, 23, 28 and 58 percent below the limit.[8] These figures reflect, in part, the widespread support for the provincial Liberals, support which continued relatively unabated during the campaign. The Progressive Conservatives and New Democrats had difficulty making any significant inroads (Starr 1987, 238–55).

Advisory Committee
The passage and subsequent implementation of the *Political Process Financing Act* had various other results. While these were not quite so dramatic, they were nonetheless significant. One result was the emergence of the multi-party Advisory Committee to the Supervisor. Each party with members in the Legislative Assembly had two members on the Committee. The Committee was very busy in the early years of the Act when understandings had to be reached and when working relationships were developing. Despite the Committee's partisan orienta-

tion, it proved a valuable forum of informed discussion. Samuel Field, the Supervisor, has publicly acknowledged the Committee's important contributions (New Bruns. Supervisor 1979, 6). If any participants entertained fears of bitter wrangling and infighting, these were soon put to rest in the cooperative environment that prevailed. This productive atmosphere continued through the years. When the New Brunswick NDP won its first Legislative Assembly seat in 1982 it too became eligible for Advisory Committee membership. Over time both the Supervisor and the various party representatives have found the Advisory Committee a useful vehicle for sharing ideas and information.

As time went on, many important understandings and definitions were arrived at. Means of treating matters that arose, such as volunteered or donated goods and services (New Bruns. Supervisor 1979, Schedule 5, 20–21), were dealt with in a generally unpublicized yet effective way. In recent years there have been fewer issues to resolve, and meetings of the Advisory Committee have become less frequent. However, participants continue to value the Advisory Committee as a means of keeping in touch with each other and learning about any emerging topics. One notable change was made to the Advisory Committee's structure in the aftermath of the complete Liberal sweep in the 1987 election. Membership on the Committee was made conditional on a party's having contested "at least one-half of all electoral districts at the immediately preceding general election."[9] This decision allowed the Advisory Committee to remain an active multi-party forum.

Tax Deductibility

Although the formation of the Advisory Committee proved a durable policy approach, this did not prove to be the case for the 1978 rejection of tax deductibility. Party fund-raisers on all sides pointed out to their partisan colleagues the examples of tax deductibility in other jurisdictions. Deductibility was cited as a way of increasing support for the provincial party system. By 1980, this sort of argument had achieved a partial triumph. Provincial Finance Minister Fernard Dubé oversaw passage of arrangements providing for individuals, but not corporations, to receive tax credits based upon political donations.

Tax credits for corporate donations came in 1981–82. In 1981, there was also an increase in the rate set for the per vote payment from $1 per vote to $1.30, and the standardization of the contribution ceiling of $6 000 for both election and non-election years. These other changes are noted, not to diminish the significance of the changing position on deductibility, but to illustrate that other components of the regulatory framework were also evolving. Like the differing donation standards for election and non-election years, the 1980 decision to allow deductibility for individuals and not for corporations did not prove a lasting solution. Standardization was welcomed by many because it made the overall regulatory regime easier to understand and explain.

The breadth of the *Political Process Financing Act*'s provisions facilitated both enforcement and compliance. The ongoing year-round system of fund-raising controls, for example, is not seen as something applicable to a limited timeframe such as the span of a campaign. The apparent good cooperation the Supervisor of Political Financing receives from the political parties also facilitates enforcement.

Campaign Contributions

Over the sweep of years, several important trends have become visible in the response of the parties to the Act's provisions and the resulting regulatory regime. Perhaps most obvious has been the ability of the Progressive Conservatives and Liberals to obtain contributions far in excess of those received by the New Democratic Party. Summary data on contributions received by party and district associations are provided in table 4.3. Note, for example, the relatively low level of contributions received by the NDP in all years reported.

Another significant trend has been the Liberal party's successful pursuit of individual donors. In this the Liberals showed keen foresight, quickly perceiving the financing opportunities offered by this group of donors. Some key Liberal party activists analysed the financing legislation and reasoned that the spirit of the evolving regime would move toward openness and greater reliance on individual donors.[10] In

Table 4.3
Summary of totals of contributions, party and district associations, 1981–87
(dollars)

	Conservative	Liberal	NDP
1981	264 282	145 155	11 052
1984	233 895	89 803	32 580
1985	282 063	467 771	38 719
1986	300 861	540 439	39 743
1987	1 084 759	1 726 745	151 876

Source: Drawn from "Summary of Contributions, Parties and District Associations" in the *Annual Reports* of the Supervisor of Political Financing 1982–88; Schedule 3, 1982–87 and Schedule 7, 1988.

Note: Figures are rounded to the nearest dollar.

Table 4.4
Donations to parties and district associations from individuals, selected years
1981–87
(dollars)

	1981	1984	1985	1986	1987
Progressive Conservatives					
$100 or less	20 362	15 507	21 762	26 443	83 160
More than $100	37 525	25 375	46 676	41 715	198 187
Total	57 887	40 882	68 438	68 158	281 347
Liberals					
$100 or less	56 148	21 768	146 141	143 632	255 728
More than $100	21 277	10 550	105 457	86 956	365 500
Total	77 425	32 318	251 598	230 588	621 228
New Democrats					
$100 or less	6 620	14 917	20 240	22 125	48 526
More than $100	4 418	12 328	15 439	17 518	47 228
Total	11 038	27 245	35 679	39 643	95 754

Sources: Drawn from "Summary of Contributions, Parties and District Associations" in the Annual
Reports of the Supervisor of Political Financing 1982–88; Schedule 3, 1982–87 and Schedule 7, 1988.

Note: Figures are rounded to the nearest dollar.

response, they improved direct mailing and began to cultivate individual donors as a target group. The Liberals were far more successful as fund-raisers than their competitors (see table 4.4). Note the marked growth in donations over time and bear in mind that the Liberals were in opposition during all of these years, with the exception of that part of 1987 following their autumn election victory.

From 1985 onward the Liberal party received far more from individual contributors than did the Progressive Conservatives and the New Democrats. As table 4.4 illustrates, the most dramatic increase for the Liberals came in the form of contributions of $100 or less. As already explained, the $100 limit is important in terms of reporting purposes. Dividing up the data this way also provides a sense of the expanding base of Liberal supporters. Future research into the average size of different types of contributions is obviously needed, but for the moment we can make a few tentative observations. The Liberal party seems to have met with significant success in its efforts to increase its base of supporters. Furthermore, one might infer from the pattern of contributions over the years 1985–87 that the Liberal party was able to maintain its general supporter base. The general increase in total contributions to the Liberals displayed in table 4.3 would appear to support this observation. Thus, what appears to have happened was a noteworthy increase in the number of contributors rather than a different mix of contributions. Such judgements remain tentative, of course, subject to further investigation into the size and distribution of contributions.

The relative proportions of contributions from the various categories of donors are reported in table 4.5. The importance of corporate donations to the Liberals and Progressive Conservatives can be readily seen. The NDP is the political party most reliant on small personal contributions (under $100).

This table clearly illustrates the importance of corporate donations. It also shows the low level of financial support for the New Democrats by trade unions. Even in 1987, when their contributions constituted over a quarter of the total contributions made to the provincial NDP, the dollar figures are not large: $2 970 in 1985 and $40 499 in 1987.[11]

The low level of political contributions to provincial parties and district associations of all parties from trade unions is the subject of ongoing debate. Reference to the annual reports of the Supervisor of Political Financing shows that this has been a trend. Under the *Political Process Financing Act* a trade union "that holds bargaining rights for employees in the Province"[12] to whom the New Brunswick *Industrial Relations Act* and the *Canada Labour Code* apply, may make political contributions. The provincial New Democrats regard these provisions as

Table 4.5
Relative share of total contributions by party, 1985–87
(percentages)

	Conservative			Liberal			NDP		
	1985	1986	1987	1985	1986	1987	1985	1986	1987
Individuals									
$100 or less	7.7	8.8	7.7	31.2	26.6	14.8	52.3	55.7	32.0
More than $100	16.5	13.9	18.3	22.5	16.1	21.2	39.9	44.1	31.1
Corporations	75.1	77.1	72.8	46.2	57.3	63.4	—	0.3	1.6
Trade unions	—	—	0.2	—	—	—	7.7	—	26.7
Donated goods and services	0.6	0.2	1.1	—	—	0.6	0.2	—	8.7

Sources: Drawn from "Summary of Contributions, Parties and District Associations" in the *Annual Reports* of the Supervisor of Political Financing 1982–88; Schedule 3, 1982–87 and Schedule 7, 1988.

Note: Totals may not equal 100% because of rounding.

too restrictive. Their current leader, Elizabeth Weir, has objected to them, citing the donations received by the Liberals and Conservatives from business concerns "resident outside New Brunswick."

> In 1983 and 1984, 71 percent of all corporate donations received by the Liberal Party and 56 percent of all corporate donations received by the Conservative Party originated from outside the province of New Brunswick. I think we have a real issue here of influence from outside the province on our electoral process and on elections in New Brunswick. We have received no corporate donations other than from owner-operated businesses; in terms of trade unions, the same rule does not apply. A trade union that makes a contribution must have a chartered local in the province of New Brunswick. That same restriction does not exist for corporations. (New Bruns. Standing Committee 1990; the author's transcript of their proceedings labels this as part of Tape 2)

Expenditure Practices

The Office of the Supervisor of Political Financing prepares an annual report which provides data on both political fund-raising and expenditure practices. On file at the Office are financial records which are available for examination, and the media have used this material periodically to examine the financial practices of the political parties. Evidence of such general openness and media access was apparent in coverage during March and April 1986 of material contained in Conservative party submissions to the Supervisor. These submissions detailed the use of party funds to pay some expenses incurred by the party leader, Premier Hatfield. (See, for example, the *Daily Gleaner* 1986a; Benteau 1986a, 1986b, 1986c.) Included in these expenses were some payments to cover part of the legal fees accumulated by Premier Hatfield when he was charged and acquitted of marijuana possession.

In explaining the decision to use a portion of the party funds for this purpose New Brunswick PC Party Executive Director Fred Blair issued a statement "to officials of the party" (the *Daily Gleaner* "Editor's Note" accompanying 1986b) wherein he argued:

> A question has been raised about the propriety of the Party paying the legal costs of defending the Premier's marijuana charge. It is my personal belief, shared by many others, that the Premier was placed in legal jeopardy as a result of an attempt by persons unknown to discredit him as Premier and Leader of our Party. This, and other considerations, were taken into account by the Financial Officers of

our Party in reaching the decision to finance the legal costs. This action falls within the guidelines of the *Political Process Financing Act*, and was cleared in advance by the Supervisor of Political Financing. (*Daily Gleaner* 1986b)

Mr. Field, Supervisor of Political Financing, reviewed the party expenditures and found them in order. Although suggestions of duplicated expenditures and/or questionable expenses surfaced in the local media (Benteau 1986a), Field's investigation found no significant problems. Fredericton's *Daily Gleaner* interviewed Field and reported that he made this comment: "In each and every instance, I found there was an allocation of expenses between the party and the government. Everything seems in order" (Benteau 1986c).

Adherence to the new regime exacted a behavioural change from those active in the political process, because it meant increased scrutiny and public knowledge of matters long considered private. Topics such as financial dealings between party and leader would not likely have become a public issue without both adherence to the regulatory regime and generally open access to information.

Compliance has been made easier for the political parties because of the provision of public funds. The amounts involved have been quite significant. Payments in 1990 were as follows: Progressive Conservatives, $254 620; Liberals, $537 810; and NDP, $93 921. As noted earlier, payment rates are based on the number of votes cast for a party's candidates at the immediately preceding general election. In 1981, the rate was set at $1.30 per vote, and since then it has been allowed to rise in relation to increases in the consumer price index.

Overall, perhaps the most striking results of the *Political Process Financing Act* and the evolving regulatory regime have been increased openness and availability of information. Also interesting have been the shifts in party financing strategies. The Liberals were the first to capitalize on the potential value of improved fund-raising campaigns directed toward individuals. Their success has not been lost on their competitors. The NDP, however, continue to have difficulty raising donations in New Brunswick.

An important feature of the regulatory regime has been its underlying consistency. The basic framework set out in the 1978 Act has remained largely in place. Tax deductibility was added later and there have been periodic amendments of donation or expenditure levels (*Daily Gleaner* 1986c), but the basic structure established with the *Political Process Financing Act* has remained functional and productive.

Debate continues, though, about the regulatory regime's strengths and weaknesses as various observers have called attention to perceived deficiencies. We turn to these voices before venturing a concluding summary.

FUTURE DEBATES – VOICES OF CHANGE

Despite the durability of the regulatory regime spawned by the *Political Process Financing Act*, there have been criticisms of the regime's perceived limitations. It is worthwhile looking at these before reaching some final judgements.

The New Brunswick New Democratic Party has periodically raised calls for amendments to the legislation. The previously mentioned discontent about the provisions for trade unions as opposed to those for corporations headquartered outside New Brunswick is only one example of NDP complaints. Former NDP Leader George Little spoke out, for example, on what he regarded as the need to prevent banks from making donations to provincial parties (Fogan 1987). Robert Hall, a former New Democrat MLA, also sought legislative amendments. For example, in May 1987 he called for changes such as controls on the influence "particularly [of] out-of-province corporations," the setting of "minimum penalties for the illegal financing of candidates and parties" and "extending financial disclosure to leadership campaigns" (New Bruns. Leg. Ass. 5 May 1987, 1409). Despite these protestations, the NDP was unable to force major changes on these points.

Another critical observer has been Professor Philippe Doucet of l'Université de Moncton. Doucet perceived a dangerous connection between the volume of money spent in a constituency and the likelihood of electoral victory. "In fact, in 1978, 60 percent of the candidates who spent the most money in their constituencies were elected. In 1982, the figure was 66 percent" [translation] (Doucet 1986, 35). Doucet cited this as evidence of a persistent link between spending and electoral success. While observers may debate the nature of this link, the question remains of how far regulation can go to assure equality of electoral opportunity.

In their report *A Comparative Survey of Election Finance Legislation 1988*, the Ontario Commission on Electoral Finances queried the ratio between the maximum permitted contribution size (then $9 000 a year from any one source) and the maximum campaign expenditure limit (now $22 000). "Theoretically, a candidate would receive his/her maximum funding from two and one-half contributions" (Ontario, Commission 1988, 69). While the evidence before the Ontario Commission indicated that the New Brunswick reality is one where "relatively few contributors contribute the maximum" (ibid.), the authors of their report may have had a point worth considering. In 1990 the provincial government endeavoured to lower the per-party ceiling to $6 000. The change would be instituted as part of a move to "per-party ceilings" rather than all-encompassing "blanket ceilings." The Honourable H. Seamans, the minister then responsible for election financing matters, endorsed the idea of such a move for reasons of administrative convenience. In the words of Seamans:

> Quite innocently, some of these donors would exceed the limit over-all. Someone might give one political party $5 000 and another polit-ical party $5 000. The political parties would receive the money; they would check and say, "Yes, it is under the $9 000 total limit; everything looks fine."
>
> The problem that the Supervisor of Political Financing was run-ning into at year-end when the returns came in was that Joe Blow had donated a total of $10 000, which exceeded the $9 000 limit in the Act. (New Bruns. Standing Committee 1990; the author's transcript of their proceedings labels this as part of Tape 3)

For reasons to be discussed below the donation ceiling was not reduced until 1991. It is now the case that an individual, corporation or trade union may contribute not more than $6 000 in a calendar year to "each registered political party or to a registered district association of that registered political party" and "one registered independent candidate"; the maximum yearly permitted contribution from any source is $6 000 per party (in an election year, this includes the party's candidates). The 1991 amendments also extended the deadline for commencing prosecutions under the Act to two years from one.

There should be periodic monitoring of the number of donors con-tributing the maximum level and of the distribution of such donations among ridings, candidates, district associations and/or provincial par-ties. Large donations would obviously have more impact at the local con-stituency level. Such monitoring would, however, be a complicated task, given the number of contributors and the differing party strate-gies toward collecting contributions. A key feature of Liberal strategy, for example, has been the centralization of collections, and the distri-bution of money from provincial headquarters to the various ridings and candidates. Meanwhile, the Progressive Conservatives and New Democrats are now monitoring the possible potential of direct mailings and other such fund-raising tactics.

Three final aspects of political fund-raising and expenditures which deserve mention are political activity at the municipal level, so-called advocacy advertising, and the impact of political financing legislation on overall campaign spending. There are few political financing controls for municipal politics. Advocacy advertising involves advertising by groups directed toward policy positions on issues deemed to be electorally divisive. This is not covered by the New Brunswick legislation and has not become a major provincial issue. Meanwhile, the complete nature of the relationship between the political financing legislation and the pattern of total campaign period expenditures can only become clear with the passage of time and elections.

Overall, despite the assorted criticisms, the regulatory regime spawned by the *Political Process Financing Act* has proven to be an impressive achievement. There is now a salutary openness about the whole issue of party financing: much information is now available to the public that was once confidential. The Supervisor's Office produces an annual report packed with interesting information, and keeps financial records on file that are available to the media and to the general public.

While regulatory regimes are not designed to meet the wishes of the regulated, it is important that those regulated feel the regime to be fair and reasonable. Political parties in New Brunswick remain supporters of the essential aims of the *Political Process Financing Act* and the associated regulatory regime. Their record of overall compliance represents an important feature of the contemporary political landscape.

One feature of the regulatory regime which deserves an added note is the Advisory Committee. Both participants and close observers have applauded the constructive spirit which has marked its deliberations. One indicator of the support shown for the Committee by the party system can be seen in the short-lived effort of the Honourable H. Seamans on behalf of the McKenna government to amend the *Political Process Financing Act* in 1990. The amendments were designed to create a per-party ceiling. NDP Leader Weir protested that the proposals had not first been reviewed by the Advisory Committee. As a result of her request for Advisory Committee discussion the government withdrew its proposed legislation. In fact, Premier McKenna and Seamans both agreed that such consultation was necessary. McKenna went so far as to admit that "the lack of consultation is not defensible" (Dunsmuir 1990). As already noted, amendments were introduced and passed amicably in 1991.

The New Brunswick experience with the *Political Process Financing Act* has been generally positive overall. Party fund-raising is no longer shrouded in the mists of cynicism and back rooms. Increased openness, generally high levels of compliance, and the development of a productive multi-party Advisory Committee are all significant products of the regulatory regime.

ABBREVIATIONS

c.	chapter
R.S.C.	Revised Statutes of Canada
R.S.N.B.	Revised Statutes of New Brunswick
s.	section
S.N.B.	Statutes of New Brunswick

NOTES

This study was completed on 10 March 1991.

The Liberal, Progressive Conservative and New Democratic parties in New Brunswick have been very cooperative. Each has provided the author with the opportunity to discuss political financing issues with thoughtful and cooperative representatives of their organization.

The assistance of Mr. S. Hoyt and Mr. S. Field has also been valuable. Both of these individuals kindly shared their experiences in regulating political and electoral activity.

The author also wishes to express his thanks to those other observers who provided advice and commentary: Dr. P. Aucoin, Dr. G. Betts, Mr. S. Field, Mr. B. Hatfield, Honourable R. Hatfield, Mr. S. Hoyt, Mr. D. Macdonald, Mr. L. Maillet, Mr. C. Sargant, Mr. A. Scott, Dr. L. Seidle, Dr. A. Sharp and the two anonymous reviewers who carefully evaluated an earlier draft of this paper.

1. Robichaud's major Equal Opportunity initiatives resulted in the transfer of a variety of government functions from the local to the provincial level. For a description of these initiatives see Young (1987).

2. The New Brunswick Legislative Library has a folder labelled "Select Committee on Electoral Reform" which appears to hold a complete compilation of all submissions to the Select Committee. The positions of the groups referred to in the text are set out on pp. 19, 23, 20, and 37 respectively. Examples of concerns voiced by individuals can be found in the presentations of Jack Keefe (22) or Leon Rideout (6).

3. Until 1980 the proceedings of the New Brunswick Legislative Assembly were recorded in the *Synoptic Reports of the Proceedings of the Legislative Assembly of New Brunswick*. Since 1980 the debates have been recorded in the *Journal of Debates (Hansard) of the Legislative Assembly of the Province of*

New Brunswick. For ease of reference, citations from the Legislative Assembly proceedings will be referred to as "(New Bruns. Leg. Ass. date, page number)."

4. For a sense of the general reaction to the purchasing legislation see, for example, "Public Tendering Bill Wins Praise," *Telegraph-Journal* (1974a).

5. See reference to this in the exchange between Hatfield and Liberal leader Joe Daigle in the Legislative Assembly on 27 June 1978. Note, for example, Daigle's comments on pages 6373–76.

6. This is from the text below the accompanying news photo.

7. Bruce Hatfield is a nephew of former Premier Richard Hatfield.

8. Adapted from "Schedule 4 – Election Expense Analysis 1987 General Election" in the Supervisor's *Annual Report* for the period 1 April 1987 to 31 March 1988, p. 18.

9. *An Act to Amend the Political Process Financing Act,* assented to 8 December 1988. See section 1 which amended the pre-existing subsection 20 (2) of the Act.

10. Author interviews with various past and present Liberal party officials and activists in Fredericton during August 1990.

11. Drawn from Schedule 3 in the *Annual Report* for 1 April 1985 to 31 March 1986 and Schedule 7 in the *Report* for 1 April 1987 to 31 March 1988.

12. See the definition of trade union found in the opening section of the *Political Process Financing Act.*

REFERENCES

Benteau, Steven. 1986a. "Hatfield's Expenses Examined – Six New Instances Reported." *Daily Gleaner,* 26 March, 1, 5.

———. 1986b. "Field Gathering Expense Documents." *Daily Gleaner,* 27 March, 1, 2.

———. 1986c. "Hatfield's Expenses Found to Be in Order." *Daily Gleaner,* 1 April, 1.

Bickerton, James. 1989. "The Party System and the Representation of Periphery Interests: The Case of the Maritimes." In *Canadian Parties in Transition: Discourse, Organization, and Representation,* ed. Alain G. Gagnon and A. Brian Tanguay. Scarborough: Nelson Canada.

Canada. *Canada Labour Code,* R.S.C. 1985, c. L-2.

Childs, Gerald. 1973. "Boundary Commission 'Very Soon' – Hatfield." *Telegraph-Journal,* 9 January, 5.

Daily Gleaner. 1986a. "Hatfield's Expenses Examined – Party Paid Law Firm $120,000." 26 March, 1, 5.

———. 1986b. "Statement Issued to New Brunswick PCs" and accompanying "Editor's Note." 2 April, 5.

———. 1986c. "Political Process Financing Act Changed." 19 June, 8.

De Merchant, E.B. 1978. "Bricklin Books Opened – Minus a Few Chapters." *Telegraph-Journal*, 16 March, 1.

Doucet, Philippe. 1986. "Les élections et l'argent." *Policy Options* 7 (7): 33–35.

Dunsmuir, Heather. 1990. "*Political Process Financing Act* Amendments Delayed." *Daily Gleaner*, 10 November, 3.

Fitzpatrick, P.J. 1978. "New Brunswick – The Politics of Pragmatism." In *Canadian Provincial Politics: The Party Systems of the Ten Provinces.* 2d ed., ed. Martin Robin. Scarborough: Prentice-Hall.

Fogan, John. 1987. "NDP Wants Banks Barred from Making Political Donations." *Telegraph-Journal*, 5 May, 4.

Jonah, David R. 1971. "The Case for Patronage in New Brunswick – 'We've Waited 10 Years for These Jobs'." *Telegraph-Journal*, 30 March, 1.

Leger, Paul C. 1983. "The Cabinet Committee System of Policy-Making and Resource Allocation in the Government of New Brunswick." *Canadian Public Administration* 26:16–35.

Michaud, The Hon. J.E. 1966. *Report of The Honourable J.E. Michaud, Q.C. on Study and Revision of N.B. Elections Act.* Fredericton.

Moncton Times. 1978. "Putting Politics Back to the People." 28 June.

New Brunswick. *An Act to Amend the Elections Act,* R.S.N.B. 1973, c. 12 (Supp.).

———. *An Act to Amend the Political Process Financing Act,* S.N.B. 1980, c. 40.

———. *Elections Act,* R.S.N.B. 1973, c. E-3.

———. *Industrial Relations Act,* R.S.N.B. 1973, c. I-4.

———. *Political Process Financing Act,* S.N.B. 1978, c. P-9.3, s. 58.

New Brunswick. Chief Electoral Officer. 1974. *Report of the Chief Electoral Officer on Election Expenses.* Fredericton.

New Brunswick. Legislative Assembly. 1970–87. Selected portions of the proceedings. Fredericton.

New Brunswick. Representation and Electoral District Boundaries Commission. 1975. *Future Considerations and Recommendations of the Representation and Electoral District Boundaries Commission.* Fredericton.

New Brunswick. Select Committee on the Elections Act. 1974. *The Report of the Select Committee on the Elections Act*. Fredericton.

New Brunswick. Standing Committee on Law Amendments, New Brunswick Legislative Assembly. 1990. *Proceedings of November 8, 1990*. Fredericton.

New Brunswick. Supervisor of Political Financing. 1979 onward. *Annual Reports*. Fredericton.

Ontario. Commission on Election Finances. 1988. *A Comparative Survey of Election Finance Legislation 1988*. Toronto: CEF.

Ontario. Commission on the Legislature. 1974. *Third Report*. Toronto: Queen's Printer.

Pedersen, Mark. 1982. "The Transition from Patronage to Media Politics and Its Impact on New Brunswick Political Parties." MA thesis, Queen's University, Department of Political Studies.

Simpson, Jeffrey. 1988. *Spoils of Power: The Politics of Patronage*. Toronto: Collins.

Stanley, Della M.M. 1984. *Louis Robichaud – A Decade in Power*. Halifax: Nimbus.

Starr, Richard. 1987. *Richard Hatfield: The Seventeen-Year Saga*. Halifax: Formac.

Telegraph-Journal. 1974a. "Public Tendering Bill Wins Praise." 8 March, 2.

———. 1974b. "A Different Election." 21 October, 4.

———. 1978a. "Bob Exits, Head High." 26 January, 8.

———. 1978b. "Legislation Coming on Campaign Spending." 26 January, 2.

———. 1978c. "Election Reform." 8 June, 6.

———. 1978d. "Political Financing Supervisor: Capital CA Named to Post." 26 July, 3.

Thorburn, Hugh G. 1961. *Politics in New Brunswick*. Toronto: University of Toronto Press.

Young, Robert A. 1984. "Non-Development on the Periphery: The Case of New Brunswick Multiplex." In *Proceedings of the Atlantic Provinces Political Studies Association 1984*. Antigonish.

———. 1986. "Teaching and Research in Maritime Politics: Old Stereotypes and New Directions." *Journal of Canadian Studies* 21:133–56.

———. 1987. "Remembering Equal Opportunity: Clearing the Undergrowth in New Brunswick." *Canadian Public Administration* 30:88–102.

5

PARTY FINANCING IN ALBERTA
Low-impact Legislation

Doreen P. Barrie

POLITICAL POWER IS a prize worth fighting for and, throughout history, human beings have sought it through fair means or foul. Until recently, the sources of funding for political parties and candidates have been shrouded in mystery. The exchange of money between contributor and candidate or party was a private transaction that was shielded from public scrutiny. Within the last two decades, the veil of secrecy has been slowly lifted, shedding light on one of the most vital questions in politics: who gets what and from whom?[1] With the staggering increases in campaign costs, parties and candidates must now raise vast sums of money. Where this money comes from is of some importance.

The drive for greater openness with respect to finance has gone hand in hand with the desire to open the doors of political opportunity to a broader spectrum of the population. Consequently many jurisdictions have introduced public subsidies to candidates, tax rebates to contributors and expenditure limits in an attempt to increase participation in the political process. In Canada there is a variety of mechanisms currently in use, from limits on spending and contributions to reimbursements to candidates. This study will examine party financing in Alberta.

The genesis of Alberta's legislation and its major provisions will be discussed first. The focus will then shift to the pattern of party financing in the province, followed by an examination of the impact of the Alberta legislation. The last provincial and federal campaigns will be compared, and the study will conclude with an assessment of Alberta's legislation. The study is based primarily on interviews with elected officials at both levels of government, party officials from the three major parties, officials from the office of the chief electoral officer and former members of the Legislative Assembly. In total about 35 people were interviewed.

GENESIS OF THE LEGISLATION

The 1975 provincial election was the last that was unfettered by a legislative framework governing party finance. By that time, legislative initiatives were in place nationally and in other parts of the country. Quebec had enacted legislation introducing spending limits and subsidies; Nova Scotia, Manitoba and Saskatchewan had also implemented expenditure controls in provincial elections; the federal *Election Expenses Act* was in place; Ontario's legislation regarding election finances had just come into effect (Ontario, Commission on Election Finances 1988, 34). Thus it could be argued that the "contagion effect" was at work when the Alberta caucus first considered legislative measures connected with party financing.

Tom Chambers, one of three Alberta MLAs who studied the matter and introduced the bill into the legislature, stated that after the 1975 election, the Conservative caucus decided "it was time" to look into the whole question of financing election campaigns. Dave King, another member of the committee, recalled that although then-Premier Lougheed's preference was for minimal statutory intervention, he realized that the public "expected some statutory paradigm on election financing and contributions."[2] The question ceased to be whether or not there should be legislation, but rather what form it should take.

Both Chambers and King recalled discussion in caucus regarding the desirability of such an initiative, and although they were given no directives per se, they were aware of the opinions of their colleagues. Caucus members favoured complete disclosure but were not convinced of the need for statutory limits on contributions. The consensus from caucus discussions also appeared to be that there should be no expenditure limits in election campaigns, nor should candidates be subsidized by the public purse. King stressed that although caucus predisposed the committee to a particular outlook, there was no admonition against other models. It appears that while caucus did not present the committee with a detailed road map, it was aware of the preferred route in the quest for the best legislation for Alberta.

Against this backdrop, committee members studied legislation in other jurisdictions in Canada as well as initiatives in the United States.

Ontario's *Election Finances Reform Act* was most influential and hence it served as the model for Alberta's legislation. The fruits of the committee's labours, Bill 24, the *Election Finances and Contributions Disclosure Act* (*EFCDA*), was introduced into the legislature in March 1977 and came into effect 1 January 1978.

Although the Alberta Act was patterned on that of Ontario, there were some important exceptions. The Ontario legislation provided for a commission to administer the Act (s. 2), limitations on advertising expenses (s. 39) and subsidies to candidates (s. 45). Alberta opted to require the chief electoral officer (CEO) to administer the *EFCDA* and the *Elections Act*. The legislation did not impose limitations on spending, nor was there any provision for reimbursement of candidates' expenses. According to Dave King, the committee had discussed spending limits because they were embedded in some of the legislation the committee had examined. However, spending limits were not considered seriously because of the perceived difficulty in enforcing the limits.

In an exchange in the legislature when the Bill was being debated, Walter Buck, a Social Credit MLA, raised the question of expenditure limits. He expressed concern that it was "now becoming almost a rich man's hobby to be elected to the Legislature or the House of Commons, or to be the leader of a major party in this province or this country" (Alberta, Leg. Assem. 1977, 1397). In response, Tom Chambers quoted from an Ontario royal commission report that recommended no limitations on spending because of the great difficulties with their enforcement. The report stated that "the enforcement of spending ceilings requires exacting reporting standards and thorough auditing, and demands of constituency organizations a competence that few of them in fact can be assumed to have" (ibid.).[3] Chambers argued that there are too many possible loopholes in attempts to impose limits on spending.

He also pointed out that the 28-day campaign that the province had adopted would curtail expenditures without "having to get into the onerous and complicated problem of trying to enforce a legislated limitation on expenditures" (Alberta, Leg. Assem. 1977, 1397). In an interview with the author, Chambers said that the possibility of limiting certain expenses such as advertising was considered impractical and unnecessary. Chambers emphasized that he and his colleagues on the committee believed that disclosure of the source of contributions and the ceiling on contributions from a single source were by far the most important provisions in the legislation. Albertans now have access to information that had hitherto been secret and are in a position to judge for themselves whether the actions of candidates or contributors are questionable. Contribution limits ensure that individuals and/or parties do not become indebted to and therefore unduly influenced by a handful of donors.[4]

The restriction of contributions to Alberta residents, Alberta corporations and trade unions was intended to limit outside influence on Alberta. It was felt that provincial elections should be funded wholly within the province.[5]

Alberta's legislation governing election financing is an accurate reflection of the philosophy of its architects. When faced with the need to draft legislation, the committee members chose a set of provisions that would sit comfortably with their colleagues in caucus. Convinced that public scrutiny is the most effective check on politicians, as the next section will demonstrate, the Act requires parties and candidates to submit to ongoing monitoring of their finances. The premise is that the public will be vigilant and any impropriety will be punished at the ballot box.

MAJOR PROVISIONS OF THE LEGISLATION

This section will focus on the most important sections of the Act rather than presenting a detailed discussion of the legislation. The major provisions contained in the *EFCDA* include registration of parties, disposition of surpluses of funds, sources of and limits on contributions, disclosure of sources of larger donations and a system of tax credits for contributions.

Registration of Parties

The Act requires registration of political parties for them to be eligible to receive contributions. To register a new party, organizers must provide the CEO with a list of names, addresses and signatures of eligible voters. The minimum number of signatures required to gain status as a registered party is 0.3 percent of electors (currently 4 653) eligible to vote in the previous general election.[6] A party can be registered if it obtains the required number of signatures. However, although it is then eligible to receive contributions, it is not actually required to run candidates in the next election. Patrick Legerwood, Alberta's CEO, pointed out that the Act will probably be amended to compel parties to run candidates in elections to maintain their party status.

The CEO maintains up-to-date records on political parties in the province, records that include information on the leader and principal officers, especially the chief financial officer. Under the Act such information is replicated at the constituency level. Registrations of parties, constituency associations or candidates may be cancelled for non-compliance with the Act, if the party no longer qualifies to be registered or obtains registration falsely.[7]

Annual financial statements must be sent to the chief electoral officer by constituency associations, but parties must file an audited financial statement annually. For a campaign period, candidates must file financial statements and here again, parties must file an audited financial statement. If registration of a party is cancelled, all funds not required to pay outstanding debts are held by the chief financial officer until the party is re-registered. If the party fails to do so within a year of cancellation, funds are transferred to the provincial treasurer.

Surpluses of Funds

If a candidate has a surplus after an election campaign, these funds may be held in trust until the next election. If the candidate does not run, the funds may be disposed of in one of five ways, to a registered party, a registered constituency association, a registered candidate, a registered Canadian charity or the provincial treasurer.

Thus the candidate is not obliged to dispose of the funds to either the party or the constituency association. Some defeated or retiring Conservative candidates have decided to turn surplus money over to the party instead of the constituency association as they did not support the person who had won the nomination. In some other instances, however, funds have been donated to universities for scholarships or to charities.[8] The CEO commented that the Act would probably be amended to eliminate the fourth option.

Sources of Contributions

Only residents of Alberta, corporations that carry on business in Alberta, and unions that hold bargaining rights for employees in Alberta are eligible to make political contributions in the province.[9] In addition, there are constraints on the transfer of funds to and from federal parties. A provincial party may, during a federal campaign, transfer a maximum of $150 to a federal party for each candidate running in the election in Alberta. Similarly, the party may accept revenue from a federal party only during a campaign period and the total must not exceed in aggregate $150 per candidate running in the campaign.[10] There are no restrictions on intraparty transfers within the province. Such transactions, even if they include real or personal property, are not considered contributions. Despite this provision, the author was given to understand that constituencies rarely share their funds with other constituencies.

Limits on Contributions

The Alberta legislation limits the size of a contribution from a single source, be it an individual, corporation or trade union. It is possible to make an annual contribution and/or contributions in any campaign period. The current limits are as follows:

1. Annually, the limit is $15 000 to a party and $750 to a constituency association. Contributions may be made to a maximum of five constituency associations, making the aggregate amount $3 750.
2. In a campaign period, the limit is $30 000 to a party and $1 500 to a candidate. Contributions may be made to a maximum of five candidates, making the aggregate amount $7 500.

Contributions to the party during an election year must be deducted from the amount given to it during a campaign period. In other words, if a $15 000 annual contribution has been made, the campaign period contribution may not exceed $15 000. Contributions may be made to candidates in addition to annual contributions to constituency associations. In an election year, then, the maximum that can be contributed by a single contributor is $41 250.[11]

Candidates are not eligible to receive contributions except during a campaign period. Conversely, constituency organizations may accept contributions at any time except during a campaign period. Candidates themselves are bound by contribution limits so it is not possible for wealthy candidates to pour money into their own campaigns.

Non-monetary contributions must be valued at the market value of the contribution at the time it is made. For example, the donation of professional services or of office space is considered to be a contribution under the Act and must be assessed at market value. Payroll deductions exceeding $0.15/month contributed to a party, constituency association or candidate are also deemed to be contributions.

Contributions cannot be made through an unincorporated organization such as a law firm. Amounts received from such organizations are attributable to individuals in that firm and a breakdown as to the individual sources and amounts must be provided.

Disclosure of Funding Sources

The Act requires disclosure of sources of funding by requiring parties, constituency associations and candidates to file returns with the CEO. For contributions below $40, only the total amount received needs to be recorded. For contributions above that amount, different rules apply. If an annual (or campaign period) contribution exceeds $40 but not $375, the total amount of such contributions must be recorded and transmitted to the CEO. The chief financial officer must record the names and addresses of contributors but does not have to submit them to the CEO.

If a contribution exceeds $375 in a year or a campaign period, the name and address of each contributor must be recorded and filed with the CEO. The latter publishes this list along with an annual/campaign report.

Receipts for contributions must be issued by parties, constituency associations and candidates. As one copy of the official receipt must be submitted to the CEO, that office does in fact have the names and addresses of those who contribute less than $375.[12]

The CEO is required to publish a statement of election expenses incurred by a candidate in a newspaper circulated in a candidate's riding.

Tax Credits

The Alberta legislation provided for a system of tax credits whereby contributors receive a tax credit for contributions. The following examples illustrate the extent of the tax credit:

Contribution	Tax Credit
$ 100.00	$ 75.00
200.00	137.50
500.00	287.50
1 000.00	508.00
1 725.00	750.00

The maximum tax credit is reached at $1 725. As the foregoing figures show, the tax credit system is geared to benefit the small donor. If individuals make contributions of $100, in reality it costs them $25, making it much easier for the party to approach potential supporters. The tax advantage declines with the size of the contribution so that whether contributors make contributions of $15 000 or $1 725 to a party, they would receive the maximum tax credit of $750. The tax credit might motivate contributors of modest amounts, but for large contributors there is less tax incentive. In 1988 the total value of tax credits for contributions to political parties and constituency associations was $2 911 124.[13]

PATTERN OF FINANCING

The pattern of financing of political parties in Alberta is not unlike that found at the federal level. Table 5.1 gives a breakdown of contributions to the three major parties during the 1989 campaign.

Table 5.1 shows that the bulk of the revenue obtained by the PCs, 80 percent of the total, comes from corporate contributions. The Liberals, who did not expect to garner even $350 000 to fight the

Table 5.1
Party financing: 1989 election campaign
(dollars)

Contribution	Progressive Conservative	Liberal	NDP
Up to $375			
Individual	104 604	138 603	402 801
Corporate	40 110	45 073	14 738
Union	—	—	3 892
Over $375			
Individual	137 968	50 316	143 068
Corporate	982 168	229 486	9 579
Union	—	—	48 087
Total	1 264 850	463 478	622 165

Source: Calculated from Alberta, Chief Electoral Officer (1990).

election, surpassed that figure.[14] Although a large portion of their revenue came from individuals, 60 percent was contributed by corporations. The vast majority of the NDP's funding, 87 percent, came from individual contributors. Contributions from unions amounted to 8 percent and the balance came from corporate donors.

Since disclosure provisions came into effect and the names of major contributors have been published, newspaper reports indicate that the Conservatives have received substantial revenue from corporations. The Liberals were in financial difficulties until fairly recently but their campaign financial statement shows that they are now receiving contributions from some corporations that also contribute to the Conservative party. Funds raised by the New Democrats are more widely based with individual contributors providing most of the revenue. Officials in the NDP commented that the tax credit makes it much easier for them to solicit funds from individuals.

Table 5.2 traces the fund-raising capabilities of the three parties during election campaigns since the *EFCDA* came into effect. It should be noted that these figures quoted apply only to moneys raised during campaign periods.

Table 5.2 illustrates that of the three parties, only NDP revenues display a consistent upward trend. The PCs took in less than $1 000 000 during the 1979 campaign and almost $1.5 million in 1982 – the largest amount raised by the party during the four campaigns.[15] In the following election, Conservative revenues declined by approximately 15 percent, and in 1989 registered an increase of less than $20 000.

No pattern emerges when examining figures for the Liberal party.

Table 5.2
Fund-raising in election campaigns: trend since introduction of *EFCDA*
(dollars)

Election	Progressive Conservative	Liberal	NDP
1979	869 847	95 039	51 634
1982	1 466 208	12 090	482 948
1986	1 245 763	72 311	519 259
1989	1 264 850	463 478	622 165

Source: Alberta, Chief Electoral Officer (for years cited).

While the initial amount is modest compared with that for the PCs, the ability of the Liberals to raise money declined sharply between the 1979 and 1982 elections. In the latter campaign the party raised one-seventh of the 1979 figure. Party finances in the 1986 campaign improved vastly, but only relative to the previous contest. The 1989 election represents a sort of financial "coming of age" for the Liberal party. For the first time since disclosure provisions came into force, campaign revenues were in the six-digit range, more than six times the 1986 level. The gap between the Liberals and the New Democrats is now much narrower.

As mentioned above, of the three parties, only the NDP has recorded ever-increasing revenues. Although the dramatic ninefold increase between the 1979 and 1982 elections has not been repeated, gains have been registered in every campaign. In 1986 the increase was approximately $36 000, and in 1989 the party experienced an improvement of some 16 percent on the previous campaign.

The Liberals improved their fund-raising capabilities considerably in the 1989 election, but it would appear that the New Democrats have been the major beneficiaries of the party financing legislation in the province. Although the amount they now receive is far below that of the PCs, it represents a substantial improvement in their fortunes.

Parties do not raise revenues only during election campaigns, so to provide a more complete picture of party revenues, table 5.3 sets out the figures provided in annual audited statements for selected years. Because parties gear up for elections ahead of time, figures are provided for election years and each year before a campaign. To make up for deficits incurred during the campaign, parties also attempt to raise revenue immediately following the campaign.[16]

Table 5.3 illustrates that political parties raise considerable amounts around election campaigns. If revenues collected in the pre- and post-election periods are considered as being part of campaign revenue, the

Table 5.3
Annual revenues of political parties: selected years
(dollars)

Year	Progressive Conservative	Liberal	NDP
1979	444 001	32 439	165 038
1982	304 701	56 247	222 210
1983	927 699	71 770	227 933
1985	943 785	194 991	349 890
1986	505 118	64 727	410 318
1988	1 324 687	190 609	348 136
1989	759 330	263 365	357 967

Source: Alberta, Chief Electoral Officer (selected years).

Conservatives amassed $1.2 million, $1.4 million and $2.0 million for the 1982, 1986 and 1989 elections respectively. This is in addition to funds raised during the campaign period.

For the Liberals, the corresponding figures are approximately $128 000, $260 000 and $454 000 for the three elections. The New Democrats accumulated about $450 000, $760 000 and $706 000 for the three campaigns.

If the funds raised during the campaign period are added to these figures, for the 1989 election period the PCs collected $3.3 million, the Liberals just under $1.0 million and the New Democrats $1.3 million.

IMPACT OF THE LEGISLATION

View from the Trenches

Moving from a regime in which there are no constraints on the type and size of contribution to one in which statutory limits are imposed naturally requires some adjustment. Although most of the people who were interviewed in the course of this study had no experience before 1978, no one complained that the *EFCDA* was particularly onerous or restrictive. While there were complaints about specific provisions, the Act was praised for its simplicity and clarity – watchwords of Alberta's first Chief Electoral Officer, Ken Wark.

Administration of the Act

Wark pointed out that simplicity was his goal in setting up his office as well as in establishing the administrative regime for everyone who had to comply with the legislation. Unlike Ontario, which had a staff of 132, the maximum number of staff members during his tenure was 11 and that was pared down to 9 after the enumeration.[17]

Forms provided to parties, candidates and constituency associations were explicitly designed to be as straightforward as possible. For instance, the return to be filed by candidates following an election campaign amounts to a simple two-column form detailing income and expenditures. While there are no limits on expenditures, candidates must document them in part, so that the extent of surplus funds can be determined.

Although the *EFCDA* does not impose limits on expenditures, provisions in the *Elections Act* permit the chief electoral officer to query expenditures. The *Elections Act* prohibits a candidate from making "an improper payment" for a number of things like rental of space, equipment, travel and living expenses, and printing. The candidate must show that expenses paid were "fair, reasonable and proper and not in excess of what is ordinarily paid for such facilities and goods" (Alberta, *Elections Act*, s. 176). Ken Wark stated that he appealed to candidates to use common sense and advised them not to hire their spouses or relatives at exorbitant rates. He felt they heeded his advice and his experience was that chief financial officers were sensible and sensitive.[18]

Wark believes that the *EFCDA* works well, that the penalties (which range from fines to prison terms depending on how serious the infraction is) are sufficiently severe to ensure compliance.[19] He argues that publicity is punishment enough in most cases because negative publicity – the prospect of having one's name splashed all over the papers – is a strong deterrent.

The CEO's office runs workshops for workers to familiarize them with the legislation, and the CEO will also speak to party workers at conventions on request. Parties also run their own workshops for their volunteer campaign workers so they will not violate the legislation. However, some people suggested that it would be useful if the CEO's office had a "post mortem" with parties after each election so that problems that had cropped up in the campaign could be discussed while still fresh in everyone's mind.

Volunteers are the lifeblood of political parties and they must be handled tactfully. Statutory requirements to maintain records make it easier for party officials or workers at the constituency level to keep abreast of events without appearing heavy-handed. Thus, from the party's point of view, the enforced record keeping is welcome. Good records also enable the party office to keep track of the numerous transactions that take place, particularly during an election campaign.

Individuals who have to comply with the legislation pointed out that keeping track of incoming money is a necessity whether it is a legal requirement or not. The only difference when there is a legal requirement is that there is the added discipline of knowing that statements have to be filed. As the financial statements are very rudimentary, and as constituency associations and candidates do not have to submit audited financial statements, compliance is not difficult.

Because the chief financial officer is authorized to issue receipts, he or she has to ensure that the contribution does not exceed the limit and that the contributor is eligible to make a contribution. In the three major parties, receipts are issued by the central party organization. Each party charges the candidate and the constituency association a "handling fee" for this service; in the Conservative party the charge is 10 percent, in the Liberal party, 15 percent and in the NDP, 40 percent.

From conversations with MLAs it became obvious that they did not have to concern themselves unduly with complying with the legislation. They were aware of limits on contributions and that tax credits are available on contributions; but beyond that, in most cases, it was their chief financial officer who ensured that nothing was done in violation of the Act.

Impact on the Campaign

As mentioned, the legislation has had little impact on the way campaigns are run. There are some constraints on fund-raising events: records must be kept of gross income from such functions and a portion of the charge to individuals is considered a contribution.

The consensus among those interviewed seemed to be that limits on contributions were high enough so that there was little influence on campaigns one way or the other.[20] There were people who felt that no limits were necessary as long as full disclosure was a requirement. A number of people interviewed pointed out that the tax credit makes it easier to solicit funds, with the result that the base of support has been broadened. Since candidates must raise most of their own money, the provision of tax credits means that they can approach people who might not otherwise have contributed.

COMPARISON: FEDERAL AND PROVINCIAL CONTESTS

The rules of the game naturally dictate the way it is played as they condition the behaviour of the players. Federal and provincial political contests in Alberta take place under very different conditions. In federal election campaigns contestants are governed by the *Canada Elections Act*, which imposes expenditure limits during election campaigns, but does not regulate contributions in any way. In provincial campaigns the opposite is true, as candidates are constrained in their fund-raising efforts but unfettered with respect to their expenses. Moreover, contribution limits are a permanent feature of the provincial political landscape, unlike expenditure limits at the federal level, which are merely creatures of the writ period.

The obvious question, then, is how these diametrically opposed regimes affect federal and provincial contests. Are provincial parties and candidates wildly extravagant because there is no ceiling on their expenditures? Are federal parties and candidates in Alberta awash in revenue as they are limited only by their ability to solicit funds successfully? In this section an attempt will be made to assess the impact of differing rules on federal and provincial elections in Alberta. But first a word of caution.

There is a problem of equivalence. As a federal campaign cannot be equated with a provincial campaign, there are limited points of comparison. In the section that follows, an effort has been made to extract roughly equivalent information from data published on the 1988 federal election campaign and the 1989 provincial election to compare revenues raised in federal and provincial contests and relative costs of such contests. It must be pointed out that the figures in the tables that follow pertain to contributions and expenditures at the constituency level only. Although political parties raise considerable amounts centrally, it is not possible from the data available for national elections to break out the figures for each province. While the resulting figures in tables 5.4 and 5.5 do not tell the whole story, they are at least an accurate reflection of the position "on the ground," so to speak.

Another point that needs to be clarified is that, given the scope of this study, it was possible to look at only one election, so what we have is a snapshot rather than a trend; but it is nonetheless the most recent snapshot. Looking only at the election period also ignores the fact that parties gear up for elections before the writ falls.[21] In any case, limits on expenditures for federal contests are in effect only during election campaigns, so a comparison of election periods is the most meaningful.

Table 5.4 is a comparison of contributions received at the constituency level of the three major parties in provincial and federal elections in the province.[22] Note first that, at both levels, the Progressive Conservatives received more revenue than the other two parties by a wide margin. At the provincial level, the Liberals raised only one-third as much as the Conservatives, and the NDP raised only one-fifth. In federal campaigns the gap is not so wide but it is still considerable, with

Table 5.4
Comparison of contribution levels
(dollars)

| Party | 1988 federal/1989 provincial election funds raised at local level* | | |
	Progressive Conservative	Liberal	NDP
Provincial	2 586 088	850 842	530 908
Federal	1 168 663	423 087	530 940

Source: Provincial figures constructed from Alberta, Chief Electoral Officer (1990). Federal figures constructed from Canada, Elections Canada (1988).

*Figures refer to contributions raised by candidates during provincial campaigns and may include moneys transferred from the constituency association and from the party.

the Liberals receiving 36 percent of what the Conservatives did, and the NDP about 45 percent. More relevant to the subject of this study is whether contribution limits choke off revenue to provincial political entities – in this case, candidates.

The figures, particularly those for the Conservatives, do not suggest that the contribution limits represent an impediment to fundraising. Albertans went to the polls a scant four months after the federal election, but it is obvious that the well had not run dry. Both the provincial PCs and Liberals were able to raise more than twice as much as their federal counterparts. The figure for the NDP is close for both contests. As the New Democrats depend on individuals for the bulk of their funding, it is perhaps not surprising that the provincial candidates, soliciting funds only a few months after the federal election, were unable to raise more revenue.

It does not appear that the statutory limit on contributions in provincial campaigns poses much of a problem to the three parties. With no ceiling on contributions in national campaigns, it would not be unreasonable to expect federal candidates to garner a great deal more from contributors, especially as their reach is so much wider – 26 federal ridings versus 83 provincial constituencies. In addition, it could be expected that since federal candidates went to the well first, this might have reduced the flow of revenue to provincial hopefuls. Yet this does not appear to have happened. From table 5.4 it could be concluded either that Albertans are more generous in provincial than in federal campaigns, or that the ceiling on contributions is high enough to make little difference to fund-raising.

While there seems to be agreement that the high ceiling on contributions at the provincial level does not present much hindrance to raising revenue, there may be something else at work too. In election campaigns it is primarily the candidate who attracts funds at the constituency level, by virtue of his or her stature in the community. Appeals for money go out to the candidate's network of colleagues, friends and family. Thus it could be argued that it is not the size of the constituency that increases the flow of funds, but rather the number of candidates drawing on their personal networks. While parties are reluctant to divulge their strategies, party officials did point out that campaigns were expected to be largely self-sufficient. In the NDP they have to be entirely self-sufficient. This being the case, the total amount collected would depend on the number of personal networks being activated rather than the number of people in a given constituency.

Table 5.5 compares election expenses in provincial and federal campaigns. Here again the Conservatives outdistanced their rivals. Spending by the Liberals in the provincial campaign was only 41 percent of the total spent by the Conservatives, and the New Democrats disbursed 30 percent of the Conservatives' outlay. Per elector spending in federal elections is 87 cents lower than the corresponding figure for provincial elections.[23] At first glance it would appear that the 1989 provincial election was far more costly than the 1988 federal campaign. However, this conclusion would be premature: the first point that must be borne in mind is that every candidate in an election campaign has certain fixed costs for items like signs, office space and telephones. Thus, with several candidates running in 83 ridings, the basic campaign costs would be considerably higher than that for candidates in 26 ridings. Another factor that might account for the lower federal figures is that these may not be an accurate reflection of the actual campaign

Table 5.5
Comparison of expenditure levels
(dollars)

| Party | 1988 federal/1989 provincial elections: constituency-level expenditures* | | | |
	Progressive Conservative	Liberal	NDP	Spending per elector
Provincial	1 999 697	810 991	579 369	2.18
Federal	987 625	479 044	582 231	1.32

Source: Provincial figures constructed from Alberta, Chief Electoral Officer (1990). Federal figures constructed from Canada, Elections Canada (1988).

*Figures refer to contributions raised by candidates during provincial campaigns and may include moneys transferred from the constituency association and from the party.

expenses. As expenditure limits apply only to the writ period, it is quite possible that campaign expenditures were incurred before the writ fell and after the writ period had expired (some individuals interviewed hinted that this was the case). There being no expenditure limits in provincial campaigns, candidates would not need to juggle their spending.

Taking the above points into consideration, it does not appear that provincial candidates spend exorbitant amounts on their election campaigns despite the absence of limits. It would also seem that spending limits in federal campaigns in Alberta are adequate for contests in this province.

The foregoing remarks must, however, be qualified, as spending in election campaigns is driven by more than the presence or absence of limits.[24] Bill Heald, Executive Director of the Progressive Conservative Association of Alberta in Calgary, pointed out in an interview with the author in October 1990 that "dogfights cost a lot of money." Just such a dogfight took place in Calgary in 1989 between the Liberal incumbent and his Conservative challenger. Kate Thrasher (PC) spent $52 774 to try to unseat her rival, and Sheldon Chumir (Liberal) spent $50 792 to fend off her challenge (the NDP candidate spent a paltry $1 283 on the contest). While on the subject of competitive campaigns, it should be noted that until 1986, Conservatives in provincial campaigns faced few serious challengers. Now that their stranglehold on power appears to be weakening, the cost of campaigns may escalate dramatically.

It is difficult to discern a pattern in spending levels. In other words, the rationale for spending large sums is not always clear. In an instance like the one cited above, escalating costs may be explained by the need to keep up with a rival. However, in many cases (21 out of 83 ridings), the differential between one candidate, usually the Conservative candidate, and the closest contender was between $10 000 and $30 000.[25] The question that requires further research is: Why do some candidates spend so much? Is it merely because they have the money or because they feel an expensive campaign is a mark of credibility? Marie Laing, NDP MLA for an Edmonton constituency, suggested that it reflects poorly on candidates if they have insufficient funds to mount a credible campaign because the public perception is that they are not serious. This is an important point because many campaign workers undoubtedly equate financial resources with credibility.[26] However, whether most voters are impressed by lavish spending is debatable. Being able to afford signs and literature to get the message out is a necessity, but it is possible that many people would be turned off by apparent profligacy. It is not obvious that those involved in campaigns are always clear as to the most effective way to translate dollars into votes.

Alexander argues that a large part of spending in election campaigns "is done solely for psychological motives." He goes on to assert that "perhaps half of all spending is wasted – but no one knows which half" (1976, 57). While the latter remark may be tongue-in-cheek, it does raise some interesting questions regarding campaign expenditures.

Seidle and Paltiel argue that the spending limit in federal campaigns "has obliged parties and candidates to assess the potential usefulness of certain expenditures and has undoubtedly helped control frivolous spending that used to occur as long as funds did not run out" (1981, 276–77). While the limits on spending may be restrictive in many areas, this does not appear to be the case in Alberta. According to the *Report of the Chief Electoral Officer* (Canada, Elections Canada 1988), in only six of the 26 federal ridings did a candidate's expenses exceed 90 percent of the limit and in the majority of cases spending was below 80 percent of the limit. In fact it is quite possible that many candidates would have spent considerably less if they were not eligible to obtain the rebates. People who had worked in federal campaigns indicated that candidates routinely factor rebates into their budgets. It could be argued that if the expenditure ceiling is generous, the discipline it imposes is negated by the provision of rebates to candidates, encouraging them to spend in the expectation of recovering some of the money.

This brief and admittedly limited comparison of provincial and federal campaigns suggests that statutory limits on contributions and expenditures present few impediments to candidates. Alberta's contribution limits are generous enough that they do not present serious obstacles to individuals. Similarly, the ceiling on expenditures in federal campaigns appears to be sufficiently high, at least in Alberta, so there is little hindrance to conducting a campaign. It is entirely possible that the costs of campaigns in Alberta will escalate when competition becomes fiercer, but more than one person interviewed pointed out that, whereas in Quebec and Ontario labour must often be bought, the spirit of voluntarism is alive and well in Alberta, particularly in Calgary.

Before concluding this section on the federal-provincial comparison, mention must be made of complaints about the complexity of the federal legislation.[27] In conversations, two Alberta MPs pointed out that the reporting procedure is unnecessarily detailed and ambiguous. Campaign workers suggested that record keeping is arduous, particularly for fairly trivial amounts. The official agent for a federal candidate pointed out that the forms for reporting could have been greatly simplified.[28]

VIEW OF THE TRENCHES

One factor that emerged during the course of this study was the variety of opinions, even within the same party. Despite having to live with party discipline in their official lives, politicians expressed their personal opinions freely, and their views were often unexpected.[29]

On the question of disposition of surplus campaign revenue, an MLA from the NDP remarked that it was good that a candidate should have the freedom to decide this matter because "parties are becoming too preponderant." Opinion was sharply divided on this question (in fact, most MLAs were not even aware of the provision in the legislation that allowed them to make the decision). Many people from the Liberal and Conservative parties believed that contributors were giving money to the individual and only incidentally to the party. Tom Chambers commented that his colleagues applauded his actions when he set up a scholarship for engineers because they had supported him, not necessarily the party. So far only Conservatives have been placed in the happy position of having to dispose of surpluses.[30]

A similar diversity of views was revealed on the issues of whether rebates should be provided to candidates and expenditure limits imposed on them. While a number of individuals (mostly, but not exclusively, Conservatives) were unequivocal in their opposition to both, ambivalence was much more common.

It was revealing that, despite the fact that candidates must become members of a cohesive group if elected, they receive surprisingly little financial and other support from the central party organization on the journey to the legislature. While it is not possible to make a blanket statement on this point, given the limited number of people interviewed, the impression gained was that parties expect candidates to raise funds themselves and to draw on personal networks for volunteers.[31] No doubt most constituencies have a core of workers who toil in every campaign, but only rarely does the party intervene to help in individual campaigns.

It must be difficult for a successful candidate to make the transition from a virtually independent, self-sufficient campaigner to an anonymous, docile backbencher in our parliamentary system. It is somewhat surprising that there are no apparent consequences of this dissonance in roles.

CONCLUSION

The study of Alberta's legislation governing party finance has led the writer to conclude that the Act has accomplished what its architects set out to achieve: a "statutory paradigm" that inspires public confidence without inhibiting the capacity of parties to raise funds.[32] Not only does the disclosure requirement permit public scrutiny but it precludes the "purchase" of an elected member by a large contributor.[33] Conversely, a ceiling on contributions must be welcomed by large contributors such as companies bidding on government contracts, which might otherwise have felt pressured into greater generosity. As Adamany and Agree aptly put it: "Extortion, or practices that differ only in being more genteel, are the Janus face of undue influence by contributors" (1975, 11).

Alberta has opted for "low-impact" legislation in its attempts to regulate political finance, so the *EFCDA* has a limited reach. The emphasis is on full disclosure, as the authors of the legislation were pessimistic about whether other measures were either appropriate or practical.

In the judgement of the writer, the disclosure provision imposes a very heavy burden, for it was felt by the architects of the legislation that by throwing the books open, the ballot box would deliver the necessary correctives. There are a number of problems with this line of thinking.

In the first place, the decision to vote for a particular party depends on a constellation of factors. If the party is the governing party, its record surely transcends all else. Second, like justice, disclosure of funding sources must be swift to be effective. Consequently, if information on the source of campaign funding is to be of use to voters, it must be timely. In Alberta and most other jurisdictions, it is not. To learn several months after an election campaign who gave what to whom will not change the outcome, nor is it likely to have an impact on the next election. Voters will have more recent matters on their minds when they mark their ballots. Disclosure during an election campaign, a practice that has been adopted for municipal elections in New York City, is perhaps the only way in which the information will be used effectively by voters (New York City 1988). Such a scheme, however, would place an added burden on parties and candidates during a period of frenetic activity, and would undoubtedly create enormous difficulties.

Third, openness assists in maintaining fairness and sunshine is indeed "a good disinfectant,"[34] but the sun in this case is very selective – it shines only on the office of the chief electoral officer for Alberta. Although newspapers carry stories about contributions to parties whenever this information becomes available, it is necessary to journey to Edmonton to see the list of contributors. If all Albertans are to have reasonable access to financial records of parties and candidates, it would be desirable to have parallel sets of records in all the major centres in the province. It would also be much more enlightening for the average person if contributions from the various arms of a corporate entity were grouped together on the list. Thus one would not need to be an expert on corporate holdings to get an accurate picture of the total amount contributed by one entity.

While it is quite true that it is ultimately the electorate that must make the judgement, it could be argued that the therapeutic effects of disclosure are a trifle overdrawn.

As to whether expenditure limits and rebates should be considered in the province, this writer is as ambivalent as many of the people interviewed. From discussions with those familiar with the federal legislation it seems that it is easy to get compliance with the letter of the law while confounding its spirit. Rebates and expenditure limits are adopted to ensure that a career in politics is attainable even by citizens of modest means. However, rebates may themselves be driving up the cost of campaigns, straining the public purse and ultimately jeopardizing the very principles that we seek to uphold. As mentioned earlier, the *Elections Act* in Alberta does permit the CEO to monitor expenses and if this surveillance function is strengthened, it might eliminate the worst abuses. As the cost of advertising is prohibitive and is likely to rise even further, a limitation on advertising costs may be appropriate.

The need to strengthen confidence in the integrity of the electoral process and the desire to provide political opportunities to a wider cross-section of society are two of the main objectives underlying attempts to regulate political finance. How to achieve these goals without injuring the vitality of other democratic values will continue to challenge those who seek to reform methods of financing election campaigns.

ABBREVIATIONS

am.	amended
c.	chapter
R.S.A.	Revised Statutes of Alberta
R.S.C.	Revised Statutes of Canada
s(s).	section(s)
S.A.	Statutes of Alberta
S.C.	Statutes of Canada
S.O.	Statutes of Ontario

NOTES

This study was completed in January 1991.

I would like to express my gratitude to party officials, federal and provincial legislators, as well as the current chief electoral officer and his staff and the former chief electoral officer, who gave so generously of their time. Their contribution was invaluable, because they brought to the study the perspective of the candidate and the constituency.

1. With apologies to Harold Lasswell.

2. Tom Chambers and Dave King were interviewed by the writer in Edmonton in October and December 1990, respectively.

3. Chambers called it a "royal commission" but presumably he was referring to the Report of the Ontario Commission on the Legislature, which studied campaign financing reform in the early 1970s.

4. Former Premier Lougheed was convinced that public scrutiny was the most effective mechanism to police candidates and contributors alike. The legislation reflects this conviction.

5. An official with the Progressive Conservative (PC) party commented that this is a useful provision as it protects the provincial party from being badgered by the PC Canada Fund.

6. This figure was cited by Patrick Legerwood, Chief Electoral Officer of Alberta, in an interview on 18 December 1990.

7. Parties may be "de-registered" for failing to file financial statements, for instance.

8. For example, former MLA Tom Chambers, who is now a professional engineer, gave his surplus funds totalling roughly $50 000 to the University of Alberta to set up a scholarship fund for engineering students. The university matched the funds.

9. The Act spells out the definition of "prohibited corporations." In addition to corporations that do not carry out business in the province, these include provincial corporations and subsidiaries thereof and "any corporation designated by the Lieutenant Governor in Council." For trade unions, all locals of a trade union are deemed to be one trade union.

10. The New Democratic Party (NDP), which has an integrated party structure across the country, does collect funds for the federal party but provincial and federal accounts are completely separate. A party official pointed out that according to an agreement with the NDP Federal Council, provincial wings of the NDP are expected to contribute 15 percent of their revenue to the federal party. As the legislation prohibits this in Alberta, the provincial wing must raise this amount separately. This target has never been met.

11. Although it is not likely to happen, a single contributor could make this maximum donation to a number of parties.

12. Although the receipts are not part of the public records, Legerwood stated that if there was a compelling reason to make them available, he would do so: interview on 18 December 1990.

13. Ibid.

14. In fact they were so short of funds that then-president Michael Henry thought he might have to ask party leader Laurence Decore and his top aide to take pay cuts (*Edmonton Journal*, 28 February 1989).

15. As 1982 was Premier Lougheed's last contest, it is likely that the figure reflects this fact.

16. Since the 1982 election was held in November, table 5.3 also gives the revenue raised in the the following year (1983). The other elections were held at the beginning of the year so the previous year's figures are given.

17. It should be noted that expenditure limits and subsidies to candidates, which are provisions in the Ontario legislation, require a much more complex administrative structure. It is not possible to monitor expenses and administer subsidies effectively without sufficient personnel. Nevertheless, as it is possible to complicate even the simplest operation, Wark's determination to "keep it simple" has paid dividends.

18. The present CEO stated that he has not had occasion to query expenses and in any case, has too little information to go on. However, if there was a complaint from someone he would investigate the matter.

19. The chief financial officer of one candidate stressed that they took the provisions of the legislation very seriously. Since she was responsible for ensuring compliance, her laugh was hollow when campaign workers joked about the possibility of her going to jail! Two *Criminal Code* charges were laid against Al Iafolla, a Liberal candidate in the 1986 election. Iafolla is alleged to have received donations that were not listed in his financial record and also to have listed contributors who denied that they had contributed to his campaign. The charges (forgery and uttering a forged document) were laid in June 1989 (*Edmonton Journal*, 26 July 1989). In April 1991, he was sentenced to one day in jail and fined $7 500 for the two charges (*Calgary Herald*, 10 April 1991).

20. Comments like "not restrictive," "generous enough," and "easy to live with," were commonplace when individuals were referring to the contribution limit. The author was also told that the pattern of financing for the Conservatives had not changed with the introduction of the *EFCDA*.

21. The trend for provincial parties is covered in the previous section on the pattern of financing since the *EFCDA* came into effect.

22. A reminder that during a writ period only candidates and the party are eli-

gible to receive contributions. The totals for each party were arrived at by adding total campaign revenue for the 83 electoral divisions as published in the *Report of the Chief Electoral Officer*. The figure for each constituency includes revenue raised by the candidate plus "Other Revenue" which, as mentioned above, includes transfers from the constituency association, the proceeds from fund-raising events, as well as revenue from the party. In the case of provincial NDP candidates, all revenue is shown under the heading of "Other Revenue," as all contributions are channelled through the party office. The party issues the receipts, retains 40 percent of each contribution, and returns the rest to the candidate – in a non-election period – to the constituency association. Consequently, NDP candidates receive only 60 cents for every dollar they raise and Mary Kennedy, Administrative Secretary of the NDP, said that campaigns are self-sufficient. Occasionally the party provides the services of a paid organizer. In federal campaigns, too, contributions are funnelled through the party office and then returned to candidates. In these campaigns candidates also have to be self-sufficient.

Michael Henry, Chief of Staff and past President of the Alberta Liberal party, explained that his party handles all receipts centrally and charges a 15 percent fee. He also said that the party provides services to candidates in campaigns and gave a total of $12 000 to candidates in targeted, winnable ridings. Bill Heald, Executive Director of the Progressive Conservative Association of Alberta, mentioned that his party provides $1 500 to each candidate during the writ period, plus all signage. Receipts are handled centrally in the Conservative party, and a 10 percent fee is charged.

23. The number of names on the Alberta voters list was 1 557 669 for the 1988 federal election; it was 1 550 867 for the 1989 provincial election, a difference of 6 802, which might account for a small amount of the difference.

24. In any case it is often fairly simple to get around the law. It is not very difficult to overcome the limit on contributions: individuals who want to contribute more than the $1 500 limit to a candidate can get friends and relatives to contribute $1 500 each. As they would get the tax credit for the transaction it is to their benefit. As mentioned earlier, in federal campaigns it is possible to spend money in advance of a campaign period or to postpone payment until after it, thus circumventing the expenditure limits.

25. The biggest spenders were usually the PCs and in four ridings, including Premier Getty's, their bids were unsuccessful.

26. While this is not to suggest that Mrs. Laing meant that it was necessary to run an extravagant campaign, extravagance is relative.

27. Although there was criticism of record-keeping requirements in the federal legislation, MP Harvie Andre's campaign manager told the author that once an individual becomes familiar with the requirements and the task becomes routine, the exercise is not much of a problem.

28. She pointed out that if the forms were sent to those who actually filled them out, it would result in a number of useful suggestions for streamlining them (interview with Penny Stone, Chief Financial Officer for MLA Marie Laing).

29. Alberta's Minister of Consumer and Corporate Affairs has a self-imposed limit of $500 on contributions. He told the author that when he was first elected not many large contributions were forthcoming. However, the situation has since changed and in accordance with his policy, he must now turn down some contributions.

30. The party itself would prefer to see the revenue remain in the hands of either the central party or the constituency association. It is quite possible, then, that charitable causes will soon be ineligible to receive surplus funds.

31. Information on election strategies is hard to come by. For example, it is almost certain that some ridings are targeted and receive injections of money and volunteers. Yet the author got the impression that parties would discuss the matter only in the most general terms.

32. In fact, by broadening the base of support through the provision of a tax credit, the number of people making modest contributions to all parties has likely increased considerably.

33. This point was made so often that the author must assume that large contributors did, in fact, try to control politicians.

34. This comment is contained in the submission of Edward R.R. Carruthers to this Royal Commission. He expressed similar sentiments in a conversation with the author.

REFERENCES

Adamany, David W., and George E. Agree. 1975. *Political Money: A Strategy for Campaign Financing in America.* Baltimore: Johns Hopkins University Press.

Alberta. *Election Finances and Contributions Disclosure Act (EFCDA), 1977,* S.A. 1977, c. 18.

———. *Election Finances and Contributions Disclosure Act,* R.S.A. 1980, c. E-3; am. S.A. 1984, c. 48.

———. *Elections Act,* R.S.A. 1980, c. E-2, s. 176.

Alberta. Chief Electoral Officer. Various years. *Annual Report of the Chief Electoral Officer: The Election Finances and Contributions Disclosure Act.* Edmonton.

Alberta. Legislative Assembly. 1977. *Hansard,* 17 May.

Alexander, Herbert E. 1976. *Financing Politics: Money, Elections and Political Reform.* Washington, DC: Congressional Quarterly Press.

Canada. *Election Expenses Act*, S.C. 1973–74, c. 51.

Canada. Elections Canada. 1988. *Report of the Chief Electoral Officer Respecting Election Finances, Thirty-Fourth General Election 1988.* Ottawa: Minister of Supply and Services Canada.

New York City. 1988. *A Local Law to Amend the Administrative Code of the City of New York in Relation to Optional Partial Public Financing of Election Campaigns in the City* (3–708 (9)).

Ontario. *Election Finances Reform Act, 1975*, S.O. 1975, c. 12, ss. 2, 39, 45.

Ontario. Commission on Election Finances. 1988. *A Comparative Survey of Election Finance Legislation 1988.* Toronto: CEF.

Ontario. Commission on the Legislature. 1974. *Third Report.* Toronto: Queen's Printer.

Seidle, F. Leslie, and Khayyam Z. Paltiel. 1981. "Party Finance, the Election Expenses Act, and Campaign Spending in 1979 and 1980." In *Canada at the Polls, 1979 and 1980: A Study of the General Elections,* ed. H.R. Penniman. Washington, DC: American Enterprise Institute for Public Policy Research.

CONTRIBUTORS TO VOLUME 3

Doreen P. Barrie	University of Calgary
David Johnson	McMaster University
Louis Massicotte	Université de Montréal
Hugh Mellon	Brock University
Terry Morley	University of Victoria

Consistent with the Commission's objective of promoting full participation in the electoral system by all segments of Canadian society, gender neutrality has been used wherever possible in the editing of the research studies.

THE COLLECTED RESEARCH STUDIES*

---

* The titles of studies may not be final in all cases.

SYLVIA BASHEVKIN	Women's Participation in Political Parties
LISA YOUNG	Legislative Turnover and the Election of Women to the Canadian House of Commons
LYNDA ERICKSON	Women and Candidacies for the House of Commons
GERTRUDE J. ROBINSON AND ARMANDE SAINT-JEAN, WITH THE ASSISTANCE OF CHRISTINE RIOUX	Women Politicians and Their Media Coverage: A Generational Analysis

VOLUME 7
Ethno-cultural Groups and Visible Minorities in Canadian Politics: The Question of Access
   Kathy Megyery, Editor

DAIVA K. STASIULIS AND YASMEEN ABU-LABAN	The House the Parties Built: (Re)constructing Ethnic Representation in Canadian Politics
ALAIN PELLETIER	Politics and Ethnicity: Representation of Ethnic and Visible-Minority Groups in the House of Commons
CAROLLE SIMARD	Visible Minorities and the Canadian Political System

VOLUME 8
Youth in Canadian Politics: Participation and Involvement
   Kathy Megyery, Editor

RAYMOND HUDON, BERNARD FOURNIER AND LOUIS MÉTIVIER, WITH THE ASSISTANCE OF BENOÎT-PAUL HÉBERT	To What Extent Are Today's Young People Interested in Politics? Inquiries among 16- to 24-Year-Olds
PATRICE GARANT	Revisiting the Voting Age Issue under the *Canadian Charter of Rights and Freedoms*
JON H. PAMMETT AND JOHN MYLES	Lowering the Voting Age to 16

VOLUME 9

Aboriginal Peoples and Electoral Reform in Canada
Robert A. Milen, Editor

ROBERT A. MILEN	Aboriginal Constitutional and Electoral Reform
AUGIE FLERAS	Aboriginal Electoral Districts for Canada: Lessons from New Zealand
VALERIE ALIA	Aboriginal Peoples and Campaign Coverage in the North
ROGER GIBBINS	Electoral Reform and Canada's Aboriginal Population: An Assessment of Aboriginal Electoral Districts

VOLUME 10

Democratic Rights and Electoral Reform in Canada
Michael Cassidy, Editor

JENNIFER SMITH	The Franchise and Theories of Representative Government
PIERRE LANDREVILLE AND LUCIE LEMONDE	Voting Rights for Inmates
YVES DENONCOURT	Reflections concerning Criteria for the Vote for Persons with Mental Disorders
PATRICE GARANT	Political Rights of Public Servants in the Political Process
KENNETH KERNAGHAN	The Political Rights of Canada's Federal Public Servants
PETER MCCORMICK	Provision for the Recall of Elected Officials: Parameters and Prospects
DAVID MAC DONALD	Referendums and Federal General Elections
JOHN C. COURTNEY AND DAVID E. SMITH	Registering Voters: Canada in a Comparative Context
CÉCILE BOUCHER	Administration and Enforcement of the Elections Act in Canada

VOLUME 11
Drawing the Map: Equality and Efficacy of the Vote in Canadian Electoral Boundary Reform
David Small, Editor

KENT ROACH	One Person, One Vote? Canadian Constitutional Standards for Electoral Distribution and Districting
HOWARD A. SCARROW	Apportionment, Districting and Representation in the United States
ALAN STEWART	Community of Interest in Redistricting
MUNROE EAGLES	Enhancing Relative Vote Equality in Canada: The Role of Electors in Boundary Adjustment
DOUG MACDONALD	Ecological Communities and Constituency Districting
ALAN FRIZZELL	In the Public Service: Representation in Modern Canada
DAVID SMALL	Enhancing Aboriginal Representation within the Existing System of Redistricting

VOLUME 12
Political Ethics: A Canadian Perspective
Janet Hiebert, Editor

PIERRE FORTIN	Ethical Issues in the Debate on Reform of the *Canada Elections Act:* An Ethicological Analysis
VINCENT LEMIEUX	Public Sector Ethics
IAN GREENE	Allegations of Undue Influence in Canadian Politics
WALTER I. ROMANOW, WALTER C. SODERLUND AND RICHARD G. PRICE	Negative Political Advertising: An Analysis of Research Findings in Light of Canadian Practice
JANE JENSON	Citizenship and Equity: Variations across Time and in Space
KATHY L. BROCK	Fairness, Equity and Rights
JANET HIEBERT	A Code of Ethics for Political Parties

VOLUME 23
Canadian Political Parties in the Constituencies:
A Local Perspective

R. KENNETH CARTY

Canadian Political Parties in the
Constituencies: A Local Perspective

COMMISSION ORGANIZATION

CHAIRMAN
Pierre Lortie

COMMISSIONERS
Pierre Fortier
Robert Gabor
William Knight
Lucie Pépin

SENIOR OFFICERS

Executive Director
Guy Goulard

Director of Research
Peter Aucoin

Special Adviser to the Chairman
Jean-Marc Hamel

Research
F. Leslie Seidle,
  Senior Research Coordinator

Legislation
Jules Brière, Senior Adviser
Gérard Bertrand
Patrick Orr

Coordinators
Herman Bakvis
Michael Cassidy
Frederick J. Fletcher
Janet Hiebert
Kathy Megyery
Robert A. Milen
David Small

Communications and Publishing
Richard Rochefort, Director
Hélène Papineau, Assistant
  Director
Paul Morisset, Editor
Kathryn Randle, Editor

Assistant Coordinators
David Mac Donald
Cheryl D. Mitchell

Finance and Administration
Maurice R. Lacasse, Director

Contracts and Personnel
Thérèse Lacasse, Chief

EDITORIAL, DESIGN AND PRODUCTION SERVICES

ROYAL COMMISSION ON ELECTORAL REFORM AND PARTY FINANCING

Editors   Denis Bastien, Susan Becker Davidson, Ginette Bertrand, Louis Bilodeau, Claude Brabant, Louis Chabot, Danielle Chaput, Norman Dahl, Carlos del Burgo, Julie Desgagners, Chantal Granger, Volker Junginger, Denis Landry, André LaRose, Paul Morisset, Christine O'Meara, Mario Pelletier, Marie-Noël Pichelin, Kathryn Randle, Georges Royer, Eve Valiquette, Dominique Vincent.

LE CENTRE DE DOCUMENTATION JURIDIQUE DU QUÉBEC INC.

Hubert Reid, *President*

Claire Grégoire, *Comptroller*

Lucie Poirier, *Production Manager*
Gisèle Gingras, *Special Project Assistant*

Translators   Pierre-Yves de la Garde, Richard Lapointe, Marie-Josée Turcotte.

Technical Editors   Stéphane Côté Coulombe, *Coordinator*;
Josée Chabot, Danielle Morin.

Copy Editors   Martine Germain, Lise Larochelle, Elisabeth Reid, Carole St-Louis, Isabelle Tousignant, Charles Tremblay, Sébastien Viau.

Word Processing   André Vallée.

Formatting   Typoform, Claude Audet; Linda Goudreau, *Formatting Coordinator*.

WILSON & LAFLEUR LTÉE

Claude Wilson, *President*

DUNDURN PRESS

J. Kirk Howard, *President*
Ian Low, *Comptroller*
Jeanne MacDonald, *Project Coordinator*

Avivah Wargon, *Managing and Production Editor*
Beth Ediger, *Managing Editor*
John St. James, *Managing Editor*
Karen Heese, *Special Project Assistant*

Ruth Chernia, *Tables Editor*
Victoria Grant, *Legal Editor*
Kathleen Harris, *Senior Proofreader*

Editorial Staff   Michèle Breton, Elliott Chapin, Peggy Foy, Elizabeth Mitchell, John Shoesmith, Nadine Stoikoff, Shawn Syms, Anne Vespry.

Copy Editors   Carol Anderson, Elizabeth d'Anjou, Jane Becker, Diane Brassolotto, Elizabeth Driver, Curtis Fahey, Tony Fairfield, Freya Godard, Frances Hanna, Andria Hourwich, Greg Ioannou, Carlotta Lemieux, Elsha Leventis, David McCorquodale, Virginia Smith, Gail Thorson, Louise Wood.

Formatting   Green Graphics; Joanne Green, *Formatting Coordinator;*
Formatters   Linda Carroll, Mary Ann Cattral, Gail Nina, Eva Payne, Jacqueline Hope Raynor, Carla Vonn Worden, Laura Wilkins.